The Raiders of 1862

The Raiders of 1862

James D. Brewer

Westport, Connecticut
London

Library of Congress Cataloging-in-Publication Data

Brewer, James D.
    The raiders of 1862 / James D. Brewer.
      p. cm.
    Includes bibliographical references (p.   ) and index.
    ISBN 0–275–95404–8 (alk. paper)
    1. United States—History—Civil War, 1861–1865—Cavalry
operations. 2. Confederate States of America. Army. Cavalry.
I. Title.
E470.4.B74 1997
973.7'3013—dc20   96–24333

British Library Cataloguing in Publication Data is available.

Library of Congress Catalog Card Number: 96–24333
ISBN: 0–275–95404–8

First published in 1997

Praeger Publishers, 88 Post Road West, Westport, CT 06881
An imprint of Greenwood Publishing Group, Inc.

Printed in the United States of America

The paper used in this book complies with the
Permanent Paper Standard issued by the National
Information Standards Organization (Z39.48–1984).

10 9 8 7 6 5 4 3 2 1

Copyright Acknowledgment

Grateful acknowledgment is given for permission to quote from Lt. O. C. Ayers, "Pursuing
General Forrest: This Looked But Little Like Trying To Catch The Enemy," *Civil War Times
Illustrated* (September 1984), published by Cowles History Group, 741 Miller Drive, SE, Suite
D-2, Leesburg, VA 22075. Subscription # (800) 829-3340—Outside the US (904) 446-6914.

This book is dedicated to my great-grandfathers:

Private Louis Washington Moody
J.B. Williams Independent Cavalry, C.S.A.

Sergeant Andrew Whitney Vance
5th Illinois Volunteer Cavalry, U.S.A.

and to all the cavalry troopers, north and south, who acted according to the following battle monument inscription:

Not for fame or reward
Not for place or rank
Not lured by ambition
Or goaded by necessity,
but in simple obedience to duty
As they understood it
These men suffered all
sacrificed all
dared all
and died.

Contents

Illustrations   ix

Acknowledgments   xi

Introduction   1

Part I: Brig. Gen. Frank C. Armstrong's West Tennessee Raid, August 24–September 4, 1862

1. General Situation   9

2. The Movement on Bolivar   19

3. Medon Station and the Camp at Estanaula   31

4. The Battle of Britton's Lane   47

Part II: Brig. Gen. Nathan B. Forrest's West Tennessee Raid, December 13, 1862–January 3, 1863

5. General Situation   69

6. The Crossing at Clifton and the Fight at Lexington   75

7. Salem Cemetery   85

8. Up the Railroad   93

9. The Treacherous Withdrawal   99

10. Parker's Crossroads and Forrest's Escape   109

**Part III: Brig. Gen. John H. Morgan's Christmas Raid,
December 22, 1862–January 5, 1863**

11. General Situation   133

12. Glasgow, Bacon Creek, and Nolin   139

13. Harlan's Pursuit and the Battle of Elizabethtown   147

14. The Muldraugh Trestles and the Battle at the Rolling Fork
     River   159

15. Lebanon and Home   171

Closing Thoughts   179

Appendix: "Whatever Happened to . . . ?"   187

Works Cited   193

Index   201

Illustrations

MAPS

1.1	The Area of Armstrong's Raid	16
2.1	Armstrong's Action near Middleburg 8:00-12:00 A.M.	21
2.2	Armstrong's Action near Middleburg 12:00-4:00 P.M.	23
2.3	Positioning Prior to the Saber Battle with Col. Hogg	26
2.4	The Cavalry Drill for "Right Front Into Line"	28
4.1	The Battle of Britton's Lane 9:00 A.M., September 1, 1862	50
4.2	Britton's Lane: Armstrong's Initial Attack	53
4.3	The Battle of Britton's Lane 10:00-11:30 A.M., September 1, 1862	56
4.4	The Battle of Britton's Lane 12:30-1:30 P.M.	59
5.1	The Area of Forrest's Raid	72
6.1	Forrest's Crossing at Clifton, Tennessee, December 15-16, 1862	76
6.2	The Battle Against Col. Ingersoll at Lexington, Tennessee	82
7.1	The Fight at Salem Cemetery: Daylight, December 19, 1862	87
7.2	The Fight at Salem Cemetery: 8:00 A.M., December 19, 1862	89
8.1	Forrest's First West Tennessee Raid	95
9.1	The Federals Tighten the Noose	106
10.1	Parker's Crossroads: Daylight, December 31, 1862	114
10.2	Parker's Crossroads: 8:00 A.M., December 31, 1862	116
10.3	Parker's Crossroads: 9:00 A.M., December 31, 1862	118
10.4	Parker's Crossroads: 10:00 A.M., December 31, 1862	119
10.5	Parker's Crossroads: 12:00 P.M., December 31, 1862	121
10.6	Parker's Crossroads: 1:00 P.M., December 31, 1862	125

14.1   Route of Morgan's 1862 Christmas Raid   162
14.2   Col. Duke's Rearguard Action at the Rolling Fork, December 29,
        1862   168

FIGURES

4.1   Order of Battle: Armstrong and Dennis   50
5.1   Order of Battle: Forrest's First West Tennessee Raid   72
11.1   Order of Battle: Brig. Gen. John Hunt Morgan's Cavalry   137
14.1   Order of Battle: Col. John M. Harlan's Brigade   163

PHOTOGRAPHS

Brig. Gen. Frank C. Armstrong   11
Col. Harvey Hogg   25
Col. Elias S. Dennis   37
Brig. Gen. Nathan B. Forrest   70
Col. Robert G. Ingersoll   80
Brig. Gen. John Hunt Morgan   135
Col. Basil Wilson Duke   143
Members of the 2nd Kentucky Cavalry   146
Col. John M. Harlan   149
The Hamilton-Hall House   166

Acknowledgments

I began researching Armstrong's Raid in 1977, Morgan's Christmas Raid in 1980, and Forrest's First West Tennessee Raid in 1982. The years have brought me the fascinating company of so many gifted researchers, historians, relic hunters, reenactors, and community members that it would be impossible to name them all. I hesitate to name any, lest some be offended by my omission, yet I clearly must thank the following people whose insights, attention to detail, and love of history combined to make this book possible.

Jerry Lessenberry, President, Britton's Lane Battlefield Association

Charles Richards, Armstrong's Raid historian and friend

Jim Cupples, late historian, friend, and scholar of Parker's Crossroads Battlefield

Steve McDaniels, government official, reenactor, and friend

B. R. Hall, landowner, Hardin County, Ky.

Mrs. Susie Hill, landowner, Lexington, Tenn.

Fonville Neville, late historian of Denmark, Tenn.

Mrs. Judy Stephenson, research librarian, Fort Knox, Ky.

Dan Kennerly, author and historian of Parker's Crossroads

The Raiders of 1862

Introduction

To the young men asked to choose sides and enter the army upon the outbreak of the War Between the States, the cavalry may have offered the most exotic, interesting, and potentially glorious duty of the various service branches. The infantry required less equipment, and there was certainly no shortage of such units looking for recruits, but the cavalry offered the lure of travel and an esprit de corps and camaraderie unequalled in the other service branches.

That the ranks of the cavalry quickly filled in 1861 is not surprising, but nowhere was that more true than in the western theater of the south, where the predominance of agriculture and the absence of urban density meant that young men were often reared in the saddle, and consequently felt the cavalry to be a natural choice for their military service. In *Glory at a Gallop*, William Brooksher and David Snider write, "The average Confederate had been born to the horse and gun. Accustomed to a life of riding and shooting, war meant only a change in locale and game. The skills he had developed over the years coincided beautifully with the demands now placed upon him. Fiercely independent, [he was] proud to a fault, and possessed of boundless confidence in his ability" (Brooksher & Snider 1993, xv).

In this book we shall examine the 1862 cavalry expeditions of three important Confederate commanders: Frank C. Armstrong, Nathan Bedford Forrest, and John Hunt Morgan. We shall note the tactics, leadership procedures, and results obtained during each of their most important raids between the months of August and December, and we shall attempt to determine what made them successful or what led to their defeat.

"History is not merely what happened but rather what happened in the context of what could have happened" (Costello 1994, 331), and it is in this light that we shall examine the *Raiders of 1862*, always maintaining a view of how critical events developed, how opportunities were seized or lost, and how the personalities of the commanders impacted upon mission accomplishment.

CAVALRY ROLE AND ORGANIZATION

The United States neither authorized nor manned a regular mounted force in the army between the Revolutionary War and 1833. Even after 1833 and the origin of the U.S. Dragoons, American officers seldom led a mounted force numbering more than fifty troopers in a unit. Thus, when the War Between the States began, leaders on both sides had little precedent for cavalry maneuver other than the tactics and performance of Napoleonic Cavalry. Since Napoleonic thinking dominated the theory of warfare during the first half of the nineteenth century, it is little wonder that the hostilities of 1861 began with cavalry being viewed in a European sense as "parade units, sporting beautiful uniforms and executing intricate close-order maneuvers actually suitable only for reviews" (Emmert 1993a, 44). Dismounted action found little place among cavalry leaders, for they viewed such tactics as contrary to the cavalry spirit and tradition of mounted shock action.

Unfortunately, the theory of cavalry did not keep up with the technological development of weaponry, for the invention of the conical Minie ball for the rifled musket extended the range of infantry from one hundred yards to almost one thousand yards, thus rendering massed bodies of cavalry subject to a devastating fire from a disciplined infantry unit. Mounted warfare had to change, and gradually it did, as soldiers and forward-looking leaders began to transform saber-wielding, lancer-bearing, massed units into what moved and fought as mounted infantry. Change would come slowly, however, for Col. Phillip St. George Cooke's 1862 *Cavalry Tactics, or Regulations for the Instruction, Formations, and Movements of the Cavalry of the Army and Volunteers of the United States* virtually reproduced the "Formation for Attack" as shown in the French manual of the Napoleonic period.

While our focus in this book is Confederate cavalry, many of the same preconceived notions about the employment of cavalry plagued the north and south alike. Confederate units, as well as Federal, were initially formed with each trooper furnishing his own mount. Since the government of the Confederate states made no effort to raise a supply of horses to perpetuate their cavalry, the force was only viable as long as good horses remained available throughout the south. Consequently, southern cavalry, which early in the war had an edge on Federal cavalry both in the experience of the riders and the quality of the mounts, eventually succumbed to the drought of available mounts and attrition within the ranks.

The southern soldier did not take well to the discipline required to maneuver large bodies of cavalry in Napoleonic fashion, and that resistance may well have been one of the south's best assets. The lack of appreciation for tightly controlled, close-order drill, coupled with taking some heavy casualties as they fought in mass formations early in the war, led southern cavalry leaders to seek other means of employing their mounted force outside of set-piece maneuver in support of infantry. During the War Between the States, the most effective use of cavalry by the south, and arguably by either side, was the independent raid. According to the U.S. Army's field manual on military operations, the raid in its modern sense remains unchanged from the definition applied during 1861–65. A raid constitutes a

> limited-objective attack into enemy territory for a specific purpose other than gaining and holding ground. Commanders conduct raids to destroy key enemy installations and facilities, to capture or free prisoners, or to disrupt enemy [command and control] or support functions. The raiding force withdraws from its area after completing its mission (*Operations* 1993, 7–8).

The year 1862 would feature a number of effective cavalry raids, with one of the most studied and discussed Jeb Stuart's "Ride Around McClellan," in October. In three days, Stuart's eighteen hundred cavalrymen rode 130 miles, destroyed a quarter of a million dollars' worth of Federal supplies, captured and paroled 275 prisoners, destroyed railroad and telegraph lines, and appropriated clothing and small arms along the way. Stuart's accomplishment damaged Union morale and gave the southerners in the eastern theater something to cheer about during the fall of 1862 (Brooksher & Snider 1993, 68). But while much has been written about this daring raid, many readers will be surprised to realize that Stuart's mission pales in comparison to any of three cavalry raids conducted in the western theater during the same period of time: Brig. Gen. Frank C. Armstrong's Raid into west Tennessee; Brig. Gen. Nathan Bedford Forrest's Raid into west Tennessee; and Brig. Gen. John Hunt Morgan's Christmas Raid into Kentucky. Each of these leaders would epitomize the dash and daring of cavalry in its newfound mode of operation, and the actions and decisions of each can teach us much about the role of cavalry, not only during 1862, but for now and in the future.

The company was the basic, primary-level administrative and tactical unit of southern cavalry in 1862, a holdover most likely from frontier operations against Plains Indians. Even though organized into regiments, and most often referred to by the name of the regimental commander rather than a numerical designation, for example, "Jackson's Regiment" as opposed to the "7th Tennessee Cavalry," the company was the integral level of organization. Companies had a natural integrity, the result, no doubt, from many men from the same or nearby counties joining up together, for example, Brig. Gen. John Hunt Morgan's original unit was a company-sized militia force composed of men from in and around Lexington and bearing the name "Lexington Rifles." A squadron generally consisted of two companies affiliated for operations, with the standard organization of Confederate cavalry reflecting a ten-company, five-squadron system. As regiments shrunk by attrition during the war, company strengths were kept as high as possible, while the number of squadrons and companies were reduced (Emmert 1993a, 45). Therefore, in 1862 a regiment generally consisted of five squadrons of two companies each, or a total strength of 480 men; however, given desertions, illness, and casualties, a figure around 400 would be closer to reality.

The cavalry troopers of Armstrong, Forrest, and Morgan differed from much of the Napoleonic-influenced northern cavalry, and even some of their southern counterparts in the eastern theater, in that they fought primarily as mounted infantry, their horses being a means of arriving at the battlefield as opposed to a true battle-mount. Perhaps earlier than their counterparts in the eastern theater, western cavalrymen had relegated the saber to a secondary role, if they carried sabers at all, preferring instead the revolver, carbine, and in some cases the Bowie knife. Many western cavalrymen had to settle for the double-barrelled shotgun until they could capture rifles from the enemy, and those who did carry rifles often fought with what must have been a quartermaster's nightmare—a mixture of Enfield, Belgian, or Austrian muskets (Lord 1993, 47). But while the revolver was clearly more advantageous in a close fight than the saber, the more the western cavalryman dismounted to fight as infantry, the less suitable his revolver or his shotgun, and the more he prized a rifle or carbine.

A WORD ABOUT RAILROADS—A PRIMARY TARGET

The Federal supply network, in particular the railroads, and the communication system, for example, telegraph lines, constituted the primary targets of the Confederate cavalry raids of 1862. The next chapters will reveal how hundreds of miles of railroad track was torn up and twisted into a useless mess, while Federal reinforcements rushed to meet the enemy and halt the destruction. But the rails and the locomotives of 1862 were different than those transporting the Amtrak of today. Wrought iron, rolled to a T-shape, varying from eighteen to twenty-four feet in length, and weighing between thirty-five and sixty-eight pounds per rail constituted the tracks of the 1860s. Those rails weighed less than half that of modern rails, thus the act of ripping them from their supports, heating them until red hot, and twisting them into a radiating pile of metal was not the construction effort one would think of when considering a modern rail. When T-rails were not available, the railroads consisted of "strap," a stretch of soft iron on a wooden stringer, nailed to the crossties. Strap was even lighter than T-rails, making destruction all the more simple (Rogge 1995, 53).

Locomotives of 1862 were usually 21-ton, wood-burning, 8-wheelers, with two pairs of five-foot high driving wheels and two pairs of smaller front wheels. All rolling stock was wooden, again lending itself to easy destruction by burning, and the top speed for a locomotive was about sixty miles per hour, but "forty miles per hour was reckoned a good passenger train speed—on good track" (Rogge 1995, 80).

Thus, it was against such targets that the cavalrymen under Armstrong, Morgan, and Forrest operated. Listen to their call for service as shown in the extract from recruiting posters listed below, and then examine how each of them approached the task.

A CHANCE FOR ACTIVE SERVICE—MOUNTED RANGERS

Having been authorized by Governor Harris to raise a battalion of mounted rangers for the war, I desire to enlist five hundred able-bodied men, mounted and equipped with such arms as they can procure (shotguns and pistols preferable), suitable to the service. Those who cannot entirely equip themselves will be furnished arms by the State. When mustered in, a valuation of the property in horses and arms will be made, and the amount credited to the volunteers. Those wishing to enlist are requested to report themselves at the Gayoso House, where quarters will be assigned until such time as the battalion is raised.

N. B. FORREST

KENTUCKIANS!

I am authorized to raise a
CAVALRY COMPANY

for service for three years, or during the war. You now have an opportunity to vindicate the ancient reputation of the old Commonwealth. The Confederate Armies are rapidly driving the enemy toward the Ohio. You must FIGHT FOR the South or AGAINST HER. There is no other alternative. Will you be forced into the ranks of your enemies when a glorious opportunity offers to defend your hereditary friends?

Headquarters at Frankfort, Ky.

J. A. GRANT

PART I
BRIG. GEN. FRANK C. ARMSTRONG'S WEST TENNESSEE RAID

August 24–September 4, 1862

1

General Situation

To move northward at a moment's notice . . .

—Gen. Braxton Bragg

Frank C. Armstrong was the only general officer in the War Between the States to have fought for both the north and the south. A competent young captain in the 2nd U.S. Cavalry, Armstrong fought a frantic rearguard action to protect the retreating Union army at the first Battle of Bull Run in July 1861. His duty performance drew no criticism, in fact, his commanding officer, Maj. Innis Palmer, would cite in his report that Armstrong's "conduct . . . was in the highest degree praiseworthy" (Palmer 1887, 393). Yet, less than one month later he resigned his commission as a U.S. Army officer, and offered his services to the Confederate States of America. Armstrong's action was certainly not unique. Men of the stature of Robert E. Lee and Albert Sydney Johnston had led the way. But the fact that Armstrong would fight a pitched battle as a Union officer *before* deciding to change his loyalties is nothing short of bizzare.

Frank C. Armstrong's strange arrival into the ranks of the south created much speculation during and after the war, and to this day no one can say with certainty why Armstrong switched sides. With the whipping the Federal Army took at Bull Run, Armstrong may have been convinced that the south would win the war and simply wanted to be on the winning side. Having served in the U.S. Army after his graduation from Holy Cross, Armstrong must have known many of the prominent officers who had gone south to tender their services to the fledgling Confederacy, and perhaps his acquaintance with these officers led him to change his mind. Armstrong may have reexamined his own values and attitudes about the war, and finding himself in sympathy with the southern cause, resigned his commission. Whatever the reason, Frank C. Armstrong ceased to be a Union officer on August 13, 1861, when he and twelve others declared in writing to Secretary of War Simon Cameron that they intended to ride south and fight for the Confederacy. Thus began a series of events that slightly more than a year later would pit a young, aggressive, newly promoted Brigadier General Armstrong against a crusty old Kansas marshal-turned Union colonel, Elias S. Dennis, in the decisive battle of what would be later known as Armstrong's Raid.

Armstrong's career as a Confederate soldier, and thus his road to a rendezvous with Dennis, began in Arkansas. Less than a week after wearing a blue uniform, now *Confederate* Lieutenant Armstrong had obtained a position with Col. James McIntosh. He participated in the battle of Elkhorn Tavern and was present when Brig. Gen. Ben McCulloch was killed in March 1862. He and several competent staff officers next reported to a receptive Gen. Earl Van Dorn who recommended Armstrong be promoted for his service at Elkhorn Tavern. Not satisfied to wait for the slow, grinding wheels of military bureaucracy, the ever aggressive Armstrong managed to get himself elected colonel of the 3rd Louisiana Infantry; but he held the position less than three months before a series of events would lead the Confederate high command in the west to select Armstrong for yet another promotion.

After Confederate defeats at Fort Henry, Fort Donelson, and Island Number Ten during the winter and spring of 1862, the heart of the western Confederacy lay exposed for invasion. At the bloody struggle of Shiloh (April 6–7, 1862), the Confederate army in the west succeeded in punishing the Federals, even slowing them, but not in stopping their progress into northern Mississippi and Alabama. Thus, as General P. G. T. Beauregard consolidated the Confederate army's position near Corinth, Mississippi, the chronically cautious Union commander, General H. W. Halleck, crept his army toward a confrontation with Beauregard in late May. Beauregard, however, slipped through Halleck's grasp with a surreptitious retreat virtually in the face of the enemy. While a frustrated President Abraham Lincoln searched for a fresh commander of his Army of the West, the Confederate States also replaced Beauregard with Gen. Braxton Bragg. This change of commanders ultimately drew Frank C. Armstrong closer to his meeting with Dennis.

General Bragg believed the Confederate military effort should be directed toward eastern Tennessee, conceiving a grand plan to take the offensive and ultimately invade Kentucky. By June, he had persuaded President Jefferson Davis of the soundness of his plan, and began moving his army to its new headquarters in Chattanooga, Tennessee. Bragg could not leave Mississippi and Alabama unprotected, so to oppose the threat of an attack upon Vicksburg by Adm. David Farragut's Union fleet, he left Gen. Earl Van Dorn in command of the Confederate forces in and around

Brig. Gen. Frank C. Armstrong. Photo courtesy of General Sweeny's Museum, Republic, Missouri.

Vicksburg. Bragg next appointed Gen. Sterling Price to take command of fifteen thousand poorly armed, sickly, and minimally trained men that would compose the Army of the West (Johnson & Buel 1982, 725). This arrangement was not to General Price's satisfaction, for he echoed the desires of many of his men, that is, since his force was made up largely of men from Missouri and Arkansas, he should return with his command across the Mississippi River and carry the fight back home. Price even made a futile trip to Richmond to sell his view to President Jefferson Davis. In spite of his strategic plea, he found himself back in Mississippi trying to sort out his new command while a formidable Union army stood poised less than fifty miles north.

After dividing his army into two divisions, placed under the able leadership of Gen. Henry Little and Gen. Dabney Maury, Price realized immediately that his army lacked a significant cavalry force. What mounted men he had were interspersed throughout his army as scouts. Many of the units, though recruited as cavalry, were serving as infantry, either for military expediency or for lack of mounts. Price needed an officer who could gather a mounted force, supervise their training, and lead them as an effective fighting unit. With General Bragg in full support, Price sent the following order:

SPECIAL ORDERS NO. 8

HEADQUARTERS ARMY OF THE WEST
Priceville, Miss., July 7, 1862

I. The cavalry of this army will be, until further orders, under the immediate command of acting Brig. Gen. Frank C. Armstrong, to whom the commanding officers of all regiments, battalions, unattached companies, and squads of cavalry in the Army of the West will report forthwith.

By command of Major-General Price:

THOS. L. SNEAD
Assistant Adjutant-General
(Snead 1887, 642)

The Union captain at Bull Run had now become a general officer for the Confederacy.

Frank C. Armstrong's job would not be easy. The cavalry he was to gather and train presently served in an army suffering from disease, desertion, and despondence. Shiloh had suddenly shattered the grandiose dreams of glory held by the average soldier in the go-to-war euphoria of the previous year. While many men had sensed the war would not be won in a matter of months and settled in for the long haul, others became disillusioned and homesick, having witnessed enough human suffering to last them a lifetime. So while Armstrong was working to build an effective cavalry force in north Mississippi that June, a 33rd Alabama soldier from Tupelo was writing home, "I am tired of camp life. There is a great deal of sickness in our company and it makes the duty very hard on the rest. What time we are not on guard nor on detail to work we have to drill" (Daniel 1991, 84). And in one of the last corporal incidents of its kind in the war, three men of Company G, Tennessee Artillery, were lashed and branded for desertion at Tupelo (Daniel 1991, 188).

One antidote for lying around camp and waiting to get sick, or make a run for home and suffering the consequences, was a real military mission. Perhaps the hope of actually doing something to contribute to the war effort helped Armstrong in his recruitment, or perhaps the fact that cavalrymen have never been particularly fond of masquerading as infantry worked in his favor. Either way, once the general order to consolidate cavalry was issued, the troopers came quickly to Brigadier General Armstrong. Even the possibility of combat had to be better than "constantly patrolling . . . to arrest all stragglers and persons improperly absent from their regiments" whom General Price sought for beseiging the "gardens, corn fields, and property of our citizens" (Jordan 1887, 646). That was not what these southern horsemen had signed on to do.

Many of the Arkansas and Missouri cavalrymen had, for lack of river transport, been forced to leave their horses west of the Mississippi. Turning to private sources, Armstrong began rounding up mounts for his gathering force from the available pool of horseflesh not yet depleted by the war effort (Richards 1990, 7). In his report to General Price on July 12, 1862, Armstrong seems to have made considerable progress, drawing into his new brigade and mounting almost seven hundred men; and though his troops were spread along a twenty-mile picket line, he reported the presence of these cavalry units:

Forrest's Cavalry, Lieut. Col. D.C. Kelley commanding

McCullouch's battalion (Missouri), Lieut. Col. McCullouch commanding

2nd Tennessee Battalion, Lieut. Col. C. R. Barteau

Louisiana Squadron (though only company-size), Capt. Webb commanding

Hill's Company (Mississippi)

Sanders' Company

Two detachments (on general officer escort duty)

The level of training among his new brigade varied greatly, with most of the men possessing little or no experience operating as a large body of cavalry. Since Armstrong's initial mission was to screen against the Federal army vicinity of Corinth, and ultimately to fight them in conjunction with General Price's infantry, Armstrong had to whip his new brigade into fighting shape. Perhaps this was the primary reason Price selected Armstrong for command—his military experience and his understanding and appreciation for close-order cavalry drill. Armstrong went to work over the next month, bringing his cavalry "to an excellent condition, and restrict[ing] the Federals pretty closely to Corinth" (Evans 1987, 66). His reputation as a strict drillmaster spread quickly, making a mixed impression on the young recruits under his relentless mentorship. Sergeant Edwin H. Fay,[1] of the Louisiana Squadron mentioned above (later to become part of Balch's Battalion), wrote, "[Armstrong] is in the habit of cursing men and if he should curse me without a cause I should be tempted to shoot him" (Fay 1958, 166).

ARMSTRONG'S FIRST CHALLENGE

The initial test of Armstrong's leadership came with a brief raid to harass and disrupt Federal operations just across the Alabama line, east of Corinth, Mississippi. On July 17, General Price ordered Armstrong to advance on Decatur, Alabama, and the Tennessee River, operating "at his own discretion, doing all practicable things to harass the enemy and cut off any detachments or supply trains" (Jordan 1887, 729). Moving out with orders that granted him the independence of a classic cavalry mission, Armstrong led his seven hundred men over a ten-day raid that culminated in a victory at Courtland, Alabama. The tactics employed here by Frank C. Armstrong are particularly interesting as they foreshadow what he would do in less than one month against Elias S. Dennis in the decisive battle of his west Tennessee raid.

Armstrong's brigade was spotted near Courtland, Alabama, as it approached the camp of Companies A and H of the 10th Indiana Infantry, along with a detachment of the 1st Ohio Cavalry. Leaving the cavalry to form a line of battle in the camp, the two Federal infantry companies, under the command of Capt. Henry G. Davidson, sought cover behind a railroad embankment that shielded them from the view of the approaching Confederates. Holding their fire until Armstrong's men were almost upon them, they emerged from behind the embankment and "fired two volleys into [Armstrong's] ranks as they charged," with the Federal cavalry detachment remaining in camp (Harlan 1887, 823). Armstrong's horse was shot from under him, but he still managed to direct an envelopment of the outnumbered Federals. "I immediately pushed around some dismounted men to charge them on foot. Seeing this they ceased firing, threw down their arms, and surrendered" (Armstrong 1887, 827). Armstrong's men captured two wagons and teams, five hundred bushels of sacked corn, fifty mules, ten good horses, ammunition and small arms, and six day's supplies (Hancock 1887, 206; Armstrong 1887, 828). The Federal commander indicates that Armstrong was enraged at the captured Captain Davidson, denouncing him and "threaten[ing] to kill them all . . . because he did not surrender, without fighting, to such a superior force" (Harlan 1887, 824). Armstrong's behavior in this instance appears presumptuous, if not immature, in the ways of war. Perhaps Davidson did not initially know how many men Armstrong had, but the Federal commander is hardly to be faulted or threatened with his life for setting up what in modern terms would be called an "L-shaped ambush," and at the very least compelling Armstrong to fight. In the brief affair, three of Armstrong's men were killed and perhaps ten wounded (reports disagree). Three Federals were killed, six wounded, and 133 captured. The commander of the 10th Indiana Infantry, Col. John M. Harlan,[2] was not present with the two detatched companies when they were captured; but he will appear in chapter 13 of this book when he encounters another Confederate raider by the name of John Hunt Morgan.

That Armstrong had successfully stung the Federals did not escape Sterling Price's notice, nor that of General Bragg, who commended "the conduct of [Armstrong] and his gallant command" (Snead 1887, 662). Bragg's observation that the raid proved "what a few resolute men intelligently handled can accomplish" may very well have prompted Gen. Sterling Price to develop the plan that would thoroughly test Armstrong's leadership and his newly formed brigade's readiness.

CONCEPTION OF THE RAID

When the last of Bragg's army left Tupelo, Mississippi, on July 29, 1862, General Price's Army of the West began what amounted to a supporting mission for Bragg's Kentucky invasion. Bragg was depending upon Price to keep General Grant, and to the extent possible, General Rosecrans, from reinforcing the Union forces under Buell in middle Tennessee. Should Rosecrans or Grant vacate north Mississippi to reinforce Buell, Price was to "keep his men well in hand and ready to move northward at a moment's notice" to invade west Tennessee (Castel 1968, 94). By August 4, Bragg declared that "West Tennessee is now open" for General Price to invade, thus he ordered General Van Dorn in Vicksburg to join Price for a consolidated effort.[3]

If Price was to invade west Tennessee, he would require intelligence on the enemy's strength, disposition, and movement. Frank C. Armstrong's successful expedition into Alabama had not only given the young general confidence in his new cavalry brigade, it had convinced his commander, Sterling Price, that the unit was ready for a bolder, more aggressive mission. Thus, Price conceived a plan for Armstrong's brigade to link up with approximately eleven hundred cavalry under the command of Col. William H. "Red" Jackson, for "[an] intended reconnaissance . . . [to] make the circuit of Corinth, striking at whatever points may appear most available" (Price 1887, 687). That Price expected Armstrong to push into west Tennessee seems clear from his discussion with General Van Dorn about the efficacy of the latter joining forces with him and moving "our combined armies

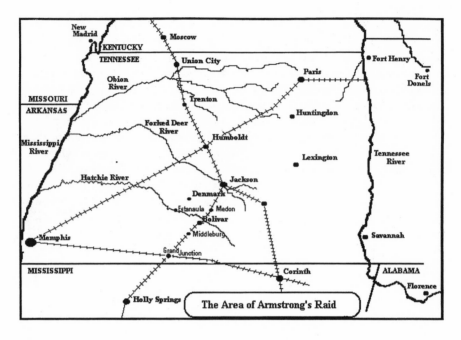

Map 1.1

through Western Tennessee toward Paducah, and thence wherever circumstances may dictate" (Price 1887, 687).

On August 15, 1862, R. R. Hancock, 2nd Tennessee Cavalry in Armstrong's Brigade, records in his diary, "an order was read at dress parade
requiring us to drill on horseback in the morning, foot in the evening, go
on a dress parade once a day, and prepare as fast as possible for a more
vigorous campaign" (Hancock 1887, 207). At (appropriately named) Guntown, Mississippi, Armstrong conducted the final drills in preparation for
his raid into west Tennessee, and two days later pared down his supply
train by ordering his regiments to prepare ten days' rations and to march
with only one wagon for every two companies.

Armstrong's command was joined in Guntown by Col. W. F. Slemons'
2nd Arkansas Cavalry and Col. Wirt Adams' Mississippi Cavalry Battalion,
increasing his strength to almost sixteen hundred. Leaving Guntown at
daybreak on August 22, he marched toward Holly Springs, moving primarily at night to avoid detection by Federal cavalry. Riding into Holly Springs
on August 26 just as the town clock struck 9:00 A.M., Armstrong's unit was
"generally speaking . . . a well mounted and fine looking bunch of men"
(Hancock 1887, 208). In less than half an hour, Armstrong's raiders were
riding north again, where they bivouacked five miles north of town on the
banks of the Coldwater River (Alexander 1962, 32). Here Armstrong linked

up with Col. William H. "Red" Jackson's cavalry, swelling the total force to approximately twenty-seven hundred men. Jackson contributed Colonel McColloch's 2nd Missouri (originally with Armstrong, then detached, now returned), Jackson's own 7th Tennessee, and Col. Richard A. Pinson's 1st Mississippi. Armstrong shared with Jackson his plan to raid northward, "threaten Bolivar [Tenn.], and, if possible, take Jackson and destroy the Mobile and Ohio Railroad" (Armstrong 1887, 688). Resting in camp until 3:00 P.M. on August 27, Armstrong's cavalry column moved out, stretching for miles as it snaked northward toward La Grange, Tennessee. Riding nonstop for almost sixteen miles, Armstrong encamped on the bank of the Wolf River, just four miles outside of La Grange, where he rested until the 28th. Thus began the whirlwind mission that would be known as Armstrong's Raid, but the young general would have to accomplish his mission without the benefit of surprise; for already, word of mouth from pro-Union citizens competed with the telegraph wires to warn the Federal army of Armstrong's approach.

NOTES

1. A careful reading of Edwin H. Fay's letters in *This Infernal War* may lead one to the conclusion that Fay spent as much time trying to get out of the Confederate army as he did trying to function within it. A schoolteacher by vocation, Fay seems to have joined the army as much out of peer pressure as out of any ideological beliefs. Only weeks after his enlistment, the Confederate government granted a service waiver to teachers, and Fay's letters contain many references to his attempts to obtain a discharge in light of the new government policy. Fay was not the only trooper who sought to go home, but while his desire to leave the cavalry did not make him a bad soldier, it certainly made him a distracted one.

2. In his official report, Colonel Harlan goes to great length to explain the tardy march rate of his regiment subsequent to the affair with Armstrong, attributing his slow progress to his men's sore feet. A man of very precise words, as will be demonstrated in chapter 13 of this book, Harlan still appears to take a whining tone in much of his correspondence with higher headquarters.

3. By the fall of 1862, the south was hungry for good news, particularly in the western theater. The people anticipated a victory that would stem the tide of Federal successes at Fort Henry, Fort Donelson, Island Number 10, Shiloh, and Corinth. A joint effort by Price and Van Dorn might provide this victory, and its attending success might, as Edwin H. Fay noted in his letters home, bring about the much anticipated European intervention on the side of the Confederacy.

2

The Movement on Bolivar

Give them cold steel, boys!

—Col. Harvey Hogg

"Four or five thousand horses raise no small amount of dust," declared Edwin H. Fay in describing Armstrong's brigade on the march. And while the numbers may be slightly inflated, even allowing for lead mounts, anyone who has ever ridden in column can surely appreciate Fay's observation that "the dust is oppressive" (Fay 1958, 147). Among those observing Armstrong's dusty column as it left camp on the Wolf River around noon on August 29 were a number of slaves and pro-Union citizens. As Armstrong's command crossed the Memphis and Charleston Railroad at La Grange and rode toward Bolivar, Tennessee, these Federal sympathizers set out to warn the Union army garrisoned there. By the time the Confederates had reached a campsite that night some nine miles from Bolivar, every Federal detachment and outpost for miles had been alerted (Alexander 1962, 34). Col. Marcellus M. Crocker, commander of Federal troops at Bolivar, had received word that some four hundred southern cavalrymen appeared just south of Middleburg (about five miles away) along the Grand Junction Road. This report may well have prompted Crocker to conclude that little more than a Confederate patrol threatened his post; but early the next morning, the Federal Provost Marshal in Bolivar had a local plantation owner by the name of John H. Bills brought into town to identify four slaves arrested that night for attempting to cross Federal lines. When the slaves told their story about being run off from their work detail south of town by Confederate cavalry, Crocker suspected more than an enemy reconnaissance at his doorstep. With some seven thousand Union soldiers available in and around Bolivar, Crocker resolved to determine exactly who and how many enemy cavalry were approaching.

Col. Mortimer Leggett commanded the First Brigade at Bolivar, consisting of his own 78th Indiana Infantry, the 20th Ohio Infantry, the 11th Illinois Cavalry, and a gun section of the 9th Indiana Artillery. Leggett received a reconnaissance-in-force mission from Crocker at 7:00 A.M. (August 30) and immediately set out from Bolivar toward Middleburg. Col. Manning Force, commanding the 20th Ohio, had anticipated such an order, and by the time Leggett linked up with him, Force had already dispatched two companies of the 20th Ohio, under Maj. John Fry, to "guard the lines and feel [for] the enemy" (Leggett 1887, 46). Leggett immediately sent forty-five of his mounted infantry to support Major Fry, and followed shortly thereafter with the remainder of the 20th Ohio and three companies of his own 78th Ohio Infantry. Henry Dwight, a 2nd lieutenant with the 20th Ohio Volunteer Infantry, describes the mounted infantry as follows:

> Colonel Leggett . . . organized a body of mounted men . . .taken from the regiments of our brigade . . . infantry soldiers [who] but for the sake of quick movement they were mounted, mostly on mules. In the camp they were known by the euphonious name of "Jackass Cavalry." A peculiar bugle caused them to rally at Brigade headquarters by day or night. This call was always greeted with derisive laughter by all the rest of the force (Dwight 1980, 33)

Leggett also ordered two companies of the 11th Illinois Cavalry and a two-gun section of the 9th Indiana Artillery to meet him at the picket post along the Grand Junction Road. He kept the remainder of the 78th Ohio on a short string with orders to be ready to march from Bolivar at a moment's notice.

Upon reaching the linkup point on the Grand Junction Road, Leggett discovered that the cavalry and artillery had not yet arrived. Sensing trouble, he left the 20th Ohio and the three companies of the 78th under Colonel Force's command, with instructions to escort the cavalry and the guns forward when they arrived. He rode south to find Major Fry and "to prevent, if possible, an engagement until my main force could come up" (Leggett 1887, 46). About five and one-half miles from Bolivar, on the Van Buren Road, Leggett found the two companies of the 20th Ohio, under Fry, along with the mule cavalry he had dispatched earlier, in a brisk skirmish with considerably more Confederate cavalry that he was expecting. "I immediately discovered that we had been deceived as to the number of the rebels, and [I] sent back for the balance of my command to come forward as rapidly as possible," Leggett reported (Leggett 1887, 46).

Two companies of the 11th Cavalry were the first to join him, probably about 9:00 A.M., but the heavy timber on both sides of the road made mounted men of little use. Still, Leggett had about twelve or fourteen of these men, armed with carbines, dismount and join the 20th Ohio skirmish

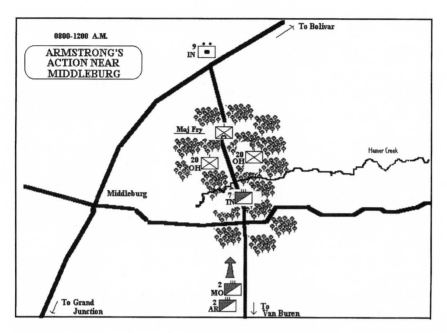

Map 2.1

line. Advancing slowly, the Federal skirmishers pressed the Confederates back some three-fourths of a mile, enabling Leggett to gain a clear view southward from a high piece of terrain. What he saw confirmed his worst fears. Leggett sent a staff rider to Crocker reporting "a force of over 6,000 instead of 300 or 400," and calling for reinforcements. As previously stated, Armstrong had only twenty-seven hundred men in his entire command, and most of those were barely out of camp. But the dry conditions that Edwin H. Fay described must have produced a dust trail that stretched for miles in the direction of Grand Junction. That dust cloud, coupled with the rumors circulating for the past two weeks of a massive Confederate invasion by General Bragg or General Price, led Leggett to overestimate the enemy strength. Leggett now had a decision to make: fight or flight. As he reported to Colonel Crocker after the battle,

> At this time I would have withdrawn my little force from the contest, having less than one man to twenty of the enemy, but the nature of the ground over which I would have been obliged to retreat was such that my force must have been annihilated had I attempted to escape from such overwhelming numbers. I had not men enough to retreat, and consequently had no choice left but to fight until support could reach us" (Leggett 1887, 47)

Leggett's dilemma, albeit with a much smaller force, would mirror that faced by Elias S. Dennis two days hence, when he, too, would meet Frank C. Armstrong in battle.

THE BATTLE NEAR MIDDLEBURG

The Confederate force that Major Fry's advance guard encountered that morning was an element of Colonel W. H. "Red" Jackson's 7th Tennessee Cavalry. Made up largely of men from west Tennessee (Company E was raised from Hardeman County, where Bolivar is the county seat), Jackson's cavalry were among the battle-tested veterans in Armstrong's brigade, and thus a logical choice to ride the point of his column. The 7th Tennessee, followed by McCulloch's 2nd Missouri and Slemons' 2nd Arkansas, would be used that day to fix any isolated Federal resistance and avoid decisive engagement of Armstrong's main body, allowing his force to continue the raid northward. Thus, when the 7th Tennessee encountered Fry's men, who fired upon them from long range and killed some horses (Young 1976, 45), they immediately deployed into a skirmish line. Armstrong quickly rode forward to weigh the situation. If the force opposing him was small enough, and could be overpowered without bringing on a full-scale battle, Armstrong might well decide to fight his way through and continue to Bolivar. Based upon intelligence gathered as late as the 27th, Armstrong believed the Federals were moving forces from Bolivar and Jackson to strengthen the defense of Memphis. He had even suggested in a message to General Price on that same day that the enemy may have evacuated Bolivar entirely. If he still held this belief on the morning of the 30th, it must have been severely tested by the resistance the 7th Tennessee encountered. Still, Armstrong's plans never called for the capture of Bolivar. All along, he had planned to "*threaten* Bolivar, and, if possible, take Jackson and destroy the Mobile and Ohio Railroad" (Armstrong 1887, 688). The only way Armstrong would know for certain about the vulnerability of Bolivar, and consequently the vulnerability of Jackson, was to develop the situation.

Brigadier General Armstrong must have recalled his success at Courtland just a few weeks before, for in a tactic mirroring his flank attack against the 10th Indiana, he ordered McCulloch and Slemons to sweep to the west and turn north in an attempt to envelope the Federal companies defending the Van Buren Road. Ordering the 7th Tennessee to delay southward, he apparently hoped to lure the Federals toward him, exposing them even more to his envelopment. And with the enemy pressing slowly forward, they seemed to be taking the bait. Little damage was done to the 7th Tennessee during the skirmishing along the Van Buren Road. If fact, after hours of exchanging fire with the Federals, the only member of the regiment to even be wounded was Lieutenant W. L. Duckworth, a man who would become colonel of the regiment later in the war (Young 1976, 174).

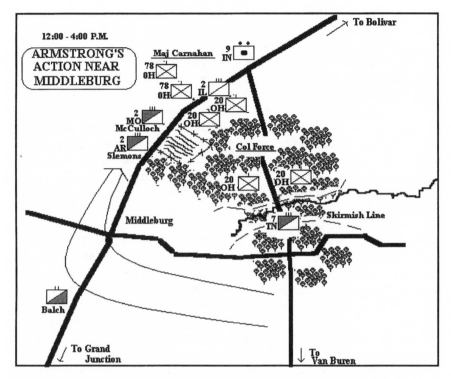

Map 2.2

Economy of Force

By noon, Col. Manning Force had joined Leggett with six companies of the 20th Ohio and two pieces of artillery. Sending the infantry forward to relieve-in-place the infantry and Jackass Cavalry that had been skirmishing for almost three hours, Leggett kept the artillery back at the junction of the Van Buren and Middleburg Roads, as he had, as yet, no adequate infantry support to protect the guns. From his vantage point on high ground, Leggett realized from the dust signature that the Confederates were attempting to flank his position from the west. Henry Dwight writes, "The long lines of grey heaved and trembled and wound off toward the right, like great serpents lashing up the dust in immense clouds as they went" (Dwight 1980, 34).

Leaving Colonel Force in command of the troops on the Van Buren Road, Leggett took the two companies of the 11th Illinois Cavalry, plus his Jackass Cavalry, and rode to the Middleburg Road, where he encountered "the enemy advancing in large numbers" (Leggett 1887, 47). Again he dismounted his cavalry and his mule infantry and used them as a fixing force until he could bring forward reinforcements. After "a desperate struggle of over an hour," two companies of the 20th Ohio, and two companies of the 78th Ohio, under a Captain Chandler, reached Leggett's position, deploying on both sides of the Middleburg Road and joining in the skirmish. Despite Chandler's arrival with help, Leggett realized the critical moment of the fight was upon him. "It was evident," Leggett said, "that the enemy were organizing for the purpose of making a determined effort to break our lines to reach our rear" (Leggett 1887, 47). Sensing that he would soon bear the brunt of the Confederate assault, he sent word for Colonel Force to shift his men from the Van Buren Road to support him on the Middleburg Road. But even with Colonel Force's men on the march, and remnants of the 78th Ohio rushing from Bolivar to support him, he needed help immediately.

While Leggett had been developing the situation along the Van Buren Road earlier that morning, a train from Jackson arrived in Bolivar at 9:00 A.M. bearing seven companies of the 2nd Illinois Cavalry. Unrelated to Armstrong's appearance and the escalating conflict, the 2nd Illinois, commanded by Bloomington, Illinois, lawyer Harvey Hogg, had been ordered to Bolivar several days before to patrol the railroad south of town. Hogg's men had recently completed just such a mission by clearing the railroad north of Jackson of partisan rangers who had been harassing troop and supply movements (Richards 1990, 39). Hogg's men, veterans of Fort Donelson and Shiloh, found themselves barely off the train before they were ordered by Colonel Crocker to reinforce Leggett. Crocker feared that Bolivar was the enemy's objective, thus he did not want to empty the city's defenses to support Leggett, whom he still considered to be conducting a reconnaissance-in-force. Crocker's plan seems to have been for Leggett to delay back to Bolivar where Crocker could fight the Confederate force from entrenchments on the outskirts of the town. Leggett's exaggerated report of six thousand cavalry probably confirmed Crocker's suspicion that he was encountering the advance of a major invasion—perhaps Price's army—thus his decision to fight from the protection of the town.

Sometime around 1:00 P.M. Colonel Hogg arrived at Leggett's position on the Middleburg Road with four companies of his cavalry—precisely as the Confederates were massing to overwhelm Leggett's blocking force. Before he could position Hogg's men, the Confederates charged down the line of the railroad and were repulsed by Captain Chandler's infantry firing from behind the railroad embankment. Twice more the Confederates attempted to sweep down the road, but they were stopped both times. Throwing down the fence rails on the southern end of a broad cottonfield, the Confederates opened fire on the Federal's left flank. Hogg's men and two companies of the 20th Ohio Infantry under Captain Chandler returned fire as the enemy began massing for a charge from the far side of the cottonfield. Colonel Leggett rode up to Colonel Hogg and warned him that if he had any doubts about being able to hold his position, "he had better fall back and not receive their charge" (Leggett 1887, 48).

Col. Harvey Hogg. Photo courtesy of McLean County Historical Society.

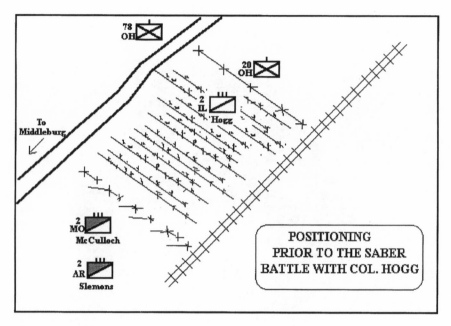

Map 2.3

"Colonel Leggett," Hogg declared, "for God's sake don't order me back."

"Meet them with a charge, Colonel," Leggett replied, "and may Heaven bless you."

Harvey Hogg, a believer in the efficiency of the saber as a primary weapon of cavalry, ordered his men to draw their sabers. According to Leggett, he then ordered his men forward and, leading the charge himself, shouted, "Give them cold steel, boys!"

Battle Drill

C. Y. Ford's unit, Company G, 2nd Missouri Cavalry, was riding at the head of Armstrong's flanking column when it reached the Middleburg Road and turned north. As the unit moved up the road, the Federals opened fire from the railroad embankment paralleling the road. "General Armstrong ordered the bugler to sound the charge," writes Ford, "and we thundered down a dusty lane by platoons, with drawn sabers. Capt. Rock Champion was at the head of the troop, Colonel McCulloch riding by his side, and our sabers glittering in the bright sunshine made an imposing line of battle" (Ford 1922, 290).

This charge was met by Chandler's[1] Federals and repulsed, the charismatic Capt. Rock Champion of the 2nd Missouri being killed instantly in the fight. Upon reforming, McCulloch ordered some of his men to throw down the fence rails in the cottonfield opposite the Federal left, and then gave the following command: "Right-front into line, March!"

The chief of the first platoon would then have commanded, "Forward, March," and continued straight ahead for about thirty paces, where he would order his platoon to "halt" and "dress left." The chiefs of the other platoons would have commanded, "Right Oblique, March," and as each platoon reached its place opposite the line, it would have been ordered "Forward" until its horses reached the croups of the horses on the left, where the platoon would be halted and dressed to the left. Once the regiment was aligned, McCulloch would have commanded, "Front" (Cooke 1862, 190).

Col. Robert "Black Bob" McCulloch ordered his 2nd Missouri to draw sabers and charge the Federal cavalry on the opposite side of the cottonfield. Slemons' 2nd Arkansas followed McCulloch's regiment through the gaps in the fence, but halted just inside the cottonfield. As if playing out a grand drama upon a stage, McCulloch's and Hogg's regiments charged toward each other, with their respective commanders in the lead, while the Federal infantry on one side, and Slemons' cavalry on the opposite side watched what Mortimer Leggett would describe as a "sublimely terrible" spectacle.

While the accuracy of rifled weapons, coupled with the availability of breech-loading carbines, had rendered the saber to a limited role in cavalry operations thus far in the war, the *arme blanche* would have its soliloquy amid the theater of battle near Middleburg that afternoon.[2] Col. Harvey Hogg, his white dress shirt flapping in the breeze, his blue cavalry shell jacket tied to the pommel of his saddle, his saber raised high, rode directly to engage McCulloch. McCulloch was driving his mount toward Hogg, his entire regiment behind, their voices blending in the eerie, high-pitched tone of the rebel yell. Soon the two forces closed upon each other, and the respective commanders, as well as their units, engaged in cutting and slashing one another in a malestrom of dust, random revolver shots, and bellowing animals. Harvey Hogg was prevailing in his fight with McCulloch when one of the latter's men, Tom Turner, rode past and shot Hogg in the side (Hubbard 1911, 33). Within moments his horse took a round in the forehead and collapsed in the fray. Hogg, though wounded, struggled to his feet to continue the fight, his saber in one hand, the reins of his dead horse in the other. He was soon cut down, however, and his body—upon examination after the fight—revealed nine distinct bullet wounds (Richards 1990, 46). Disheartened by the loss of their popular commander, the men of the 2nd Illinois Cavalry appear to have passed completely through the charging Missourians, and it was several minutes before Captain Musser of the Company F could rally them. In the meantime, McCulloch pressed ahead to continue his attack against Companies G and K of the 20th Ohio at the northern end of the field.

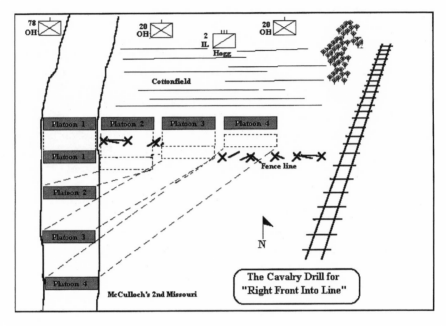

Map 2.4

Slemons, with his command drawn up just inside the cottonfield, witnessed the now leaderless 2nd Illinois emerge from the dust of the 2nd Missouri. When Musser was finally able to rally the Federals, he turned them back toward their own lines in an attempt to cut their way through McCulloch and rejoin the 20th Ohio. Slemons took offense at what he mistakenly interpreted as an affront to his unit's ability—the enemy was turning their backs on him. Furious at such audacity, he drew his saber and rode toward the Illinois cavalry, remembering only moments later to order the rest of the regiment to follow.

"Charge them, damn their American hearts, charge them!" Slemons shouted, and the 2nd Arkansas followed him (Slemons 1862, 1).

Though some of Hogg's command managed to extricate themselves from between two Confederate regiments, many were killed or captured.[3] Leggett began a slow retreat back toward Bolivar, and when McCulloch and Slemons' men attempted to press the withdrawal, the Federal artillery opened up "with shot and shell [causing the Confederates] to break and disperse in great disorder" (Leggett 1887, 48). While the 2nd Missouri appears to have reeled from the sudden artillery fire, Slemons was critical of McCulloch's hesitancy to exploit success. Writing to his wife less than a month later, he claimed that "they [McCulloch's 2nd Missouri] gave way and left men in the field alone" (Slemons 1862, 1). In fairness to the

Missourians, the decision not to pursue the withdrawing Federals, or attempt to turn a retreat into a rout, was, in all probability, not McCulloch's decision to make. Frank C. Armstrong ordered the flanking action and the subsequent attack along the Middleburg Road, and it was ultimately Armstrong who must bear the praise or blame for not carrying the fight into Bolivar.[4] Even though he brought up Balch's Battalion to reinforce McCulloch and Slemons as they were being shelled near the end of the fight, at no point in what turned into a seven and one-half hour struggle did Armstrong ever commit more than a third of his entire command. The occupation of Bolivar, as stated previously, was simply not on the young brigadier's agenda; and regardless of the possibility of exploiting an immediate tactical advantage, Armstrong seems to have been determined not to allow his brigade to become decisively engaged. The grander strategic notion of taking Jackson must have kept Armstrong from the temptation to get his command involved in a prolonged battle over Bolivar. In his report to General Price, Armstrong says,

> Just finished whipping the enemy in front of Bolivar; ran into town. I believe they will leave the country. West Tennessee is almost free of the invaders. All needed is advance of the infantry. They estimate their force at 10,000. I believe they have only about 6,000. . . . There are strong works in the rear of Bolivar, and I did not enter the town as it would only cause them to shell it without giving me any advantage. You will hear of us again in a day or so (Armstrong 1887, 51).

Colonel Leggett reported five killed, eighteen wounded, and sixty-eight missing. Armstrong made no report of losses.

The Federals were not evacuating west Tennessee as Armstrong had predicted, nor was the area anywhere near being "free of the invaders." On the contrary, the Federals were drawing their forces toward Jackson in an effort to protect their supply lines and communication hub, and with any luck, to cut off and isolate Armstrong's cavalry. Armstrong would soon discover a determined Union resistance to his raid, and he would rapidly realize that despite his optimistic reports, no infantry support in the form of an invasion of Price's army was forthcoming.

Whatever the consequences of Armstrong's decision not to become decisively engaged at Bolivar, Colonel Slemons believed that at long last his 2nd Arkansas, armed primarily with shotguns and pistols, and held by some in less esteem than McCulloch's regiment, had performed well under the command of their "long-haired, ugly Arkansas Colonel" (Slemons 1862, 1). But Slemons' celebration of his unit's effectiveness was tempered by sorrow when, from a captured Federal soldier, he learned of the death of an old friend. He and Harvey Hogg had been law students together at Cumberland University before the war; and while Slemons quite naturally mourned Hogg's death, even the rank-and-file Confederate soldiers found the gallant Union colonel's demise a sobering affair. C. Y. Ford wrote, "We all felt some sorrow at seeing so young and brave a soldier fall" (Ford 1922, 290). In his report, Leggett said of Hogg, "A braver and truer man never lifted his arm in defense of his country. He was brave to a fault, and fell while leading one of the most gallant cavalry charges of the present war." And in a final irony not uncharacteristic of this brutal war, Colonel Harvey Hogg's body[5] was recovered from the battlefield by the 2nd Missouri and returned to Illinois under a special pass granted to a Confederate soldier of McCulloch's unit. That soldier was Harvey Hogg's only brother (Evans 1862, 213).

NOTES

1. Henry Dwight had no praise for Capt. Zachariah M. Chandler, indicating that he had "run away with his two companies," leaving two of Dwight's 20th Ohio companies to be captured. "For this feat he was promoted to be Major of the regiment," though Dwight's men "were of the opinion [Chandler] ought to have been drummed out of camp for cowardice" (Dwight 1980, 34).

2. Until now, scholarship about this raid has placed the battle between Armstrong and Leggett in the town of Middleburg. The author, however, through careful mapwork, examination of diaries and firsthand accounts of the fight, and battlefield relic recoveries, has determined the fight to have taken place east of Middleburg along the Van Buren Road, and north of the town along the road leading to Bolivar.

Throughout the course of the war, the railroad depot town of Middleburg was the host of at least four different battles. Its crucial location made it a constant target, and local legend indicates that upon the occasion of the fourth battle at or near the town, a female citizen lost her mind and set a fire that burned the town to the ground.

3. Armstrong sent seventy-one prisoners back to Mississippi immediately after the fight near Middleburg, many of them troopers from the 2nd Illinois Cavalry.

4. According to the reports of Colonel Leggett, and generally confirmed by Henry Dwight's diary, the Federals were "all fagged out" upon their withdrawal to Bolivar that evening. They may well have been vulnerable to a thorough pursuit.

5. The handling of Harvey Hogg's body is one of those poignant stories of the war that seems to epitomize the tragedy of families divided. Colonel Hogg might easily have lost his life prior to the first shot had a plan to kill him materialized in Tennessee. Hogg's wife was visiting relatives in the state when Harvey came to join her and "settle up some matters before the war broke out." News of Hogg's antislavery beliefs preceded him thanks to a "bloody, fiendish, treacherous letter" sent to Tennessee by persons unknown. The postmaster where Mrs. Hogg was visiting alerted Harvey Hogg of the conspiracy to kill him and he managed to avoid the trap (*Pentagraph* 1862, 6).

3

Medon Station and the Camp at Estanaula

Into the beseigers with a yell.

—*Chicago Tribune* (1862)

"Bolivar being strongly fortified and garrisoned, the command moved around it," explained 7th Tennessee cavalryman J. P. Young, "and the next day attacked the detachments guarding the railroad between Bolivar and Medon, skirmished at Toone's Station, destroyed the bridge and one mile of trestle, and captured 40 prisoners" (Young 1976, 45). J. P. Young's explanation of Armstrong's next move in this martial chess game seems closer to Gen. Sterling Price's intent for the raid than did the action of the previous day near Middleburg. At last, the interdiction of the Federal supply line was beginning in earnest. Edwin H. Fay of Balch's Battalion writes that after the Federals retired into Bolivar to hunker down for what they suspected would be a renewed attack the following day, Armstrong's command "struck south six or seven miles turned west and north rested and fed one hour from 10 to 11 and moved on . . . " (Fay 1958, 149). That rest stop, along the banks of Clear Creek some six miles from Bolivar and south of the Hatchie River, would be one of the last chances Armstrong's men would have to refresh themselves; for the next three days would hold only hard riding and bloody fighting, with scarcely time for man or beast to sleep or eat. Because the Hatchie River was unusually low, the Federals stationed at fords and bridges to prevent the enemy from crossing up and down the river from Bolivar created no obstacle to Armstrong. The entire command slipped across the Hatchie River near the mouth of Clover Creek during the early hours of the morning, August 31 (Hancock 1887, 210). By midmorning, the full Confederate force was driving up the Mobile and Ohio Railroad line burning trestles and bridges, "scouting around" (probably a euphemism for foraging), and ambushing trains (Fay 1958, 149).

As the sun rose that morning, the Federals in Bolivar anxiously awaited the onslaught. Gen. Leonard Ross, commander of the entire District of West Tennessee, had arrived on the train from his headquarters in Jackson during the night. Assuming command of the forces in Bolivar—a post he himself had held until a few weeks earlier—Ross conferred with Colonel Crocker and determined that Bolivar could be held against the Confederate force he still believed numbered more than five thousand. In fact, Ross was yet to be convinced that Armstrong's men were not the vanguard for an invasion under General Price or perhaps General Villepugue. Having gathered during the night the equivalent of a division of troops, Ross decided to make a show of force. The long roll sounded through the regiments in Bolivar, and at sunrise, Ross marched almost seven thousand men into line of battle along the Middleburg Road, just a mile out of town ("From Jackson" 1862, 6). They waited for the Confederate attack . . . and waited . . . and waited. When no enemy troops appeared, Ross ordered a patrol to move south and find them. Instead, they returned to report no sign of the Confederates. Ross was not long in determining that he had been bypassed, and that the enemy had a bigger target in mind than Bolivar, so commandeering the first available train, he started north toward Jackson, the new suspected target of Armstrong's force. Ross had effectively robbed troops from the defense of Jackson to meet the enemy in Bolivar, and now he had to call in every detachment he could muster to stop the enemy from reaching the Federal supply depot there. Fearing that the enemy might have already crossed the river and reached the railroad ahead of him, Ross took Company H, 11th Iowa Infantry as an escort. But before leaving Bolivar, he sent a dispatch rider to Estanaula—some fourteen miles down and across the river from Bolivar—to the camp of Col. Elias S. Dennis, in command of a small brigade of two infantry regiments, an independent cavalry company, and a section of artillery. The rider had orders for Dennis to "return at once to Jackson" to assist in the defense of the city (Ross 1887, 44).

If General Ross had known how close he would come to being captured by Armstrong, he might well have chosen to remain in Bolivar. Ross' train had reached Toone Station, located between Bolivar and Medon Station, where Col. Jasper Maltby commanded five companies of the 45th Illinois Infantry. Ross warned Maltby that the Confederates were approaching, and taking Maltby's adjutant, Captain William Frolock along, he had the engineer take them north to warn other elements of the 45th guarding Treadger and Medon Stations (Richards 1990, 55). Ross' departure from Toone Station was delayed, however, as an advance element of the Confederate cavalry (or perhaps a local citizen of southern sympathies as the *Chicago Tribune* suggested when it referred to this as "the work of some underhanded abettor of treason") had during the night sabotaged the water tower right under the noses of the guards ("From Jackson" 1862, 6). Realizing the enemy was likely upon them, Colonel Maltby immediately set up barricades of cotton bales and prepared to defend Toone Station. Luther Cowan of the 45th Illinois at Toone Station wrote, "It is the time for the greatest anxiety for us. We are well fortified with cotton bales, two hundred and ten fighting men. We can hold the place against any number of infantry that can be sent against us, but if they get us with artillery, they will surely clean us out" (Cowan 1862, 1). Ross' train, having finally been watered and fueled, had scarcely left the station when the telegraph wire south to Bolivar went dead (Richards 1990, 55).

BYPASS AND MAINTAIN MOMENTUM

Upon crossing the Hatchie River in the hours just before daylight, Brig. Gen. Frank C. Armstrong divided his command. His scouts having informed him of a Federal force guarding the crossing at Estanaula, Armstrong sent the 1st Mississippi Cavalry under Colonel Pinson, along with Wirt Adams' Battalion, to cut off the Federals there and secure the crossing. Armstrong seems to have been taking steps to guarantee a safe route of egress from west Tennessee once he had accomplished his mission.[1] With the remainder of his command he pushed north along the Mobile and Ohio Railroad, where he found the Federal garrison at Toone Station drawn up for battle behind cotton bales surrounding the depot. Despite the overwhelming force that Armstrong presented before the two hundred plus defenders at Toone Station, the Confederate leader neither attacked nor demanded their surrender. Instead, he was satisfied to sever the telegraph lines both above and below the station, and march his entire command, in parade formation, past the bewildered Federals. That they had been spared a bloody fight and almost certain capture confounded them; indeed, as Col. Jasper Maltby watched in amazement at the Confederates bypassing his beleaguered garrison, he believed he was witnessing some kind of "rebel trick" (Richards 1990, 56).

Next stop for Armstrong was Treadger Station (referred to by the Federals as Teague's), about four miles north of Toone. Here, as was the case all along the Mobile and Ohio Railroad that supplied the Federal army, were isolated detachments of troops given the mission of keeping small guerrilla bands and partisan ranger outfits from harassing the trains and interdicting communications. At Treadger Station, Company C, 45th Illinois under Captain Rouse, was detailed for defense, but they were ill-matched to encounter the kind of force Frank C. Armstrong was leading toward Jackson. Balch's Battalion, lead element of the raiders, came charging up the railroad bed, but they did not gain complete surprise against Company C.

The train steaming north just seconds ahead of Balch's Battalion contained Gen. Leonard Ross and Adjutant Frohock. Not bothering to stop for fear of capture, Frohock warned the defenders at Treadger Station by tossing off a piece of cordwood with a note detailing the Confederate force approaching from Bolivar (Maltby 1862, 1). Scarcely had the note been read when Captain Rouse saw the southerners galloping toward him. Ordering his company to cover behind some nearby railroad crossties stacked against a fence with a ditch in front, he determined to put up a fight. When Balch's Battalion charged, Ross held fire until the Confederates were within one hundred yards, then "poured into them a volley which checked them" and forced them to deploy (Maltby 1862, 1). The September 9 *Chicago Tribune* indicates that Company C "fought for one hour before [the] little band was overpowered. Spartans, everyone of them, or *Illinoisians*, which means the same" ("From Jackson" 1862, 6). Armstrong never committed more than Balch's Battalion to the skirmish at Treadger, surrounding and capturing Rouse's men. A short distance north, near a trestle, a Sergeant Williams of Rouse's company and five men did manage to extend the resistance by gaining an abandoned log cabin as the Confederates approached. From here they distinguished themselves by holding off Balch's men for about three hours before surrendering. Game fight though they offered, Sergeant Williams did not prevent Balch's Battalion from immediately burning the trestle, the woodyard, and two railroad cars loaded with cotton; and it is likely that the Confederates were not particularly concerned about a half-dozen Federals held up in a cabin.

Meanwhile, Col. Jasper Maltby,[2] having been bypassed at Toone Station, busied himself by sending out couriers to keep an eye on the enemy and to determine the status of the remainder of his regiment spread along the railroad back toward Medon. Two of these couriers, a Lieutenant Adais and a Sergeant Arnett, disguised themselves as citizens and managed to ride some distance with Armstrong's scouts, from whom they gleaned valuable information.

From Treadger Station, Armstrong's men continued north toward Medon Station, moving directly up the rail line toward Jackson. Thus far, Armstrong was having his way—busily cutting telegraph communications and destroying the track as he went. He had successfully slipped past the Federals at Bolivar, determined the weakness of the enemy garrisons at Toone and Treadger, and he must, by now, have been assessing his chances of riding into Jackson and laying waste to the heart of the Federal supply depot. But then an incident occurred that might, if heeded, have offered Armstrong a taste of what lay ahead. Edwin H. Fay, riding with Balch's Battalion, encountered a train coming south from Medon. He writes, "Heard a train coming ambushed it and if the goose in command had only torn up the track behind would have burned it but he only fired on it as it stopped *to land reinforcements* [author's italics] and a great many jumped back and the train ran back" [toward Medon] (Fay 1958, 149). Edwin Fay of Balch's Battalion offers the only account of this incident, but what may appear as merely a missed opportunity at a small engagement, offers insight into a fundamental truth about Armstrong's Raid. The railroad, left undisturbed north of the Federal detachments he was encountering, would become the lifeline of the enemy. Just as Harvey Hogg's 2nd Illinois arrived by rail just in time to aid Colonel Leggett at Bolivar, forces were already in motion to support Armstrong's next target—Medon Station. And although the Federals that Edwin H. Fay encountered chose to retreat and offer no fight, the very fact that Federal troops could be rushed by rail into the face of Armstrong's command, raises an interesting question. Why, upon encountering yet another reinforcement by rail, did Armstrong not dispatch one of his regiments to slip past the defenders he knew to be at Medon, and destroy the railroad in spots between Medon and Jackson? A regiment of his cavalry had the advantage in mobility, being easily able to outmaneuver and outdistance any infantry units sent to stop them. Outside of the force he had met and defeated at Bolivar, no enemy cavalry anywhere close to his strength appeared present to oppose such a move. As demonstrated by his willingness to dispatch Pinson and Wirt Adams to Estanaula, Armstrong had no aversion to splitting his command. Such an action would have prevented any further reinforcement, allowing him to continue gobbling up company-sized detachments stationed along the track. But Armstrong executed no such plan, continuing to Medon with his command intact, less Pinson and Adams.

AN ON-ORDER MOVE TO REINFORCE

The Hatchie River bottoms offer one the hottest, most humid, and squalid places an army could camp in the month of August. The days are sultry, as are the nights, and the moist air makes a man's skin feel sticky even in the early hours of the morning. The bottoms are host to all manner of insects, thick undergrowth, snakes, and varmints. In the midst of these bottoms lay an important crossing point of the Hatchie River—*Estanaula*, a Cherokee word that means "here we cross." Estanaula was well known among the people of west Tennessee, for it had been a major fording and ferry site for almost fifty years. Cotton planters would harvest their crops and bring them by wagon to Estanaula where they would load them on flatboats and send them down the Hatchie to the Mississippi, then on to Memphis for sale. Boasting a hotel, a cotton warehouse, a mill, and a small street of stores, Estanaula had been a major center in the commerce of the 1830s and 1840s. But with the coming of the railroad, the planters found a new way to ship their cotton, and Estanuala, like many such river villages, simply dried up. In August 1862, only the shell of the old hotel remained, and perhaps two or three small buildings. Across the Hatchie, on the southern side, extended a long, narrow embankment, built by slave labor decades earlier, that supported the road across the bottomland up to higher ground and on toward Whiteville (Durbin 1992, 1).

For the last two weeks of August 1862, Estanaula was home to the 20th and 30th Illinois Infantry, a handful of cavalry, and a two-gun section of six-pounder artillery. Col. Elias S. Dennis, a former Kansas marshal during the wild and wooly days of the 1850s, was the commander of the light brigade stationed to guard this critical crossing site. He had been there with the two infantry regiments since August 15, being joined sometime later by the artillery and the cavalry. According to Alan Morgan Geer, 20th Illinois Infantry, prior to marching for the Hatchie River, his regiment manifested "a great deal of discontentment . . . caused by long inaction and contempt-ible carelessness on the part of the petty officers" (Geer 1977, 47). He indicated that several men had deserted. For now, at least, these two veteran regiments would have a mission that involved the entire regiment and that got them out of the cycle of being fragmented by company to patrol the railroad—tedious duty for a regiment that had fought at Fort Donelson and under General McClernand at Shiloh (Reece 1900, 182). The 30th Illinois, though having seen somewhat less combat, had fought at Belmont, Mis-souri.

Upon arriving on the Hatchie, Dennis placed a sentinel at the main ford (Estanaula Landing), as well as at two minor fords—one downriver and the other a few miles upriver toward Steam Mill Ferry. He camped his infantry regiments in the timber about a mile from Estanaula. Within two days of arrival Dennis had evaluated the terrain himself, and he realized that he would need cavalry to effectively patrol the stretch of river he had been assigned. But the unit sent to him by the Federal high command, the 4th Ohio Independent Cavalry, under command of thirty-five-year-old Capt. John S. Foster, brought considerably less skill and experience than Dennis required. Organized in Georgetown, Ohio, in July 1861, with each man furnishing his own horse and equipment, the 4th Ohio Independent Cav-alry had been assigned to Missouri, where the unit served first at St. Louis and then at subsequent locations, as General Henry Halleck's escort (*Sol-diers* 1883, 703). Captain Foster had been the postmaster in Brown County, Ohio, prior to the war, and outside of a minor role in a small battle at Silver Creek, Missouri, his 4th Ohio presented itself at Estanaula as a garrison company lifted from the lap of luxury (escort duty) and dropped into the Hatchie bottoms.

In correspondence with General McClernand in Jackson during mid-Au-gust, Dennis indicated that Foster's men were "wholly unacquainted" with the "roads, paths, and country" around Estanaula (Richards 1990, 29). Tasked with feeling his way around the myriad of trails and cowpaths leading through the bottoms, Dennis discovered that even a cavalry unit was ineffective if it spent a majority of its time lost. So Dennis asked McClernand to send him a Captain Curtis who reputedly knew the terrain

Col. Elias S. Dennis. Photo courtesy of the U.S. Army Military History Institute.

and road system in that section of the Hatchie bottoms. When the Federal high command did not respond, Dennis, ever the resourceful commander, determined to remedy his lack of geographical familiarity by having his own map drawn up. Sending an artillery officer, Lieut. Emil Steger, to accompany Foster on his patrols, Dennis eventually received from Steger a rough map of the area he was assigned to guard. That map survives today, though some 130 years later it is still a source of controversy.[3]

An additional forty-three cavalrymen arrived at Estanaula around August 23, as Company H, 12th Illinois Cavalry under the command of Capt. Franklin Gilbert joined Dennis. These men, together with Foster's, used Lieutenant Steger's map to patrol the Hatchie River bottoms during the last two weeks of August. While on one of these patrols, the cavalry discovered that the Hatchie, normally a deep, swift river, was unusually low—so low as to allow any number of fording points where Confederate cavalry might take advantage. One particular crossing that Dennis called to General McClernand's attention was near the mouth of Clover Creek—the precise fording spot that Armstrong would use after fighting at Middleburg and skirting Bolivar (Richards 1990, 32).

In addition to his own thorough area reconnaissance, Dennis had access to special intelligence on the movement of Confederate forces. A Unionist citizen[4] of the vicinity—a man Dennis was careful never to name in his correspondence, lest it be captured and the man suffer reprisals—gleaned word-of-mouth information from runaway slaves and other Unionist farmers. Thus, by August 29, while Armstrong paused at La Grange, Tennessee, Col. Elias S. Dennis at Estanaula seems to have had more accurate intelligence about the size of Armstrong's approaching force than either the defenders of Bolivar or his commanding officers in Jackson.

But visitors to the Union camp at Estanaula were not the exclusive privilege of the brigade commander. Sergeant Ira Blanchard, Company H, 20th Illinois, offers not only an insight into the openness of the Federal camp, but also a revealing glimpse into a typical Union soldier's view of the Negro. Blanchard's comments, like those of numerous Federal soldiers documented during the war, call into question the often repeated mantra that Union soldiers held the Negro in high regard and thus fought the War Between the States to free slaves. The very night the 20th Illinois arrived at Estanaula, after a two-day march from Jackson, Blanchard writes, "About 12 o'clock I was awakened by Johnny Rurdon, a little Englishman of our Company shaking me and saying, "Blanch, wake up; see what a nice nigger I've brought you." Johnny had been out on some of the neighboring plantations—I requested Johnny to leave me alone; let the darkey lie down until morning and I'd see what the animal looked like" (Blanchard 1992, 63). Rurdon had "jerked" the Negro from a local slave owner, and Blanchard "put him at work taking care of my gun, knapsack, canteen and haversack, and made him quite useful for about two weeks, but when the first fighting began Mr. Nigger, traps and all, were gone" (Blanchard 1992, 63).

Over the next two weeks the Illinois soldiers "plundered the neighboring plantations" Blanchard notes, naming off all manner of livestock, fruit, and personal property liberated from its owners. At one point his unit even terrorized one of the camp Negroes to the point of madness in what appears to be a purely sadistic act (Blanchard 1992, 63).[5]

The frequent effort of runaway slaves to join the Federals in their camps, was a problem common to many such outposts as Dennis commanded. And with his small brigade already on a heightened alert in anticipation of the Confederate invasion General Grant and the other ranking Union officers were expecting, a confrontation like the one described by G. B. McDonald of the 30th Illinois was bound to happen.

> We had quite a scare one night, some darkeys were trying to cross the river and come into our camp. The pickets fired on them and broke a horse's leg, and he got down in the water and made such a noise, the pickets thought the whole rebel army was coming and the pickets kept up the firing for awhile. The drum major was ordered to beat the long roll. He got out in his shirt tail and it being a still night, it would have almost raised the dead to hear that drum through the beech trees. The boys were soon in line, some dressed, some half-dressed and some not dressed at all, but all had their fighting traps on ready to lick any number of Johnnies. . . . This is what we call a false alarm (McDonald 1916, 27).

Using his covert sources of intelligence, Elias S. Dennis knew Armstrong's force to be approximately two thousand strong and moving north from La Grange; thus, he was not surprised when General Ross' courier arrived from Bolivar at three o'clock on Sunday morning, the 31st, with orders to destroy "such stores and baggage as he was unable to carry," and march for Jackson. Dennis wasted no time in preparing for the move, ordering supplies to be burned or tossed into the river—a particularly unfortunate waste as the regiments' quartermaster teams had only two days before returned with wagons fully loaded with provisions. G. B. McDonald records that among the supplies Dennis ordered destroyed, some were more difficult to part with than others.

> We hurriedly packed our knapsacks and loaded the wagons with camp equipage. The two barrels of whiskey [brought by the Friday resupply] was cumbersome for troops on a forced march. The heads were knocked in and the barrels upset and the whiskey went on the ground. The boys could not stand to see such a waste as that, and they got busy dipping it up in their hands and drinking it, and went on their way rejoicing (McDonald 1916, 28).

Exactly how much rejoicing was actually occurring probably depended upon how close a soldier was to the spilling alcohol; indeed, the brigade was supposed to have risen leisurely that morning and to muster for pay at 10:00 A.M. Instead, Dennis' command was marching from Estanaula at sunrise (Ichabod 1862, 1). They continued for approximately ten miles, arriving in the village of Denmark at 1:00 P.M., still some twelve miles short of Jackson. "The day was close and sultry, the dust intolerable, water scarce, and our progress necessarily slow and laborious" (Ichabod 1862, 1). That afternoon, after a rest halt, the lead of Dennis' column had moved five miles northeast of Denmark when they encountered a courier from Jackson. The courier bore a change of mission from Col. Michael K. Lawler, second in command of forces in Jackson under General Ross. Instead of reinforcing Jackson—the suspected target of Armstrong's raid—Dennis' force was to march for Medon and become the hammer that would slam down on Armstrong's rear and "intercept the enemy near that point" (Lawler 1887, 50). G. B. McDonald in his history of the 30th Illinois Infantry indicates the change of mission came around noon and was received while in Denmark. While the 30th may have received its order in Denmark, as it was the trail regiment in the order of march, it was most likely midafternoon when the courier intercepted Dennis.[6] Since the change of mission was a direct result of Armstrong's impending attack on Medon Station, it is unlikely that either Ross or Lawler would have changed Dennis' destination until they were certain of Armstrong's intent. Should Armstrong have bypassed Medon and gone directly for Jackson, altering Dennis' course would have made no sense. Ross and Lawler could only have been certain once Armstrong actually attacked Medon, and that was not until 2:00 or 3:00 P.M. at the earliest. Thus, it is unlikely that Dennis received the order at noon as McDonald indicates. Lawler says in his report that "Colonel Dennis countermarched his command, arriving in the vicinity of Denmark that night" (Lawler 1887, 50). Dennis' men camped in and around the Presbyterian church, where they ate hardtack, rested their aching feet after a daylong forced march, longed for a drink of the whiskey that had soaked the soil at Estanaula, and wondered what tomorrow would bring.

REINFORCEMENT BY RAIL

General Ross, his train having safely returned him to Jackson on Sunday morning the 31st, continued orchestrating the defense against Armstrong's cavalry. He sent the train south again just before noon, with the Iowa Cavalry aboard, to assist in interdicting the enemy's progress up the Mobile and Ohio Railroad. The train passed through Medon, where they were joined by Captain Palmer and Company A of the 45th Illinois—a unit sent to find out what had happened to Captain Rouse's garrison at Treadger Station. Already reports were filtering into Medon of Confederate cavalry burning nearby trestles; and traveling no more than two miles south of the village, the Federals encounted Armstrong's lead element in just such a venture. Dismounting and moving forward to engage the enemy, Palmer's Illinois men, along with the Iowans, ran squarely into an ambush. As they retreated toward the train, they found the engine steaming rapidly north *without them*, leaving the two companies to fight a slow, deliberate, delaying action for some two miles back into the village of Medon (Richards 1990, 59).

Colonel C. R. Barteau's 2nd Tennessee Cavalry was the lead unit in Armstrong's march to Medon, and having driven the two Federal companies back into town, the 2nd Tennessee dodged enemy snipers posted among the houses on the edge of town and skirted to the northeast. From that direction, at about 3:00 P.M., the 2nd Tennessee, now under command of Maj. George Morton (Barteau having taken ill and returned to Mississippi) attempted a mounted charge at the depot hastily fortified by cotton bales. The four companies of the 45th Illinois Infantry stationed in the makeshift fort were now under command of Adjutant Frolock, the officer who had accompanied Ross from Bolivar and remained in Medon (Ross 1887, 44). Frolock took command after Captain Palmer was wounded during the withdrawal into town, but under his leadership the defenders of Medon Station successfully forced the 2nd Tennessee to fall back. Morton's men dismounted and, in house-to-house fighting, captured a number of snipers and pressed toward the depot. First Lieut. Pleas A. Smith took charge of the regiment's sharpshooters and kept up a steady fire as the 7th Tennessee and the 1st Mississippi closed upon the town from the south.

To support the 2nd Tennessee, Colonel Jackson ordered two companies of the 7th Tennessee to dismount and charge the depot, which rested on a slightly raised platform. But from their cotton bale fort, enough of the 145 Federals massed their fire and stopped Jackson's men with heavy losses. John Milton Hubbard of Company E, 7th Tennessee, rightly observed that "*without artillery* we found it impossible to dislodge them, so well were they protected in and about the depot with cotton bales and other material" (Hubbard 1911, 33). Hubbard expressed an opinion apparently shared by many of his fellow troopers. "Nothing was accomplished by the attack and several Confederates were either killed or wounded" (Hubbard 1911, 33). "Several" was an understatement, as the 7th Tennessee paid dearly for its assault on Adjutant Frolock's Union depot defenders. A review of the company rosters in J. P. Young's *Seventh Tennessee Cavalry* reveals an appalling number of men killed or wounded at Medon Station, particularly the rolls of Company E, the unit designated to charge on foot past an old brick church. Where the daylong skirmish at Middleburg had left the regiment virtually unscathed, their considerably shorter engagement at Medon had blistered the boys from west Tennessee.

As soon as telegraph reports reached Jackson in mid-afternoon of a Confederate force attacking Medon, General Ross sent the 7th Missouri Infantry (730 strong), under the command of Maj. W. S. Oliver, on the first train south. Ross began orchestrating what he believed would be the destruction of Armstrong's force, as he ordered "Colonel Dennis, who was moving toward this place [Jackson] to change his direction toward Medon, attack the enemy in the rear, and if possible cut them to pieces and capture them" (Ross 1887, 44). Not only did Ross realize the garrison at Medon was all that stood between Armstrong and the city of Jackson, but he also knew that the longer he engaged Armstrong at Medon, the more time he bought Colonel Dennis to arrive in support. While the train bearing reinforcements rushed south, Ross ordered the garrison troopers of Jackson to barricade the streets with cotton bales and prepare to defend the city should the Confederates bypass Medon and continue north. *Chicago Tribune* correspondent, T. B. Robb, reflected the mood in Jackson. "Saturday night [August 30], Sunday [31], and Monday [Sept. 1] we were in hourly expectation of being attacked, and made all possible preparation to repel them. Our force here is small on account of our having to send so many of our regiments to guard the railroads and reinforce two small commands at Medon and Toombs [Toone] stations. We have great confidence in Gen. Ross, and believe that he has got the 'bars all put up'" (Robb 1862, 6).

About 5:00 P.M. that afternoon, the relief train carrying the 7th Missouri stopped north of Medon. That their arrival had not been detected by the Confederate scouts must have puzzled Major Oliver, the commander. Perhaps Oliver feared an ambush; perhaps he feared the train cruising unmolested into the middle of the enemy lines and having his men pinned onboard with enemy fire. Whatever his reason, he rapidly unloaded his regiment, dressed them in line of battle, and with fixed bayonets began moving toward the gunfire coming from the depot. Upon seeing their comrades in their makeshift fort on the railroad platform, Oliver's men "went into the besiegers with a yell" ("From Jackson" 1862, 6)

AVOIDING DECISIVE ENGAGEMENT

Frank Montgomery, commander of the 1st Mississippi Cavalry, was first to see the Federal reinforcements arriving. Having been ordered by Colonel Jackson to take five companies of his regiment and conduct a mounted charge down Main Street against the Federals occupying the depot, Montgomery balked. Such a charge would have exposed his men to enemy rifle fire for "at least two hundred yards, without shelter and unable to fire a shot [in return]" (Montgomery 1901, 85). Whether the notion of the charge was original to Colonel "Red" Jackson[7], or simply one of Armstrong's orders being relayed by Jackson, Montgomery, having seen what happened to the 7th Tennessee, was determined to find a more survivable plan for the assault. Leaving his command behind, Montgomery reconnoitered a covered and concealed route around the west side of town, using houses to screen his movement, that would bring his men within seventy-five yards of the depot—a considerably superior distance for mounting a charge. But while planning his approach to the depot, Montgomery "observed several hundred men approaching it [the depot] from the direction of Jackson, my first thought being they were a part of our force about to attack from that direction, but I was soon undeceived, for before I could get back to the line the cheers of the force in the depot, as well as those advancing, gave notice of reinforcements, which compelled us to retire" (Montgomery 1901, 86).

As darkness approached, Frank C. Armstrong realized he had allowed the 7th Missouri to fight its way to the relief of Frolock's garrison at the Medon Station depot. Now, reinforced to almost nine hundred strong, the Federals presented a formidable obstacle—a force to be reckoned with in his further strategic decisions about the raid. How had a loaded train, at least a dozen cars in length, steamed unseen to within a mile of the town his force was supposedly surrounding? How could an entire regiment dismount, form a line of battle, and advance into town before anyone saw them? What can only be described as ineffective reconnaissance now left Armstrong with an identical dilemma to the one presented by Colonel Leggett's defense of Bolivar. Should he concentrate his forces, accept decisive engagement, and renew the assault the following morning? To capture or defeat a regiment-plus, and destroy the depot and the track around Medon, would certainly have been a major tactical accomplishment. But the beating the 7th Tennessee took that afternoon proved it would have been costly, and what may have been even more significant in Armstrong's mind, it would have tied up his forces for at least half a day, perhaps longer. Such a fight would have allowed the enemy longer to mobilize its defenses in Jackson—a target Armstrong must have yet hoped to achieve during the raid.

That night the Confederates drew off from Medon and camped on the Casey Savage farm, just east of town. William Witherspoon, a private in the battered 7th Tennessee Cavalry, wrote, "We were ordered not to make any big fires, we gathered the brush and started our fires, not that it was cold, but the corn in the field was getting hard . . . and we wanted to make embers and ashes to roast the corn. Our horses fared well [always the true cavalryman's first concern] and we did not grumble, like philosophers it was what would happen sometimes in a soldier's life" (Witherspoon 1956, 86).

Many men in Armstrong's command went to sleep the night of August 31, 1862, figuring they were headed for home the next day. When Colonel Pinson's and Wirt Adams' regiments rejoined the main body that night with word that the Estanaula crossing was clear, the troopers must have been even more convinced they were returning to Mississippi. While this anticipation of return could be overlooked as wishful thinking among the line troopers—who were constantly circulating rumors of returning to garrison—the words of Colonel Frank Montgomery, commander of the 1st Mississippi Cavalry, indicate that even the officers believed they had "accomplished all we could by our raid. . . . No one expected any further fighting, and all anticipated a quiet though fatiguing march to camp" (Montgomery 1901, 86). They could not and did not anticpate the "terrible Monday" that would follow (Fay 1958, 150).

NOTES

1. A critical axiom of cavalry raids declares "it is always easier to get in [behind enemy lines] than to get out," and the truth of this statement shall be validated throughout all three raids.

2. Researcher and friend Charles Richards has discovered a very telling quote about Maltby's personality and sense of self-worth that originated from one of his men. "Colonel Maltby," the soldier says, "wouldn't fart unless there was someone there to smell it."

3. The author learned in 1993 that Elias S. Dennis' map of Estanaula, known to exist from records and reports, and long sought by the author and other researchers, had come into the hands of Madison County (Tennessee) Historian, Harbert Alexander. The map had been found in the possession of two individuals apprehended by Federal authorities for using a metal detector on the Shiloh National Military Park—an act that is anathema to conscientious relic hunters and historians. According to Alexander, the men had given up the map to authorities in hopes of helping legitimate researchers, and quite probably, to mitigate against their sentencing. The relic hunters received jail terms and fines, and the map was passed on to Harbert Alexander.

The author has since learned that another historian had located the map as early as 1992, and upon sharing a copy of Dennis' map with a magazine publisher (who shall remain nameless) located in the same geographical area as the Shiloh felons, the historian had received neither the map returned, nor a published article based upon the map. How did the criminals apprehended at Shiloh get the map?

The area of Dennis' camp is currently being registered as an archeological site, and based upon careful relic recoveries already conducted, young Lieutenant Steger did a remarkably accurate job of recreating the terrain around Dennis' Estanaula camp.

4. Local tradition in and around Denmark, Tennessee, identifies this Unionist citizen as Henry Duncan.

5. Ira Blanchard relates an incident in which a young Negro staying among the Federals began playing with a weapon—something strictly forbidden—and accidently shot another Negro, severely wounding him in the face. The Union soldiers tied the man to a tree and told him "he had better make his peace with God" for he was to be shot at noon. For more than an hour the Negro begged and pleaded with his captors, "his eyes protrud[ing] from their sockets as the time of execution drew nigh" (Blanchard 1992, 64). Blanchard says he "never looked upon a picture of such utter despair," and when he and the other Federals finished toying with the man, they let him go, the Negro man disappearing quickly into the wilderness. Sadly, such were the pastimes of the army of liberation.

6. Reports disagree, however, and there may have been *two* different couriers reaching Dennis that afternoon. "Ichabod," the anonymous reporter of Britton's

Lane for the *Carlyle Weekly Reveille*, indicates that a courier arrived ordering the brigade back to Estanaula, only to be countermanded by a second courier changing the mission to Medon. No other eyewitnesses indicate more than a single courier, however, given the uncertainty of the developing situation with Armstrong, General Ross in Jackson may well have issued an order only to change his mind.

7. William H. "Red" Jackson was the only West Point officer (Class of 1856) in Armstrong's command. Twenty-seven years of age during the raid, Jackson came from a prominent west Tennessee family. Serving with the U.S. Third Cavalry, Jackson was fighting Apaches when the war began, and resigned his commission in May 1861 to join the Confederacy. Fellow West Pointer, Thomas Claiborne, who served with Jackson prior to the war, writes, "He knew how to get the best out of his troopers in a gentle way and yet displayed, in lofty manner, his concept of official bearing. He loved to lead in attack, and counted success as certain. . . . I know he was a good officer" (Claiborne 1904, 33).

4

The Battle of Britton's Lane

New earth everywhere. . .

—Miss Murchison

Despite the beating the 7th Tennessee took the previous evening at Medon Station, indeed, perhaps *because* of it, Pvt. John M. Hubbard seems to have been spoiling for a fight on the morning of September 1. When his unit, along with the remainder of Armstrong's force, began to move at sunrise, Hubbard indicates that Armstrong passed up a good chance to whip the Federals. Upon leaving the Casey Savage farm, the Federals "presented a bold front . . . when we passed west of the railroad. Here was a fine chance for a fight of which we did not avail ourselves, though the enemy were in an open field. With our force we could have driven them to shelter or effected their capture" (Hubbard 1911, 34). While Armstrong could have chosen to renew the fight that morning at Medon, his ability to capture the depot is questionable. Driving the Federals to shelter would simply have reproduced the stalemate of the previous afternoon.

Even if Armstrong had eventually prevailed against the more robust Federal force, the time involved in prosecuting such a victory would have surely enhanced the opportunity for the gathering Federal detachments to tighten the noose around his raiding party. Defending along the railroad line gave the Federal commanders not only the advantage of rapid reinforcement, but also the ability to immediately telegraph Armstrong's direction of movement and troop strength to Jackson. Thus, as the Confederates rode west from Medon, the telegraph wires to Jackson, and subsequently in every cardinal direction, were immediately humming with fast, relatively accurate word of Armstrong's route of march.

Lieut. Col. Frank Montgomery, 1st Mississippi Cavalry, says that "the whole command was worn out, and decidedly hungry" (Montgomery 1901, 86). His is not the only reference to Armstrong's force as being saddle-weary and exhausted. William Witherspoon, in one of the more stinging barbs—directed perhaps at Colonel W. H. "Red" Jackson, the only West Point officer on the raid, though more likely targeted at the regular army approach of Frank C. Armstrong—wrote that under West Point tactics "we marched all day without rations for the men or provender for the horses. At a time, 1862, when the country was full of both. . . . Our supper, exclusively a parched corn diet, breakfast ditto" (Witherspoon 1956, 87).

Perhaps because of the casualties they had received the previous day, the men of 7th Tennessee—though they were more familiar with the terrain— were not at the head of Armstrong's march column. Instead, McCulloch's 2nd Missouri lead, followed by Balch's Battalion, Pinson's 1st Mississippi Cavalry, Jackson's 7th Tennessee, Barteau's 2nd Tennessee (under Morton), Slemons' 2nd Arkansas, and Wirt Adams' Cavalry. Company D, 2nd Tennessee, along with a detachment of the 7th Tennessee, remained in the vicinity of Medon to act as a rear guard. They watched in fascination as Major Oliver, in command of the defenders of the Medon depot, marched his men after them, trying in vain to draw Armstrong into a battle. But infantry chasing cavalry rarely succeed, and a disappointed Oliver had to return to his makeshift fortifications in Medon. In fact, Armstrong may have sensed that he was being lured into a fight designed to delay him, or fix him in place, while reinforcements arrived to cut him off. Or, he may simply have determined that taking Medon wasn't worth the cost. Most likely, he sought, like water, to flow around the rock. If he could reach Jackson without becoming decisively engaged, raid the depot, burn the Union's supplies, and destroy the railroad and communication center, he would be successful beyond even his own expectations. So it is likely that Armstrong intended to sweep west to Denmark, and from that point, based upon Federal resistance, either strike Jackson from the west, or move to Brownsville, or attempt to penetrate even further north into west Tennessee. Some researchers have argued that Armstrong entertained none of those options. They insist that Armstrong was going home. They argue that the raid was over, the Federal trap was closing upon him, and Armstrong knew it. But Frank C. Armstrong's subsequent actions on the morning of September 1 are inconsistent with such a theory.

If the telegraph notification from Medon that Armstrong was riding west had not been enough to alert the Federals, the rising dust trail that had haunted his column from the start of the raid certainly revealed his intentions. With still no rain to relieve the choking dust, the Confederates pulled scarfs over their mouths, ducked their heads, and rode in column; but one of the riders was preoccupied with death that morning. Lieut. Col. Frank Montgomery tells the story.

While marching along it so happened I was riding by the side of Captain Beall, and I observed he was unusually quiet. He was always the life of the camp, a genial, jovial gentleman. At last he told me he was impressed by a presentiment he would be killed before we got back to Mississippi. I laughed at him and told him his presentiment would come to nothing, and that he himself would laugh at it on the morrow, that there would be no more fighting on this raid" (Montgomery 1901, 86).

While the two men were talking, gunfire erupted at the front of the column, and the 1st Mississippi was ordered forward at the gallop.

A MEETING ENGAGEMENT

Sore and stiff from the previous day's forced march, Elias S. Dennis' command moved out of Denmark, Tennessee, at daylight on Monday, September 1. Company H, 12th Illinois Cavalry (the "Clinton Rangers"), led the column, followed by the 20th Illinois, the artillery, the baggage trains, and the 30th Illinois. Foster's 4th Ohio Independent Cavalry was scouting toward Estanaula with the ultimate intention of closing upon the body and riding as a rear guard. Colonel Dennis, along with Captain Foster who was not with his company, rode with the 20th Illinois ("The Fight" 1862, 8). About two miles south of Denmark, the Federals came to a fork in the road. Upon the advice of a Unionist citizen, Dennis elected to take a shortcut known as Britton's Lane—a fourteen-foot-wide country road named after the farmer, Thomas Britton, who lived at the southern end. This route would cut off several miles from Dennis' march and speed his arrival to Medon—the last known location of the Confederate cavalry.

Shortly after 9:00 A.M., the 12th Illinois Cavalry approached the southern end of Britton's Lane—a crossroads intersecting the Steam Mill Ferry Road and the Medon Road (today known as Collins Road). When the Federal cavalry spotted a huge cloud of dust rising from the south, Lieut. Charles O'Connell sent a courier back to advise Colonel Dennis, and pending his commander's decision to fight or run, O'Connell deployed the Clinton Rangers, about forty strong, into a skirmish line amid a grove of trees near the road ("From Capt." 1862, 2). O'Connell knew that his men had been spotted by the Confederates, for their pickets "immediately turned and fled to convey the news to the main body of our approach" ("The Battle" 1863, 4). Selecting a private named Charles Prindle, reputedly the best marksman in the unit, to fire the first shot, O'Connell prepared to delay the Confederate advance. Prindle, upon observing a Confederate officer at some distance, drew his carbine on him and remarked that it was "hard to shoot a man, but here goes," and the officer fell ("From Capt." 1862, 2). Lieutenant O'Connell noted the time on his watch: 9:00 A.M. (Richards 1990, 69). The enemy detected the smoke from the rifle and returned fire immediately; thus sporadic firing erupted all along the Federal skirmish line. Some of the Confederates dismounted and began to spread out on both sides of the

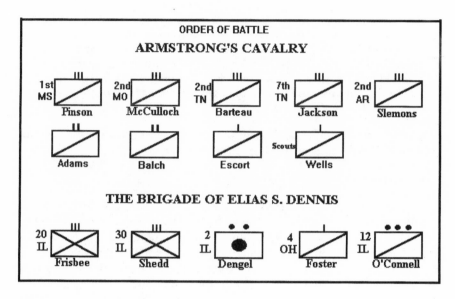

Figure 4.1

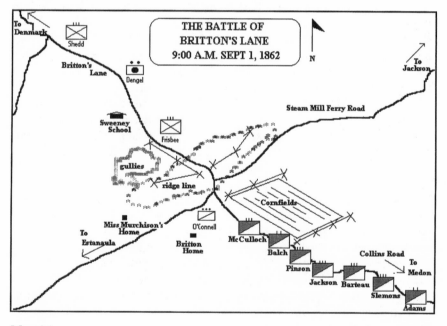

Map 4.1

road, but most of the lead regiment remained mounted. O'Connell's duty was clear: delay the enemy advance until the 20th Illinois could double-quick to the sound of the guns.

Col. Elias S. Dennis now found himself in the unenviable position of being forced into glory. And though historians have made much of Dennis' audacious decision to block Britton's Lane and fight outnumbered against Frank C. Armstrong's cavalry, the reality of the matter is that Dennis had no other choice. His small brigade stretched out five miles behind him. The enemy was mounted and probably mustered double his force. His only options were to fight or run, and the latter would have been futile. Forty cavalrymen could not delay twenty-seven hundred—at least not for very long—and should he have chosen to make a run for Denmark, his infantry-men would have been ridden down and slaughtered. Dennis had a classic meeting engagement on his hands, and the individual who chooses the best ground tends to be most successful in this situation. Realizing this, Dennis selected a position four- to five-hundred yards behind his cavalry skirmish line, along a tree-covered ridge. Cornfields and an occasional potato field stretched southeast from the base of the ridge, and Britton's Lane ran across the cornfields and up the ridge, disappearing into the treeline. This would be his initial position, and as Capt. Orton Frisbee, acting commander of the 20th Illinois Infantry, led the nose of his column up the lane to where Dennis was posted, the ex-Kansas marshal deployed Companies B and G on the left side of the road, and the remainder of the regiment on the right. Battery E closed upon the ridge line as the 20th was hustling into position, taking cover behind a stake and rendered fence that ran perpendicular to the road at the edge of the woodline. Dennis ordered the two guns unlimbered and positioned just to the right of the road and slightly forward of the regiment. Within minutes, Lieutenant Dengel began firing over the heads of the 12th Illinois Cavalry, his fused cannister rounds exploding above the dust trail that stretched for miles to the southeast.

DIRECT ASSAULT

Pickets from "Black" Bob McCulloch's 2nd Missouri Cavalry returned to the head of the column and warned that a detachment of Federal cavalry were posted near the crossroads up ahead. Scarcely had that intelligence been communicated before the Confederates began receiving rifle fire from a grove of trees to the northwest. McCulloch threw out a skirmish line and had part of his regiment dismount for a brief rest while a company-sized force developed the situation. Outside of the limited engagements before Bolivar, and the short-lived attack against Medon Station, McCulloch was used to encountering only isolated companies dispatched to guard the railroad. Perhaps he thought he had encountered only a Federal patrol; and being some eight miles from the nearest railroad, with no major town nearby, the likelihood of meeting a sizeable infantry force must have appeared small. Whatever their reasoning, neither McCulloch nor Arm-strong, who had begun riding to the front of the column at the first sound of firing, seems to have enjoyed a sense of urgency about the skirmish with the Federal force ahead of them. Any complacency the Confederate leaders may have had was quickly erased when Union cannister rounds began exploding over their heads. The sense that they had been ambushed permeates the writing of several eyewitnesses, and their surprise seems to come not from the small-arms fire, but from the sudden entry of artillery into the battle. C. Y. Ford, among the lead troopers of the 2nd Missouri, writes, "We dismounted to rest a short time and were standing by our horses, when two pieces of artillery let loose two charges of grapeshot into our column at point-blank range" (Ford 1922, 290). Edwin H. Fay, trailing the 2nd Missouri in Balch's Battalion, notes that "hardly had the first half-dozen shots been fired when a cannon opened on us with grape and canister. The Yanks were ambushed for us . . ." (Fay 1958, 150). Fay alludes to some pro-Union citizens ("acursed Union Tories") having "let us rush right into it," but no other eyewitnesses support the notion of such a conspiracy.

A Lieutenant Brotherton of Armstrong's staff reached the 2nd Missouri with orders from the commander to "draw sabers and charge the battery a few hundred yards down the road" (Ford 1922, 290). Armstrong himself had reached Balch's Battalion and communicated in person for Balch's men to support McCulloch (Fay 1958, 150). Meanwhile Pinson's 1st Mississippi, and Jackson's 7th Tennessee were riding toward the gunfire. William Witherspoon of the 7th Tennessee describes the men being ordered to load their weapons—primarily double-barreled shotguns—with "buck and ball" (a one-ounce ball and three buckshot) which he claims "did terrible execution at close quarters." According to Witherspoon, "after loading we took to the walk, shortly ordered to the trot, then to the gallop. The firing in front became more prominent and frequent" (Witherspoon 1956, 88). When the 7th Tennessee reached the front, the regiment deployed on the right of the 2nd Missouri, out to two hundred yards from the road. Several companies dismounted, and as the 2nd Missouri had at Bolivar, the 7th Tennessee began throwing down fences should they be ordered to make a mounted charge. Pinson's Regiment deployed to the left and southwest of McCulloch. Bugles sounded and McCulloch's men charged "at the Yanks with sabers and the rebel yell." On each side of them, Jackson's and Pinson's men rushed across the cornfields toward the growing number of Federal troops rushing into position behind a fence on the distant woodline. The Federal cavalry's skirmish line evaporated as they mounted up and were giving way before the Confederate charge, in a race back to their lines.

In Balch's Battalion, Edwin H. Fay's first real taste of battle turned out to be rather awkward. He had dismounted at the head of the column to throw off a fence railing when the bugler sounded "Charge." Being a well-drilled and finely trained cavalry mount, his horse took off without him, leaving Fay to charge the enemy position on foot (Fay 1958, 150). Fay mentions the

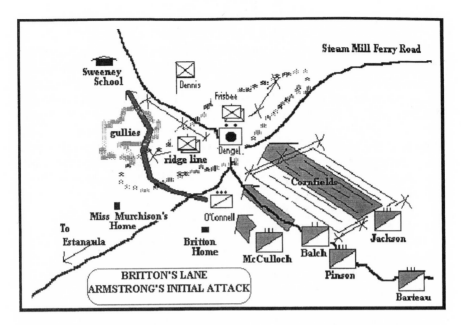

Map 4.2

tremendous obscuration created by the dust and the smoke of battle, indicating that he feared being trampled by his own men. And as the first Confederate assault made its way toward the two-gun battery, the mounted men of the 2nd Missouri and Balch's Battalion quite naturally outdistanced the dismounted regiments on their flanks. Consequently, they drew the first fire, the "Minie bullets cutting the dry [corn] stalks and our charging horses [creating] a fearful noise" (Ford 1922, 290). Closing to within fifty yards of the Federal cannon position, McCulloch's and Balch's Battalion were driven back. McCulloch's horse was shot from beneath him and several Missourians were killed, leaving the regiment in "some confusion." As the dismounted men on the flanks pressed forward, the entire fence line on the ridge before them erupted in a devastating volley fire. "A galling fire was poured into Company E," writes John Milton Hubbard of the 7th Tennessee, "but some of its men reached the fence. Dr. Joe Allen of Whiteville mounted the fences and fell dead on the enemy's side of it. John Bradford of Toone, and Willie Wendel, a school boy of Bolivar, were killed near the fence" (Hubbard 1911, 35). Hubbard goes on to mention a number of others wounded from his company and observes, "How so many men got out of that field alive is one of those unaccountable things that sometimes occur in war." Given the oppressive heat of an early September day, the sharp cornstalks striking their legs as they ran, the blinding effect of the smoke and dust, and the lead whizzing about them, the dismounted troops of Armstrong's force must have thought they were in Dante's Inferno. Pinson's men "suffered much" as well, this being their "first baptism of fire" (Montgomery 1906, 87).

McCulloch's men reformed, as did Jackson's, Pinson's, and Balch's. Twice more they charged the ridge line and twice they were repulsed with heavy losses.[1] As General Armstrong sat on his horse watching the fight develop about one thousand yards away, the Federal cannoneers took advantage of a lull in the action to shift their fire. Canister rounds began exploding above Armstrong and a company of the 7th Tennessee that had remained mounted nearby in some blackjack woods. By now, Armstrong must have realized he was being opposed by a formidable enemy force. He had flushed their cavalry, suffered from their artillery, and observed their infantry as it turned back several determined charges by three of his best regiments. Decision time had arrived, and Frank C. Armstrong's subsequent actions have been the source of debate ever since the day of the fight. Despite the enemy's resistance, Armstrong apparently did not yet fully appreciate its strength. Given the volume of fire, he might have correctly estimated a regiment. Certainly, he possessed the combat power to defeat such a force. Given the right terrain, and careful execution, he might even have concluded that he could defeat two or three regiments. Whatever his understanding of the situation, for some reason Armstrong chose to become decisively engaged at Britton's Lane—a temptation he had wisely resisted against smaller forces at Bolivar and Medon. He reasoned that the cost in time and lives to root out the relatively small Federal force blocking his route to Denmark was worth the price; thus, he began committing the remainder of his regiments, albeit rather piecemeal, into the fight.

INFANTRY IN THE DEFENSE

Riding along the line of the 20th Illinois Infantry, who were rushing to find cover behind the fence, Colonel Dennis, "apparently unconscious of personal danger, giving his whole attention to his command" ("From Jackson 1862, 8), attempted to steady the men. "In front and on the left and right were cornfields, swarming with rebels preparing for the charge. At last, on they came, the ground fairly trembling beneath their heavy tread. . . . They were repulsed and driven back. Again and again out of the cornfields on all sides they charged with like results" ("The Fight" 1862, 1).

Ira Blanchard, 20th Illinois, writes, "We had no sooner formed our line than the enemy sent up a hideous yell from the timber on the opposite side of the field. . . . Everything was hastily made ready. Boxes open, bayonets set, now as, Shakespeare would say, Then set the teeth, and stretch the nostrils wide and prepared for the inevitable. . . . Line upon line they came, with sabers lifted high in the air at full gallop (Blanchard 1992, 65). Surprised by their numbers, Blanchard describes meeting the Confederates with "a sheet of flame and a shower of lead," the cannon being particularly effective in emptying saddles; and he notes how one brave opponent reached the fence and dismounted, attempting to slash his way through the Federal line, only to be shot dead. The dust and smoke obscured the Federals' view, but eventually they could discern the field before them "now strewn with horses and men" (Blanchard 1992, 65).

Dennis needed to hold his position until the 30th Illinois could reach him and reinforce, but he sensed that time was running out, as he observed the Confederate line widening in an attempt to flank his narrowly bunched regiment. He feared the Confederates were about to renew the attack with more troops and greater vigor, thus he ordered his artillery to reposition. The guns had limbered and withdrawn about one hundred yards to a safer position behind the fenceline when the Confederates burst forth in another charge.

SEIZING THE INITIATIVE

Brig. Gen. Frank C. Armstrong had a full-scale battle on his hands, but at last he glimpsed a momentary weakness in the Federal position. When he saw the artillery limbering and withdrawing from their devastating position in front of the enemy infantry line, Armstrong realized he must act quickly. Ordering Wirt Adams' Regiment forward, along with Company L, 7th Tennessee, Armstrong determined that a mounted charge directly up Britton's Lane, while the enemy's guns were repositioning, could be the decisive blow. Having witnessed several unsuccessful assaults across the open ground, he reasoned that this approach might bring critical mass of combat power at the right spot at precisely the right moment. William Witherspoon of the 7th Tennessee writes that "the road turned south across a pretty deep ravine and then up to the lane going due west so at the mouth of the lane (east end) we made a right angle. With a yell we charged going at full gallop" (Witherspoon 1956, 89). Charging in a column of fours, Adams' regiment and the Tennesseeans crowded the narrow road, becoming intermixed as they raced toward the Federal line. Thundering down the road, a cloud of dust obscuring all but the lead troopers, the Confederates could see the enemy hastily repositioning the cannon and desperately attempting to meet them with grapeshot. "As we got fairly down the lane, we noticed they were ramming down the load . . . that cannon had to be reached before it could be fired" (Witherspoon 1956, 89).

E. B. McNeil of Wirt Adams' Regiment describes the desperate, suicidal nature of the charge Armstrong had ordered. "Not a man in the regiment could but see the death trap we were to ride into" (McNeil 1903, 442). Apparently the Federal artillerymen had managed to fire at the Confederate column before they made the right angle turn that Witherspoon describes, for McNeil writes that "we were in pointblank range and not more than a hundred and fifty yards from their guns, that were now vomiting double charges of grape and canister as fast as they could fire, while their skirmishers on both sides poured a steady fire into our charging column" (McNeil 1903, 442).

Demonstrating incredible bravery, Col. Wirt Adams, "mounted on a beautiful cream-colored mare," was at the head of the charge. "Every moment I expected to see him fall," McNeil comments. Beside Adams was his sergeant major, Lee Brisoe, a Lieutenant Montgomery, and a Captain Bondurant. The heavy volume of Federal rifle fire tore into the charging column just as it had the dismounted men who tried to cross the open fields. But by charging in a column of fours and massing their force against a single point in the Federal line, the Confederates presented a more difficult target. Men and horses at the head of the column began to fall, and in the ensuing dust and debris of fallen riders and their mounts, the troopers following began to "stumble and fall over their dead and wounded comrades . . . until the lane was completely blocked" (McNeil 1903, 442). Somehow in the melee, Wirt Adams and a handful of his troopers, along with some of the 7th Tennessee, had managed to reach the Federal cannon. "We drove in our spurs and in a mad bound were upon them," says William Witherspoon. "It was then and there the old much-derided double-barrel as an army gun done its work perfectly" (Witherspoon 1956, 89). Blasting away at the enemy artillerymen, while many of them fled along with the Federal infantry that had supported them, the southern cavalrymen captured the

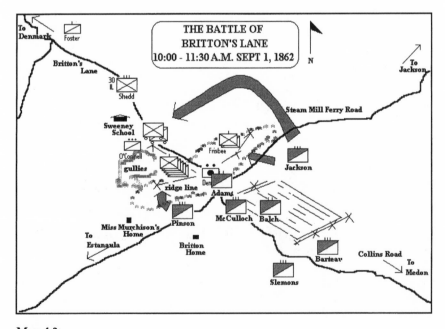

Map 4.3

two artillery pieces that had so devastated their ranks. Unfortunately, the limbers were drawn off by the fleeing Federals, leaving no way to hitch the guns and haul them to safety within the Confederate lines. Dividing up eight men to a gun, some of the men from the 7th Tennessee dismounted and attempted to roll the cannon toward their lines, while the retreating enemy kept up a brisk fire, their rounds striking the cannon and "shiver[ing] the spokes of the wheels" (Witherspoon 1956, 90). The small band of cavalry that had emerged from the dust cloud and confusion along Britton's Lane must have appeared maniacal to the Federal artillerymen and infantry posted along the road, for they certainly left an impression on E. B. McNeil that lasted a lifetime. In a 1903 article for *Confederate Veteran*, McNeil vividly recalls, "I can never forget the picture of Col. Adams as I saw him at that moment, seated on the cream-colored mare, from whose nostrils the blood spurted with each heave of her panting sides, with a smoking pistol in his hand and the light of a panther in his eyes as he looked around on his dead and dying men and the few survivors who had lived to follow him through" (McNeil 1903, 443).

Briscoe, Adams' sergeant major, and Lieutenant Montgomery were among those who gave their lives to capture the Federal artillery position. Though some of the artillerymen had fled ingloriously in the face of Adams' final onslaught, Lieutenant Dengel, along with eleven of his men, were captured with the guns.[2] With no caissons to hitch up the guns, the Confederates attempted to roll them back toward their own lines, but encountered a tangled mass of dead and dying horses that clogged the narrow road. Realizing they could never haul the guns back to Mississippi, they eventually made a cursory attempt to spike the weapons and abandoned them on the field.

W. H. Jackson's 7th Tennessee had extended its line to bend around the Federal left, and in support of Wirt Adams' assault on the guns, they again charged across the cornfields and out of the woods. Jackson's men could not dislodge the Federals on the northeast side of Britton's Lane, but they were able to capture and burn several supply wagons, taking a number of prisoners as well.[3] The 7th Tennessee had also placed the Federal left in considerable peril, and with a coordinated movement against the Union right flank, Armstrong would likely have surrounded the 20th Illinois entirely. In fact, W. H. "Red" Jackson wrote after the war that, "I thought we had whipped the fight, and Gen. Dennis afterwards[4] told me he was ready to surrender" (Gates 1897, 1).

REINFORCING THE DEFENSE

That the Federals were in trouble was clear to everyone, especially Elias S. Dennis. But while some of his men may have been ready to surrender, none of Dennis' actions that day seem to indicate that *he* considered surrendering. Still, with his artillery gone, his supply wagons, teams, and drivers captured, and the 20th Illinois Infantry fast giving ground, Dennis stared into the face of imminent defeat. Only the timely arrival of the 30th Illinois Infantry from the rear position in the Federal column kept Dennis from suffering a complete rout. The beseiged 20th Illinois sent forth a welcoming cheer as the 30th moved double-quick to join them in line of battle. G. B. McDonald writes, "Just before we got to the front the rebs captured the two guns, and had the 20th pretty well demoralized, and was making another charge just as we were climbing a little hill, and the command was on right into line, and firing as we came into line, and with a yell drove the enemy back, and just had time to form a good line with the 20th when another charge was made" (McDonald 1916, 28).

As quickly as it had materialized, the opening for Armstrong's men to isolate and capture the 20th Illinois had disappeared. The attack, with bayonets fixed, by the 30th Illinois had succeeded not only in recapturing most of the supply wagons, but the 30th Illinois' sudden appearance on the battlefield, coupled with the Confederates' failure to consolidate their newly gained position on the ridge, also resulted in Armstrong's men being driven back into the cornfields. Now Dennis had his original line back behind the rail fence, and his infantry increased to some eight hundred strong (though most of the men in the 30th were nearly exhausted from double-timing to the fight in the intense August sun). This more robust Federal line now met several subsequent Confederate mounted charges, the enemy "hanging on the far side of their horses, and firing Indian fashion" (McDonald 1916, 29). When one of the men of the 20th was captured and taken to General Armstrong, he was asked the cause of the cheering among his men. The Union infantryman told the Confederate leader his fellow Illinoisans were cheering the arrival of "Logan's Division." While Armstrong may not have taken the soldier's word at face value, he knew the enemy had been reinforced. Since he was, after all, back where he started the fight some three hours earlier, he must have at least considered the possiblility of a major Federal force joining the fight.

At any rate, Armstrong determined to make yet another assault, this one to be coordinated with an attempt to roll up the Federals' right flank. The 2nd Arkansas figured prominently in the plan, launching an attack against the Federal position in the woodline on the ridge. But Dennis had antici-pated such a move, and bending his line back upon itself like a hairpin, the commander reduced his interior lines. Thus, when the Confederates charged, "owing to the heavy clouds of dust, supposing them [the Federals] to be in their old position," they emerged through the smoke and dust to fire a volley that "never injured a man." Instantly the Federals issued an enfilading fire that "threw them [the Confederates] into confusion," emp-tying saddles and again turning Armstrong back with heavy losses ("The

Fight" 1862, 1). The 2nd Arkansas lost seventy men killed or wounded during the day's fight (Evans 1987, 294).

From this point the accounts of the battle differ widely, depending on the perspective of the two sides. The only fact that clearly emerges is that Brig. Gen. Frank C. Armstrong did not press the fight. Some eyewitnesses say that both sides tacitly agreed to call it quits, neither having gained a tactical advantage. Many Confederates report that the Federals were fleeing for Jackson in a near-rout. William Witherspoon claims that the citizens of Denmark told him that "over 200 of the Federals had returned there and were anxious to find some one to surrender[5] to" (Witherspoon 1956, 91). Alan Morgan Geer's diary indicates that initial reports flowing into Jackson that afternoon held that both the 20th and 30th Illinois had been taken prisoner. Stragglers flowed into town describing the loss of the artillery, the regiments surrounded, and the supply train wrecked, creating the "general impression . . . that the 20th and 30th were gone up except the skedaddlers who were shrewd enough to get away" (Geer 1977, 51).

The Confederate accounts, almost to a man, indicate a sense of lost opportunity—uncompleted action—as they describe the conclusion of the battle. T. J. Dupree of the 7th Tennessee writes, "Our army could have enveloped them, and should have done so" (Gates 1897, 34). Even Lieut.

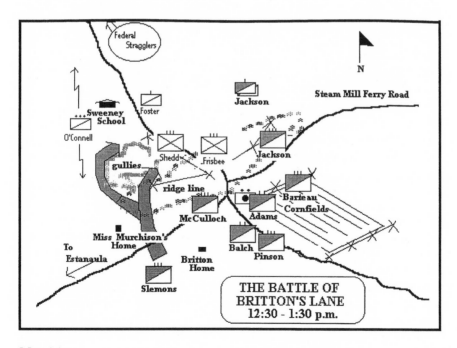

Map 4.4

Col. Montgomery of Pinson's 1st Mississippi—a regiment that had suffered fifty men killed and wounded that day—seems to have been surprised at Armstrong's subsequent actions. "While Colonel Pinson and I were consulting as to the advisability of renewing the assault on the enemy by a flank movement, which could easily have been done, as we believed, we were ordered back to the horses. To my surprise then and now, the attack was not renewed, for I am sure they were defeated" (Montgomery 1901, 88).

Ira Blanchard of the battered 20th Illinois says the Confederates withdrew "leaving 65 of their dead on the field and the hated Yankees masters of the situation" (Blanchard 1992, 66). Certainly, some isolated groups of Federals, be they stragglers or skedaddlers, were captured by the Confederate cavalry swarming Dennis' position. But other than policing up such separated forces, Armstrong made no attempt to renew the attack on Dennis' determined brigade. The Confederates did, indeed, turn south, leaving the Federals on the field. Behind them they left a number of killed and wounded—the exact figure disputed for over 130 years.

A Federal report claiming that Armstrong left "179 of his dead on the field" is characteristic of the exaggeration found in the battle reports of both sides (Lawler 1887, 51). The true casualty figures for Armstrong at Britton's Lane, based upon analyzing both regimental records and eyewitness accounts, is roughly one hundred killed and approximately two hundred wounded. Colonel Lawler's report of the Federal losses—five killed and fifty-five wounded within Dennis' command—is relatively accurate. Working independently, both this author and Britton's Lane researcher Charles Richards came to Federal casualty figures of eight killed in action (KIA) and ten KIA respectively. Anywhere from sixty to one hundred Federals were wounded, based upon Union accounts, and Armstrong appears to have captured over one hundred prisoners.

The tremendous disparity between Confederate and Federal losses is a tribute to the defensible ground Elias Dennis selected, as well as his stalwart leadership through critical moments of the battle. G. B. McDonald accurately assessed the impact of the gallant defense when he alluded to Dennis' promotion by writing, "The eagle Col. Dennis wore laid a star on his shoulder in honor of this battle" (McDonald 1916, 31). Though the actual numbers may never be known, the striking comparison in losses cannot be overlooked.

When the fight ended, Armstrong turned southwest and led his men to Estanaula, where they camped for the night. Still uncertain as to whether or not the Federals were in pursuit, he kept a security force deployed to warn him of any approaching enemy cavalry. Behind him on the battlefield, and littering the porches and bedrooms of the local community, were Confederates wounded too badly to travel. Having to leave the wounded behind—an unfortunate by-product of conducting a cavalry raid— weighed heavily on the minds of many of Armstrong's men and is reflected in their postwar accounts. Federal surgeons and local citizens teamed up to treat these men, many of whom died from their wounds. W. P. Reed of Pinson's 1st Mississippi, who was among those thought mortally wounded and left on the battlefield, tells of the care he received in the home of a local citizen. "I was cared for . . . as if I had been a member of their family. . . . Mr. Reed [no relation] . . . with his wife and daughters nursed and cared for me. One kind thing to be said about the enemy here was that they exchanged medical attention and surgical supplies with our men, and their surgeons, sent out from Jackson to look after their own men, often came by to see me and sent out plenty of supplies. These men were gentlemen and very kind" (Reed 1929, 23).

Just before dark, once assured that the Confederates had disappeared, Dennis' command began to assemble its scattered parts and march back to the battlefield from Denmark where they had rallied. They reached the scene of the fight—littered with dead and wounded men, as well as over two hundred horses—just as Major Oliver was arriving with his regiment from Medon. Having been denied his fight with Armstrong that morning at Medon, he had ordered his command on a forced march in the direction of the cannon fire, hoping to fall upon Armstrong's rear. Both Federal units spent the night on the battlefield.[6] The next day both Dennis' and Oliver's commands proceeded back to Medon to guard the railroad and to stop any Confederate infantry element that might have been following Armstrong.

By daylight on Tuesday, September 2, heat began to work upon the bodies that lay uninterred at Britton's Lane. The Federals had already buried their dead on the field, but the Confederates were left to the locals. A free Negro named Shedrick Pipkins and another Denmark citizen, William Henry, set about burying the soldiers. Some of the casualties, known personally to members of the community, were placed in individual graves in Denmark, but most Confederate soldiers killed at Britton's Lane were buried in mass graves. One such burial pit containing the bodies of twenty-three Confederates is located in the present-day Battlefield Park, honored with a monument erected by veterans after the war. Shedrick Pipkins poignantly described one such burial to the late Fonville Neville, Denmark historian, who, as a young boy, attended some of the reunions after the war. "There was something about that fresh young boy's body, its casket a coarse woolen blanket, that made the shoveling of dirt upon it a profanation that [Pipkins] never forgot and always remembered with pity" (Neville 1962, 18).

One of the most gripping accounts of the aftermath of Britton's Lane comes from the diary of a Miss Murchison, a teenage girl who lived near the scene of the fight. Her entry, dated September 3, 1862, details the carnage.

> Couldn't go to church, big fite [sic] up road, Papa says we must go and see if any of our folks in fite. Mama got some food, milk and sheet. Very hot day.

Papa got to Mr. Briton house. Lot of soldiers been hurt. A lot in his house, lot outside under tree. Mama and Me stayed. Papa went up road to see where fite was. Boys come here to get water for horses. Said they won and Yanks run. Had to carry wood fore [sic] fire. Awful smell and Boys hurting.

Papa says to Mama many died at end of lane at woods. Papa says many horses dead on top of Boys. boys to be buried in old cemetary [sic]. Cutting wood now to burn horses. Papa gone back to help. boys come and bring more hurt. some already dead in house.

Many people come to help us. Many died last nite [sic]. Put them in back yard. Papa and men got back.... Boys burned some wagons and drove Yanks off. Papa said many dead and was put in soil where they fell. Mama mad, Papa says it was too hot on bodies and many flies.

Went to where fite was. Awful smell, much sadness. Fences down, awful flies new earth everywhere. Many graves of Boys. School not hurt. Wood apart. Yanks everwhere [sic].

Among the graves that young Miss Murchison saw that day was that of Captain Beall, the 1st Mississippi Cavalry officer who had predicted his own death to Lieutenant Colonel Montgomery during the early morning before the battle.

WITHDRAWAL TO MISSISSIPPI

On the morning of September 2, Brig. Gen. Frank C. Armstrong led his cavalry force across the Hatchie River at Estanaula. A few miles beyond, at Harmony Church, Armstrong paroled the nearly two hundred Federal prisoners he had captured.[7] According to Edwin H. Fay of Balch's Battalion, "We left the field . . . being worn out and having nothing to eat for 3 or 4 days, our horses being broken down from forced marches, Gen'l Armstrong started back" (Fay 1958, 151). He led his column south toward Mississippi, reaching La Grange, Tennessee, on September 4, where the troopers, covered with thick, white dust, looked like ghosts to the locals who cheered their passing. (Fay 1958, 151; Hancock 1882, 214). Having been perpetually in the saddle or on the battlefield for five days, the soldiers in Armstrong's command were tired, sore, and hungry, and many of them were bruised and otherwise wounded. Pvt. John M. Hubbard of the 7th Tennessee reflected the mood of many. "The whole command was discouraged by the operations of this raid, and thought that, if we had gained anything at all, we had paid dearly for it" (Hubbard 1911, 35). "We were certainly on the run," confirmed William Witherspoon of the same unit.

But if the average soldier's view of the raid was less than positive, on September 2, Brig. Gen. Frank C. Armstrong offered a glowing report of his men's exploits. "I have . . . passed between Jackson and Bolivar; destroyed the bridges and one mile of trestle work between the two places, holding for more than thirty hours the road" (Armstrong 1887, 51). In referencing

Britton's Lane, Armstrong says he "captured two pieces of artillery, destroyed a portion of the train, and took 213 prisoner, killing and wounded by their own statement, over 75 of the enemy" (Armstrong 1887, 51). Had Armstrong's report ended at this point, he might be said to have presented a reasonably accurate record of the expedition. However, the next sentence in his report, though short and to the point, is clearly false. Armstrong writes, "My loss was small." Small compared to what? Certainly not to the Federal loss at Britton's Lane. After praising Colonel W. H. "Red" Jackson's cooperation, and lauding his troopers' ability to handle fatigue and hunger, Armstrong claims his men are "ever ready when an opportunity offers to punish the insolent invaders . . . I can strike across whenever needed" (Armstrong 1887, 51). In reality, Armstrong's men were ready for nothing other than rest, recuperation, and rearming. In a curious caveat to his claims of success, Armstrong closes his report with this line: "I have gone further probably than my instructions, but I hope my anxiety to render service and my success will be an excuse for my doing so."

RETURN TO JACKSON

When Col. Elias S. Dennis and his battered brigade returned to Jackson from Medon by train on September 3, they received a hero's welcome from the Federal troops stationed there. G. B. McDonald offered this stinging indictment of his fellow 30th Illinois soldiers whose premature exit at Britton's Lane made them absent from the grand arrival. "The writer [McDonald] was the only musician left, and made music for the two regiments as they marched into Jackson. *The other musicians were not killed either* [author's italics]" (McDonald 1916, 31). Marching from the train depot, the Britton's Lane veterans stood tall.

> Captain Frisbee, as usual, strutted and bellowed at the head of the 20th . . . and almost every man had some sword or gun taken from the "rebs." Colonel Shred [Warren Shedd], a modest unassuming man rode calmly at the head of the column as though nothing had happened, though one of his arms had been partly carried off by a ball . . .(Blanchard 1992, 66).

Amid ringing bells, firing cannons, and wild cheers from the garrison troops, Dennis and his men moved to the court house square where Gen. John Logan praised them as "the most undaunted heroes of the nineteenth century" (Blanchard 1992, 66). Such rhetoric leaves little wonder that Alan Morgan Geer described the 20th and 30th as feeling "invincible after their extraordinary victory" (Geer 1977, 52), and based upon the developing events at Antietam, observed that "the eastern troops are not as good fighting men as the Western boys and are discouraged" (Geer 1977, 52). Geer's comments reflect one very important aspect of the fight at Britton's Lane: The newspaper coverage that would normally have extolled such a performance for weeks following the battle was quickly overshadowed by the catastrophic casualties at the Battle of Antietam. But while the northern reading public may not have fully recognized what Dennis accomplished on September 1, his superiors did. Within months he was promoted to brigadier general primarily because of the grit and courage he demonstrated at Britton's Lane. In fact, from this relatively small engagement on a dusty Tennessee backroad emerged a total of five men who would be general officers during the war: Frank C. Armstrong, W. H. "Red" Jackson, Wirt Adams, Warren Shedd, and Elias S. Dennis.

AN ODDITY OF WAR

When Shedrick Pipkins and William Henry buried that young Confederate soldier killed at Britton's Lane, they noted that he wore a homemade uniform bearing a set of strange buttons. Perhaps moved by the fact that he would lie unknown in an unmarked grave for eternity, one of the men cut off a button and gave it to a Captain Guthrie who maintained the odd button throughout the war. During the postwar veterans' reunions, Guthrie always carried the button, showing it to other soldiers and often inquiring of anyone who might recognize it. During a reunion in Atlanta, Guthrie was staying in the home of a Mrs. Jefferson—being the custom of many southern families to open their homes to the old veterans. Guthrie and the several other veterans sat around the table one evening talking about the war, most of them indicating they "rode with Forrest." Mrs. Jefferson shared that she had lost her husband at First Manassas, and that her 14-year-old son had run away shortly thereafter to join Forrest. She said this made her feel part of the group. Mrs. Jefferson explained that her son had written her from Corinth, Mississippi, in early 1862 indicating he needed clothes, thus she made him a uniform, sewing on to it the buttons from her great-grandfather's uniform worn at Yorktown under George Washington. Having never heard from her son again, Mrs. Jefferson presumed him dead in some unmarked grave.

Hearing her story, Captain Guthrie produced the button he had received from the body of the young boy at Britton's Lane. A shocked Mrs. Guthrie knew it immediately as a match, and though many such Continental buttons were likely used during the war, the grieving mother produced a swatch of cloth that matched the piece of cloth beneath Guthrie's button. At long last, the mother knew the fate of young Sanderson Jefferson—a casualty at Britton's Lane (Neville 1962, 18).

NOTES

1. As described earlier, in the initial charge at Britton's Lane, cavalryman Edwin H. Fay suffered the martial embarrassment of losing his horse. His behavior may

have resulted in some fellow troopers accusing him of shirking, for in a letter to his wife, Fay sheepishly admits that he located his horse "on the fourth charge, but did not get into the fight at all on account of losing him . . . I am sorry it happened as it looks as if I kept out of danger. My conscience is clear on the subject however and whatever may be said will not affect either you or me. I know however I shall not let down another fence preparatory to a charge but shall be at the head of it certain" (Fay 1958, 151).

2. The mysterious "Ichabod," a soldier of the 20th Illinois who wrote an account of Britton's Lane for the *Carlyle Weekly Reveille*, is the only chronicler of the battle who indicates anything but praise for Lieutenant Dengel's two-gun artillery section. "I cannot speak of them creditably," Ichabod writes. "Their guns might make good bells; that is all that they are fit for." Perhaps "Ichabod's" position on the battlefield obscured his view of Dengel's battery, for given the Confederate reports of their devastating fire, and the degree of effort Armstrong spent to take them, Dengel's cannoneers must have rendered highly effective service.

3. O'Connell's men of the 12th Illinois (Clinton Rangers) had been ordered to cover the flanks once they withdrew through the Federal infantry line along the fence row. After rushing from point to point to repel attempted enemy flanking actions, they eventually found themselves overwhelmed by Jackson's men who slipped in behind the 20th Illinois and captured the Federal wagon train. O'Connell himself was captured, but after yielding his weapon and being ordered to the Confederate rear, he declared, "Thank you, [but] I generally take the *front*," and spurring his horse, made "good his escape, followed by a shower of bullets" ("From Capt." 1862, 1).

4. Apparently Colonel Jackson and Colonel Dennis crossed paths several times during the war and may have had an opportunity to discuss the details of Britton's Lane. At the cessation of hostilities, Dennis was present to sign the paroles of several officers and men who had fought against him at Britton's Lane. Among the Britton's Lane opponents Dennis encountered during the war was Col. Wirt Adams, whom then-Brigadier General Dennis entertained at his camp while commanding a large force at Monroe, Louisiana. In a series of events nothing short of bizarre, Dennis conducted a strange barter of supplies with Confederate forces in Mississippi that allowed Wirt Adams, in Confederate uniform, to ride about Dennis' camp in the company of the general, and to even dine with him at his officer's mess (Bedford 1877, 125). Britton's Lane, the battle that made Dennis' career, would most certainly have made for interesting dinner conversation.

5. The Federals that the Denmark citizens found ready to surrender were most likely the stragglers from Dennis' column who had fallen out of the march from Estanaula the previous day. Some may have been the shirkers and deserters that Alan Morgan Geer described as running for Jackson at the first sound of a fight and declaring "the 20th and the 30th [Illinois] all gobbled up" (Geer 1977, 51).

6. A soldier of the 20th Illinois found a pouch belonging to Colonel McCulloch on the battlefield that night, probably dislodged when McCulloch had a horse shot from beneath him early in the fight. The discovery led to the erroneous report that McCulloch had been killed. The *Chicago Tribune* also falsely reported that Col. Wirt Adams had been killed.

7. Armstrong had little choice but to parole his prisoners, as his cavalry force would rapidly outdistance the infantry detainees walking under guard behind his

column. Almost every Federal account of Britton's Lane indicates that Union prisoners were treated humanely during their removal from the battlefield. The degree of respect and courtesy extended to the Federals is best demonstrated by the one "outrage" detailed in the September 13 issue of the *Chicago Tribune*. Chaplain Charles Button (erroneously reported as "Mutton") of the 20th Illinois was relieved of his horse and equipment, and would likely have lost even more "had not the chaplain bravely asserted his private rights, even as a prisoner." A Confederate officer to whom Button appealed stepped in to save the chaplain from "so gross a personal outrage" ("West Tennessee Army" 1862, 2).

PART II

BRIG. GEN. NATHAN B. FORREST'S WEST TENNESSEE RAID

December 13, 1862–January 3, 1863

5

General Situation

New men, imperfectly armed and equipped . . .
—Gen. Braxton Bragg

By December of 1862, the soft underbelly of the Confederacy lay exposed in the western theater, and Ulysses S. Grant launched a campaign against Vicksburg, Mississippi, that he hoped would bring a rapid end to the war. If Vicksburg could be captured, the Mississippi would be opened from Cairo to the Gulf of Mexico, effectively splitting the Confederacy, isolating the armies of the trans-Mississippi, and providing a moral victory that would keep the war-weary citizens of the north behind the U.S. government effort. Having advanced as far into Mississippi as Oxford, General Grant positioned his forces to fix Confederate Lieut. Gen. John C. Pemberton's twenty-four thousand–man army near Oxford. Grant's plan was simple. He would occupy Pemberton while Maj. Gen. William T. Sherman steamed south out of Memphis with thirty thousand men aboard river transports to strike a blow against the depleted defenses at Vicksburg. Sherman would be augmented by a supporting attack from a small force out of Helena, Arkansas, under the command of Brigadier General A. P. Hovey (Martin 1990, 72). Pemberton realized that a major Union invasion was imminent, and fearing he would be attacked on several fronts and possibly cut off from reinforcing Vicksburg, he withdrew his army to Grenada, Mississippi, on December 5, 1862, appealing to Gen. Braxton Bragg for help.

General Bragg's response to Pemberton's request for assistance materialized in the form of a December 10 order to Brig. Gen. Nathan Bedford Forrest to conduct a cavalry raid into west Tennessee for the purpose of destroying the Union supply and communication lines that supported Grant's offensive into Mississippi. Forrest was a forty-one-year-old cotton,

Brig. Gen. Nathan B. Forrest. Photo courtesy of the Library of Congress.

livestock, and slave trader who enlisted as a private in Memphis in 1861, only to be selected colonel of his own regiment. He established a reputation for daring and initiative at Sacremento, Kentucky, in 1861, at Shiloh the following spring, and most recently in economy of force operations against the Federals in middle Tennessee. Many of the units he had raised and trained the previous year had been transferred to other commands, leaving him with only about twenty-five hundred men, many of them raw recruits and poorly armed. Forrest realized what a difficult mission Bragg was ordering him to undertake—make a crossing of the Tennessee River in the face of patrolling Federal gunboats, conduct offensive operations behind enemy lines amid a total enemy force of some fifteen thousand to twenty thousand troops, interdict the Union supply line, and return his command safely to middle Tennessee. Commenting on Bragg's order, Lieut. John W. Morton, who joined Forrest prior to the raid, wrote, "whether [Bragg] meant to sacrifice General Forrest to make a diversion in the direction of Memphis between General Grant and General Rosecrans, or whether he trusted to General Forrest's skill to provide for himself, is not clear . . .(Morton 1992, 47). Forrest already held little appreciation for Bragg, and he would have even less by the end of the war, yet it seems Bragg believed he was sending Forrest on a mission for which he was well-suited, for example, guerrilla or partisan campaigning. Scholars would argue long after the war as to whether or not Bragg ever realized Forrest's potential as a field commander, but for the type of raid being planned, Bragg knew he had the right man.

From his headquarters in Columbia, Tennessee, Forrest began to ready his men, weaving together a force armed primarily with shotguns, squirrel rifles, and flintlock muskets. Presently under his command were several new units, recruited and raised in the previous two or three months. The 8th Tennessee Cavalry under George G. Dibrell had been a partisan ranger outfit as recently as September, but now organized as regular cavalry, Dibrell's regiment was made up primarily of untested men from Overton, Putnam, White, and Jackson counties in Tennessee. Jeffrey Forrest, the general's younger brother, served as a major under Dibrell. The 9th Tennessee Cavalry, under Colonel J. B. Biffle, had formed in October and was made up of men from Wayne, Maury, Lawrence, and Perry counties in Tennessee. James W. Starnes, who had been with Forrest in his first major fight at Sacremento, Kentucky, in 1861, commanded the 4th Tennessee Cavalry, made up of men from the Tennessee counties of Wilson, Marshall, Bedford, and Rutherford. Forrest's most experienced unit was Colonel A. A. Russell's 4th Alabama Cavalry, which had embedded within it at least four companies of Forrest's old regiment under the leadership of Major D. C. Kelley. Rounding out the force gathered at Columbia, Tennessee, were two companies of Kentucky Irregular Cavalry under the command of Capt. Thomas G. Woodward, Cox's Tennessee Battalion, Capt. William Forrest's Scouts, and Freeman's Battery.

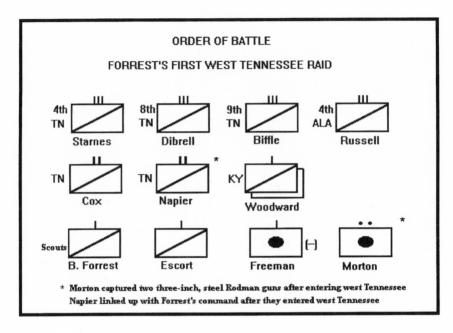

Figure 5.1

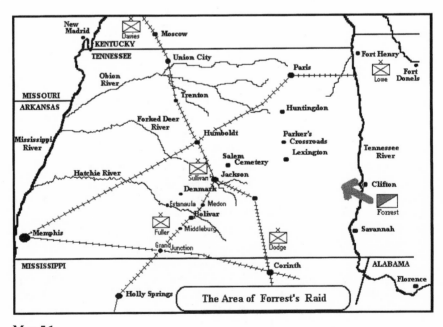

Map 5.1

Forrest protested to General Bragg that his men needed longer to train and a government issue of more serviceable weapons; but while Bragg acknowledged that Forrest had "new men, imperfectly armed and equipped," he provided no new weapons and curtly ordered him to go ahead with the mission (Bragg 1887, 592). Thus, Forrest dispatched a crew of carpenters to a small village on the Tennessee River known as Clifton, and sent a prosouthern citizen to Memphis with the mission of procuring percussion caps (in great shortage among his troops) and meeting Forrest's command once they had crossed the Tennessee River. On December 13, Forrest began the seventy-mile march from Columbia to Clifton.

6

The Crossing at Clifton and
the Fight at Lexington

"Is this your Southern Confederacy . . .?"

—Col. Robert Ingersoll

The carpenters who preceeded Forrest's main body out of Columbia had located an "old, sodden, leaky flat-boat" at the Clifton, Tennessee, river landing (Mathes 1902, 194), which they set about rebuilding in a slough that kept them out of sight of Federal gunboats patrolling the river. A second flatboat appears to have been constructed from scratch. Because a number of pro-Union citizens lived in the area, the rebuilding effort demanded the utmost secrecy, thus a small detachment of troops kept lookout and guarded the workers.

When Forrest's main body arrived at Clifton on Monday, December 15, winter weather came with them in the form of a steady rain, low cloud cover, and falling temperatures. The reduced visibility worked to the Confederates' advantage as they began the lengthy process of ferrying over the Tennessee River some twenty-one hundred cavalrymen, seven artillery pieces, and several wagon trains. Stationing lookouts both above and below the crossing to warn of approaching gunboats, the Confederate force shuttled across the Tennessee River in small loads of twenty-five men and horses on each flatboat (Lytle 1931, 124; Mathes 1902, 80). John Morton writes, "the men had not tents, and only the constant work, the desperate nature of the expedition, and the indomitable spirit of their leaders sustained them in the face of the constantly increasing difficulties" (Morton 1992, 48). Forrest's men poled the flatboats a half mile upriver on the eastern bank, then floated down and across, pioneer style, to the landing point. It took all night of the 15th, all day of the 16th, and most of that night to move the command into west Tennessee. No enemy arrived to contest the crossing, but the entire command—along with many of the percussion caps—got soaked through in the driving rain.

Starting in the predawn hours and continuing until midmorning, Forrest moved his command eight miles from the river in the direction of Lexington. The sun broke through and the skies cleared, so Forrest allowed his men the chance to dry their clothes, check their ammunition, and ready themselves for the upcoming operation (Morton 1992, 48). During this rest halt, the citizen Forrest had sent to Memphis a week earlier made a timely arrival in camp with some fifty thousand shotgun and pistol percussion caps—accomplishing no small feat of traveling almost one hundred and fifty miles through Federal-occupied west Tennessee to intercept Forrest. In addition to the caps, however, the citizen brought with him firsthand information on the Federal troop dispositions he had encountered enroute.[1]

THE FEDERAL RESPONSE

Not everyone who lived along the Tennessee River was a secessionist; in fact, the counties along the river boasted a number of pro-Union citizens. Since crossing more than two thousand men and horses over the Tennessee River was not an endeavor that could be hidden from the local populace for very long, word of Forrest's operation began to filter across west Tennessee. At Bethel along the Mobile and Ohio Railroad and some thirty

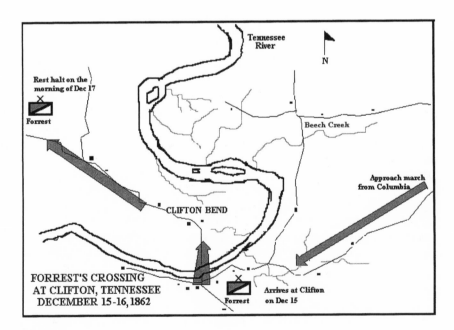

Map 6.1

miles south of Jackson, Brigadier General I. N. Haynie received a message from a Mr. Craven of Craven's Landing. Acting as a courier, Craven had left his home at 2:00 A.M. on December 15—the day Forrest's main body arrived at Clifton and began crossing—and brought a message from a Captain Carter of the First West Tennessee Cavalry (Union). "I inform you from a source believed to be reliable that a force is to cross the river at Clifton, supposed to be Forrest's cavalry, said to be 3,000 strong" (Haynie 1887, 415). It is significant to note that this early report, which Haynie promptly forwarded to Brigadier General J. C. Sullivan in Jackson, would be the most accurate estimate of Forrest's true combat power to surface among the Federals for the next two weeks. Based partly on Captain Carter's information, but supplemented, no doubt, by additional reports, Brigadier General Sullivan immediately notified Gen. Ulysses S. Grant in Oxford, Mississippi, at 6:30 P.M. that evening that "Forrest is crossing Tennessee at Clifton. A large force of cavalry is crossing above. Bragg's army is reported by scouts to be moving this way through Waynesborough" (Sullivan 1887, 415). Exactly how Carter's report got embellished to include "Bragg's army" is unknown, however it must have surely garnered General Grant's attention.

To his credit, Grant sensed immediately what Forrest would attempt. He realized the vulnerability of his railroad supply line from the depot in Holly Springs, through Jackson, Tennessee, to Columbus, Kentucky, and then to Cairo, Illinois. Despite the garrisons stationed along the track, there were hundreds of places a cavalry force could strike and destroy the line, making its escape before his troops, primarily infantry, could catch them. And if his men did resist an attack, they would likely be outnumbered at almost any point, thus being captured or killed. For Grant, the response was clear: He had to muster enough force from west Tennessee to keep Forrest from reaching his supply line, which if destroyed, would likely ruin his offensive against Pemberton, and thus against Vicksburg itself. In what amounted to field-command-by-telegraph, Grant began personally orchestrating the defense of west Tennessee, which contained in excess of twenty thousand available troops. Having heard no specifics of Forrest's location or whereabouts on the 16th, Grant received a message the following day from General Sullivan in Jackson, Tennessee, confirming that Forrest was fully across the Tennessee and seven miles inland with an estimated ten thousand men and a battery (Sullivan 1887, 423). Already Forrest's force of "three thousand" had grown to "ten thousand," and Grant made the following dispositions:

1. Brig. Gen. Grenville Dodge, at Corinth, Mississippi, was ordered to take "such forces as can be spared" and link up with Sullivan's troops in Jackson and drive Forrest east of the Tennessee;

2. Colonel W. W. Lowe, at Fort Henry, Tennessee, was ordered to take "1,500 of your command and attack [Forrest]," and to act "at once."

3. Brigadier General J. C. Sullivan, in Jackson, Tennessee, was ordered to pinpoint Forrest's location, consolidate isolated garrisons from the railroad guard, and attack Forrest; he was to accept two regiments from Brigadier General Dodge and obtain a regiment from Brig. Gen. Thomas Davies in Columbus, Kentucky, and to keep both Lowe and Dodge informed of his movements.

Jeremiah Cutler Sullivan had been a naval officer until 1854, when he resigned to practice law; but with the outbreak of hostilities he joined the army and served as a captain in the 6th Indiana Infantry and a colonel in the 13th Indiana. After serving as a brigade and division commander in the Department of the Shenandoah, Sullivan was ordered west where he took command of the Military District of Jackson, 16th Corps, Army of the Tennessee in mid-November 1862. His combat experience included Rich and Cheat Mountains in the eastern theater, and Iuka and Corinth as a brigade commander in the west (Sifakis 1988, 633). Even before receiving Grant's orders to meet and attack Forrest, Brigadier General Sullivan had, upon the initial reports of an enemy river crossing, already sent a small force toward Lexington to locate the Confederates. That force, under command of Col. Robert G. Ingersoll, consisted of the 11th Illinois Cavalry (Ingersoll's regiment), the 2nd Tennessee (Union) Cavalry under Colonel Hawkins, the 5th Ohio Cavalry, and a battery of three-inch, steel Rodman guns. While receiving Grant's instructions on the 18th, Sullivan also received a message from Ingersoll (written the previous day) confirming Forrest's presence west of the river and indicating that his pickets encountered the Confederate pickets about eleven miles southeast of Lexington. Colonel Ingersoll writes, "I have sent out two companies of Colonel Hawkins' to reconnoiter. I will keep you as well informed as possible. I intend to push on in the morning" (Sullivan 1882, 429).

Grant must have sensed that Sullivan was still hustling troops into Jackson rather than going after Forrest, for he telegraphed the following curt, yet profoundly important, directive: "Have you made preparations to get forces from Corinth? Don't fail to get up a force and attack the enemy. *Never wait to have them attack you*" [author's italics] (Grant 1885, 430).Grant's advice would prove decidedly correct in the coming days, but even as his commander demanded action, Sullivan telegraphed in reply, "Want of information from Colonel Ingersoll as to direction the enemy are marching keeps me still. I have sent out another party to find their position and will move to attack them at once." But Sullivan finished his communique with a somber reference. "A rumor here is that Ingersoll's cavalry has been whipped and dispersed; know nothing of it" (Sullivan 1887, 430).

THE FIGHT AT LEXINGTON

On Wednesday afternoon, December 17, as the remainder of Forrest's command was drying out, Colonel Starnes' Regiment moved along the Old Stage Road toward Lexington where they encountered about seventy Federals under the command of Captain O'Hara. Pickets exchanged fire and O'Hara, who had been shadowing Forrest's crossing of the Tennessee and rushing reports back to Gen. Jeremiah Sullivan in Jackson, withdrew toward Lexington. The following morning Starnes renewed his march as Forrest's advance guard, supported by Capt. Frank B. Gurley and four companies from Russell's 4th Alabama, along with a section of Freeman's Battery. At Beech Creek some five miles from Lexington, the Confederates again encountered O'Hara, but this time he was reinforced by a company of the 11th Illinois Cavalry and a company of the 2nd Tennessee (Union) Cavalry (Ingersoll 1887, 554). Although the Federals had removed the flooring from the bridge over Beech Creek, Starnes' men and Gurley's men delivered such a suppressive fire that Confederate dismounts were able to remove fence rails and refloor the bridge almost under the guns of the Federal cavalry. Realizing that the Confederates would effect a successful and rapid crossing, the Federals began a steady, ordered delay in the direction of Lexington. Starnes, Gurley, and the artillery advanced, but not without incident. As Lieutenant Morton (later to become Forrest's chief of artillery) attempted to lead the guns across the bridge, "his horse shied to one side on to the end of the plank, when the plank turned and he, horse, and plank went over into the creek, some fifteen feet below"(Morton 1992, 51). Using a rope to recover the shaken, though uninjured Morton, the Confederates crossed Beech Creek and continued to press the Federals toward the northwest. About two miles farther on they encountered the 11th Illinois Cavalry, 2nd Tennessee (Union), and the 5th Ohio in line of battle across the Old Stage Road. Again Starnes and Gurley pressed the Federals and again they withdrew toward Lexington.

Twenty-nine-year-old Col. Robert G. Ingersoll, a self-proclaimed "freethinker" and well-known agnostic in the decades following the war, had been sent by Gen. Jeremiah Sullivan to engage and defeat Forrest as rapidly as possible. The Illinois lawyer, a soldier little more than one year, had command of his own 11th Illinois Cavalry, two hundred strong, a section of Kidd's 14th Indiana Battery (3-inch Rodman rifled guns), some two hundred men of the 5th Ohio Cavalry, two hundred seventy-two men of the 2nd West Tennessee (Union) Cavalry, and the seventy or so men of Captain O'Hara's detachment. Ingersoll selected a "protected position in the edge of a wood, just over the crest of a small eminence" not more than a mile outside of Lexington (Morton 1992, 54). Two major roads leading into Lexington converged behind Ingersoll's position, the Old Stage Road on the right and the Lower Road on the left. Since Ingersoll believed Forrest would approach Lexington by the most direct route from Clifton, he positioned his entire

Col. Robert G. Ingersoll. Photo courtesy of the Library of Congress.

force to block the Old Stage Road, sending only two companies of the 2nd Tennessee (Union) under Colonel Hawkins to defend the Lower Road.

Earlier that day a fourteen-year-old runaway named V. Y. Cook had dodged Federal patrols to achieve his dream of joining General Forrest. Arriving just as Capt. Frank B. Gurley's men and Starnes' regiment were pressing Ingersoll's advance guard back toward Lexington and preparing to assault his main position along the Old Stage Road, Cook noted how "Captain Gurley formed for battle and paused for alignment, at which juncture General Forrest arrived with the main body of his command, and, with an eye and judgment equal to any emergency, ordered the position on the Federal left carried" (Ford 1922, 54).

Nathan Bedford Forrest demonstrated throughout the war no affinity for the direct assault. Whenever he could use an envelopment he would do so, and facing Ingersoll's well-deployed force, he chose just such an approach. Dispatching Dibrell's regiment to assist Starnes in fixing Ingersoll from the front along the Old Stage Road, Forrest took charge of the 4th Alabama, and bringing with him Biffle's Regiment, and his escort company, personally led the flank movement north to gain the Lower Road into Lexington. In boyish admiration still echoed over forty years later, V. Y. Cook described Forrest as the "most inspiring personage my eyes ever beheld . . . superbly mounted upon a spirited animal, which seemed to catch the inspiration of its master as he led his battalions by our position" (Cook 1907, 54).

Raising the Rebel Yell, the force under General Forrest reached the Lower Road and fell upon the 2nd West Tennessee (Union) Cavalry under Hawkins occupying Ingersoll's left. Hawkins' men "vanished like vapor" before the Confederate advance, leaving Ingersoll's flank unprotected. Ingersoll realized he was in trouble, and "learning that the enemy were in force on the Lower road, although there had been little firing in that direction, [he] ordered the guns to fall back with all possible dispatch" (Ingersoll 1887, 554). Attempting to reposition his guns to stop Forrest's envelopment, he discovered that the 2nd West Tennessee (Union) Cavalry was in a near rout, fleeing "in confusion and on the full run, pursued by the enemy. It was impossible to stop them" (Ingersoll 1887, 554). Briefly, Ingersoll was successful in using his own 11th Illinois Cavalry to protect the guns, but the Confederate force was rapidly surrounding him. Though he attempted to rally the fleeing men of the 2nd West Tennessee, they "did not succeed in making a stand"—an event Ingersoll thought would have allowed him to save his guns.

Not only did Ingersoll have high praise for his artillerymen, saying that "men could not have acted better," the Confederates also stated in their accounts that the Federal gunners "stood manfully by the guns as long as possible" (Morton 1992, 53). But with Gurley and Biffle rolling up the flank, and Starnes and Dibrell pressing from the front, the Federals could only run or surrender. A Private Kelly of Russell's 4th Alabama was cut in half in the

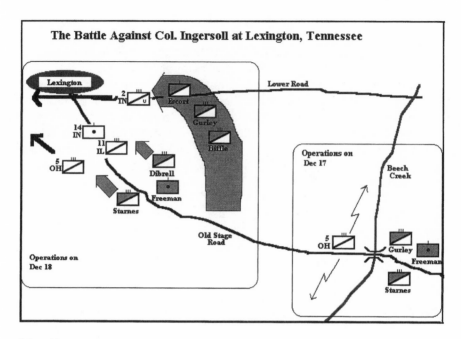

Map 6.2

final moments of the assault as one of the Federal cannons discharged. But Colonel Ingersoll, along with the guns and some 147 men surrendered—many captured as the Confederates pursued through and beyond the town of Lexington—with his composite command suffering eleven killed, eleven wounded, and many missing. Forrest also captured about seventy horses, as well as three hundred small arms (primarily Sharp's carbines) and ammunition that was immediately pressed into service (Jordan & Pryor 1977, 196).

The actual capture of Ingersoll was obtained by Captain Gurley, who upon demanding his surrender, heard Ingersoll utter the wry question, "Is this your Southern Confederacy for which I have so diligently searched?" When Gurley answered him, Ingersoll added, "Then I am your guest until the wheels of the great Cartel are put in motion. Here are the Illinoisans; the Tennesseeans have ingloriously fled" (Cook 1907, 54). General Forrest soon approached this Illinois colonel with the strange sense of humor and asked to whose command the captured forces belonged. "To Colonel Ingersoll's, if I was not the man myself," Ingersoll replied.

Forrest immediately recognized he was dealing with only a detachment of Federal troops, likely sent out from Jackson, but when he asked Ingersoll where he was from, the colonel replied, "From everywhere but here, and I hope to be from here just as soon as I can secure your genial approbation to that effect" (Cook 1907, 54).[2] Three days later, after losing most of his money and even going into debt to his captors during poker games, Ingersoll was paroled and released along with most of his men.

Forrest had whipped the first significant force sent to oppose him, and he had captured numerous personal weapons and two high-quality, rifled artillery pieces. But perhaps more importantly, he had *seized the initiative* and placed the Federals on the defensive. From now, until at least December 31, Forrest would be the actor and Jeremiah Sullivan the reactor, and that simple fact would contribute significantly to the success of his raid. One of his first goals upon the defeat of Ingersoll was to mislead the Federals as to his true strength and direction of movement. Forrest reasoned that as long as the enemy remained unaware of how small his force was, and if they were never certain of his location, they would be unable to mass an effective force to stop him. Pursuing remnants of Ingersoll's force to within four miles of Jackson, he allowed some captured Union cavalrymen to escape, having conveniently overheard an inflated figure of the Confederate strength. That misinformation, coupled with the natural tendency of a defeated force to overestimate the size of the enemy, meant that remnants of Ingersoll's command came dashing into Jackson late on the 18th with stories of "overpowering numbers." Those reports only fueled the fire of speculation among the Federal commanders about Forrest's strength (Henry 1944, 110). To further his disinformation campaign, Forrest allowed his men to speak with local citizens both pro-Union and pro-Confederate, using every opportunity to exaggerate his strength. He also ordered numerous campfires built at various points along the road from Lexington to Jackson, thus creating the appearance of a tremendous army settling in for the night. After nightfall on the 18th, Forrest's advance units had closed within four miles of Jackson and set about beating regimental drum rolls and issuing vocal commands to phantom units within earshot of the Federal defenders. These actions combined to create the uncertainty Forrest needed to keep the Federals hesitant. Now all that remained to be done was to fix the massing enemy troops presently being rushed to defend Jackson, thus enabling Forrest to move freely about west Tennessee and strike his real target—the north-south Mobile and Ohio Railroad supplying Grant in Mississippi.

NOTES

1. Tradition holds that the "citizen" who supplied Forrest with percussion caps and timely intelligence was none other than Lamar Fontaine, a famous scout. This is most likely untrue as Fontaine was at that time with the Army of Northern Virginia (Henry 1944, 507).

2. Robert G. Ingersoll possessed a quick wit, a probing mind, an expansive vocabulary, and a likeable personality, and Forrest's officers seem to have enjoyed his company as their prisoner. But while Ingersoll could command the English

language, his command of troops was less accomplished—a fact he candidly admitted to Forrest when he said, "I thought I was a soldier, but you surrounded and captured me before I knew what it was all about. I'm not a soldier and I'm not going to try to be" (Lytle 1931, 130). He soon after resigned his commission.

7

Salem Cemetery

Never wait to have them attack you.

—Gen. U.S. Grant

At 9:00 P.M. on the bitterly cold evening of December 18, Col. Adolph Engelmann, a German immigrant, took command of the 43rd Illinois Infantry and the 61st Illinois Infantry and marched them out of Jackson on the Lexington Road. His orders were to "join and take command of all the United States Cavalry [he] might find, and to feel the enemy" (Engelmann 1887, 555). About three and one-half miles from town, he came upon remnants of Ingersoll's 11th Illinois Cavalry and halted his men within sight of Confederate campfires spreading out in the distance. For a few brief moments, Engelmann entertained the notion of conducting a night attack against an unsuspecting enemy, but a consultation with Lieutenant Colonel Dengler and Lieutenant Colonel Meek (11th Illinois Cavalry) convinced him that such a move would be a bad idea, given their unfamiliarity with the ground. So Engelmann, upon "mature deliberation," and finding a defensible position about a half mile toward Jackson, deployed his troops to guard the Lexington Road. The 61st Illinois manned the north, or left, side of the road, across and through Salem Cemetery.[1] The 43rd deployed on the right, or south, side of the road, while the company-sized remnant of the 11th Illinois Cavalry crept eastward in advance along the road. Policing up the shaken remnants of the 5th Ohio and the 2nd West Tennessee (Union) Cavalry, Engelmann dispatched them to the left and right flanks, respectively, during the night. With their commander allowing no fires that might reveal their position, the Union soldiers around Salem Cemetery spent an anxious, bitterly cold night (Wood 1988, 45; Engelmann 1887, 555). Men of the 43rd, veterans of Shiloh, envied the warm glow of the Confederate campfires in the distance, knowing full well what they would likely face with the sunrise. They slept on their arms, which, as a soldier from another unit described, meant "with their belts and cartridges box straped [sic] around them, gun by their side ready to fight at a moment's warning; the officers with their sword and pistols buckled on" (Ayers 1984, 22).

Engelmann's mission constituted Gen. Jeremiah Sullivan's second attempt to stop Forrest, and this time Sullivan was convinced more than ever that the Rebel cavalryman intended to attack Jackson. Bad news had been dribbling in all afternoon and into the night—Ingersoll had been whipped. He had gotten himself, most of his men, and all of his artillery captured. The 2nd West Tennessee (Union) Cavalry had acquitted itself poorly and was scattered for miles along the Lexington Road, and to even further reinforce Sullivan's fears, stragglers brought in reports of a Confederate force numbering anywhere from five to ten thousand and *still crossing* (Grant 1887, 436).

Sullivan had ordered barricades across the main streets of Jackson, impressing slaves to "carry stores within the inner line," and he had ordered the court house walls loopholed and the doors barricaded. While storing up water and supplies and continuing to receive reinforcements from both north and south of the city, Sullivan prepared as if for a siege. Twenty-six-year-old Lieut. Oliver C. Ayers of the recently recruited 39th Iowa Infantry described the sensation of having his unit snatched from a passing train and pressed into the defense of Jackson.

> When about fifty miles north from [Jackson] we were houlted [sic] and ordered off the cars to load our Pieces. This caused a good many anxious faces and many were the conjectures as to the cause of this action. The truth was the Rebels were menancing [sic] this place and though we were under orders to Corinth, Miss. the probabilities were we might meet some Roving band of Confederates as [they were] trying to stop us by tearing up the Rail Road Track (Ayers 1984, 22)

Under orders from Grant, General Dodge hurried toward Jackson from Cornith, Mississippi, Col. John W. Fuller came from Holly Springs with a brigade, and Colonel W. W. Lowe approached from Fort Heiman. Grant would observe the following day, "I think the enemy must be annihilated, but it may trouble and possibly lead to the necessity of sending further forces from [Oxford, Mississippi]" (Grant 1887, 436). But while it may have been U. S. Grant's plan to trap and destroy Forrest, at least on the evening of December 18, it was Gen. Jeremiah Sullivan's plan to defend Jackson at all costs—just the opposite of Grant's instructions earlier that day: "Don't fail to get up a force and attack the enemy—never wait to have them attack you" (Grant 1887, 430).

THE APPROACH MARCH

With daylight on Friday morning, December 18, came the Confederate advance that Adolph Engelmann feared. A skirmish line made up of Woodward's two Kentucky cavalry companies[2] advanced and engaged the 11th Illinois Cavalry. Engelmann, who was forward with the cavalry, reports how the enemy "very leisurely reconnoitered the position of our cavalry, rarely exposing itself to a long-range shot from our carbines, and only firing occasional rifle shots at us, with the evident intention of provoking our fire, the better to be able to ascertain our position" (Engelmann 1887, 556). After holding their cavalry screen for about a half hour, the Federals were forced into a steady withdrawal as the Confederate artillery batteries of Captain Freeman opened fire from high ground on both sides of the road. As his cavalry gradually gave way back toward the two infantry regiments, Engelmann began to receive reports of "a large body of the enemy's cavalry . . . passing at the distance of a mile to the south around my right flank" (Engelmann 1887, 556). But when he attempted to counter this movement with his own cavalry, he discovered that the men he had positioned the night before were fast disappearing. Both the 2nd West Tennessee (Union) and the remnants of the 5th Ohio, having already this morning tasted the fire of the Confederate artillery, and perhaps sensing another day like the previous one, "fell back about 1 mile toward Jackson without having first

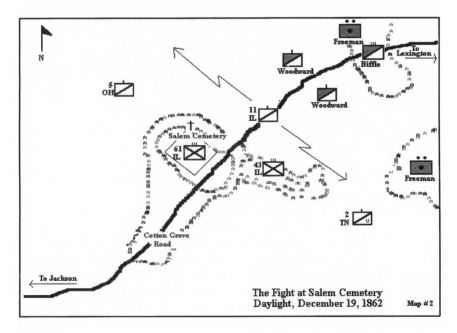

The Fight at Salem Cemetery
Daylight, December 19, 1862   Map #2

Map 7.1

obtained any orders from [Engelmann] to that effect" (Engelmann 1887, 556). Almost instantly, the Confederate skirmish line gave way to a regimental column of fours moving first at the trot walk, then the trot, then the gallop, intent on pursuing the Federal cavalry screen evaporating before them.

Colonel Engelmann's blackout from the previous night proved effective. Starnes' Regiment of Forrest's command raised the Rebel Yell and thundered down the Cotton Grove Road only to encounter a sudden volley fire from the two well-hidden and waiting infantry regiments. The 43rd opened up first catching the enemy by surprise when they were no more than thirty yards away. Lead horses and riders fell, obstructing the road, and a half-dozen riderless horses continued on madly through the Federal line.[3] The remainder of the column became jammed up behind the fallen horses and presented a momentarily opportune target. Suddenly the 61st fired a volley into the disoriented Confederates, causing them to throw down fence rails and spread out into the fields on both sides of the road. Fifteen minutes of relative quiet followed, with the two sides exchanging occasional long-range shots (Dengler 1887, 558).

Woodward's Kentucky Cavalry began working its way around Engelmann's left while Biffle moved on his right. Starnes' men deployed to the front and exchanged intermittent fire, as Freeman's batteries repositioned and began shelling the Union line. According to Lieutenant Colonel Dengler, commanding the 43rd Illinois, "the range of their guns was very exact, shells bursting all around us" (Dengler 1887, 558). Engelmann responded by deploying infantry skirmishers on the flanks and sending two companies of the 43rd Illinois into position to the right and rear of his main body, hoping that the remainder of his infantry could hold their position and entice the enemy into mounting another charge—an act Engelmann hoped to "punish." The German colonel held fast for another half hour, and although the renewed Confederate mounted attack never materialized, Engelmann reported that the enemy's "artillery began to tell among my men" (Engelmann 1887, 556). Unable to withstand the concentrated cannister fire, Engelmann ordered first the 61st, and then the 43rd Illinois Infantry, to begin a gradual withdrawal (retiring in close column, doubled on the center) to a new defensive position one mile toward Jackson—a position taking them out of range of the enemy gunners. The fight at Salem Cemetery was over, though the Federals would not realize it for several critical hours.

Neither side suffered heavy casualties, despite Engelmann's claim to have killed or wounded over sixty of the enemy. From the combined force he arrayed the previous evening, Engelmann lost only three killed and perhaps a dozen wounded. Jordan and Pryor list the Federal casualties as thirty killed or wounded, but that is likely much higher than what was actually suffered at Salem Cemetery (Jordan & Pryor 1977, 198). That figure is more likely representative of the total Federal casualties that were amassing on the 19th as a result of Forrest's next major move—dividing his

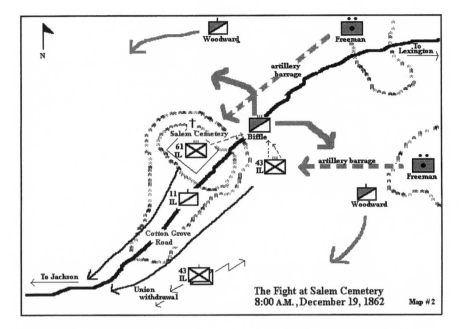

Map 7.2

command for a tactically surgical strike on the Union supply line around Jackson.

DIVIDING THE FORCE

The night previous to the fight at Salem Cemetery, Forrest had sent Colonel Dibrell on a circuitous route north of Jackson to strike the main north-south railroad supply artery leading to Ulysses S. Grant's troops in Mississippi. Simultaneously, he dispatched Maj. Jeffrey Forrest's Company and Cox's Battalion south of Jackson to strike the branch of the railroad leading to Corinth, Mississippi; and he ordered Russell's 4th Alabama south to sever the rail link between Jackson and Bolivar. Engelmann's sensation that he was being surrounded the next day at Salem Cemetery was likely fueled by late arriving reports of these very Confederate troop movements north and south during the night. In reality, Engelmann faced only a small portion of Forrest's command (probably not more than six hundred men) remaining behind at Salem Cemetery that Friday; but the Confederates' deceptive plan had created its desired effect—making the Federals believe a full-scale attack on Jackson to be imminent, while masking Forrest's destruction of the railroad. Regarding the fight at Salem Cemetery, Robert Selph Henry, in his book *First with the Most: Forrest*, asserts that Forrest "had not the slightest intention of developing more than a demonstration to keep the Union forces in Jackson busy while the real work of the day was being done elsewhere" (Henry 1944, 111). Henry is correct, for General Forrest would not have depleted his command the previous night if he had maintained any intention of seriously threatening Jackson, and from his report to General Bragg some five days later, it is clear that he held no illusions as to the enemy's strength. "The enemy had heavily reinforced at Jackson from Corinth, Bolivar, and La Grange, and numbered from the best information I could obtain, about 9,000 men" (Forrest 1887, 593).

While Freeman's Battery was pounding Engelmann that Friday morning, Dibrell struck the stockade at Webb's Station just eight miles north of Jackson along the Mobile and Ohio Railroad, where he captured 101 Federals, destroyed the track, the stockade, and the switching devices (Forrest 1887, 593). Later in the morning, Cox and Russell demolished the separate rail lines leading to Corinth and Bolivar, although in the case of the latter, the destruction would not occur until Fuller's Brigade—a force to figure largely in Forrest's confrontation at Parker's Crossroads—had passed on its way to reinforce Sullivan in Jackson.

By eight o'clock the evening of Friday, December 19, Forrest had drawn off in the direction of Spring Creek, leaving only a skeleton force to keep the campfires of a phantom army blazing so as to occupy the attention of Adolph Engelmann and his weary command. Russell's 4th Alabama and Cox's Battalion had completed their destruction south of Jackson and were rushing by a circuitous route to rejoin the main body. Colonel Dibrell's Regiment, following his success at Webb's Station, was enroute to destroy the Forked Deer River railroad bridge between Humboldt and Jackson. Colonel J. W. Starnes was riding hard with orders to attack Humboldt, and Biffle's Regiment departed sometime during the wee hours of the next morning to "get into the rear of Trenton" (Forrest 1887, 593).

While General Sullivan collected forces to defend Jackson from an attack that would never come, Forrest was setting the stage for the massive destruction of Grant's supply line and the interdiction of his entire Vicksburg campaign. But the *Chicago Tribune* did not see the matter in quite the same light, and the reader in the north received this picture of the campaign in west Tennessee:

> [Jackson, Tennessee], under the command of Gen. Sullivan, a General who knows how and who has the luck to fight, meaning to hurt the "rebs," every time, an officer in whom we all have the utmost confidence—has the forces in this district at his command, in positions to resist, to the best advantage and to the last, any attack that may be made upon the place. When the emergency demands, he will make a good report of himself and a vigorous defense of his position. (Day 1862, 2)

Unfortunately, "a vigorous defense of his position" is not what General Grant ordered, but the northern reader could not and did not know that. As a result, he was treated to the following effort at martial cheerleading: "We bide our time whether to defend or attack; and . . . it matters not which—so that we are prepared for either and the opinion is current here [in Jackson] that General Sullivan is master of his position, for his life-maxim seems to be *"Semper paratus"*—always prepared—to meet his friends or his foes" (Day 1862, 2).

NOTES

1. This cemetery held the remains of Adam Huntsman, d. 1848, the peg-leg politician whose defeat of Davy Crockett for a Tennessee congressional seat helped send the notorious frontiersman west with the declaration, "You can go to hell, but I'm going to Texas" (Wood 1988, 45; Williams 1946, 83).

2. Lieut. Col. Thomas G. Woodward had commanded a near-regimental sized force the previous spring, but a series of setbacks in guerrilla-style engagements had depleted his ranks to two companies. John H. Morgan offered Woodward a position in his command in October, but the Kentuckian refused him, preferring to join up with Forrest in middle Tennessee. Following the raid, the Confederate government tried to "regularize" his command, but "wholesale desertion followed." Choosing to operate behind Union lines, Woodward had occasional successes, but after an incident at which he ordered the killing of some Federal prisoners, Woodward was shot from his horse and killed by pro-Union citizens in Hopkinsville, Kentucky.

3. At least six of these Confederates were buried in Salem Cemetery after the battle.

8

Up the Railroad

When next it is worn . . .

—Gen. N. B. Forrest

Cairo, Illinois, December 20th, 1862—

This evening, at dusk, fighting was reported as still going on in Trenton, but as telegraphic communication is uninterrupted, it is supposed the rebels are not successful in driving off and whipping the Union troops. The city is full of rumors, none of which are deemed reliable. Some say Jackson, Tenn has been captured and our troops massacred. Others that seventeen miles of railroad track has been torn up north of that place and the country full occupied by 30,000 rebels . . . what tommorrow may bring forth cannot be said. An inference, drawn from the knowledge of facts, is that the rebels will be caught in a net of their own setting. ("Jackson Reported" 1862, 1)

This fascinating newspaper dispatch reveals just how successful Gen. Nathan Bedford Forrest had been in his campaign of deception. About the only correct information in the above account is the amount of railroad track the Confederates had destroyed and the fate of Trenton. That morning, Saturday, December 20, Forrest had launched his main body northward along the Mobile and Ohio Railroad. Starnes attacked Humboldt, capturing over one hundred prisoners, destroying the stockade, and the depot, and burning a huge trestle just outside of town. Dibrell, however, encountered heavy resistance from the recently fortified stockade guarding the Forked Deer River railroad bridge. He spent the better part of the day trying to dislodge the Federals, even using Lieutenant Morton to engage an approaching troop train with artillery. Of this affair, Morton writes, the stockade proved too strongly fortified to fall to the guns, and a move was made farther down the road, near a swamp. Hardly had this position been reached and the guns masked than a long train drew up. It consisted of flat cars, and on these were Federal soldiers. Moving slowly they made excellent targets, and their surprise was comical when Morton's guns opened on them. They tumbled off into the swamp, running in all directions, and the murky depths proved a friendly refuge, as the guns could not venture farther in. (Morton 1992, 57)

Despite the spirited engagement, Dibrell had to eventually move north, his mission unsuccessful and the bridge intact. A. H. Russell's 4th Alabama remained at Spring Creek as rear guard, while Forrest attacked Trenton with Cox's Battalion, Freeman's Battery (the escort company), and Biffle's Regiment positioned to cut off any retreat.

The Federal officer in command at Trenton, Col. Jacob Fry, had for several days been frantically gathering all available men to defend the town. He had barricaded the depot platform (150 feet by 40 feet) with cotton bales, armed the convalescents, and even impressed some seventy soldiers returning on a hospital train from Columbus, Kentucky. The hodgepodge of troops defending Trenton represented over fifteen different regiments, but even while he was preparing to defend the town, he was being gradually stripped of troops by order of General Sullivan in Jackson. When Colonel Hawkins, commander of the frequently flighty 2nd West Tennessee (Union) Cavalry reached Trenton the previous evening, he told Fry that he had observed no more than eight hundred Confederate cavalry, and to his knowledge they possessed no more than the two Rodman guns captured from Ingersoll. "This news gave us renewed hopes," wrote Fry. "Our stockade was secure against any force of cavalry or infantry unless accompanied by artillery" (Fry 1887, 561). When his scouts told him on Friday that Forrest was marching his way, Fry wired General Davies in Columbus declaring that he had "nothing left but convalescents" with which to hold Trenton, and he requested reinforcements with a battery of artillery. Davies curtly replied that he had none to spare (Fry 1887, 561). Fry also wired Sullivan in Jackson that he knew Forrest's entire command had encamped at Spring Creek, but shortly after that communication, the telegraph wire to Jackson went dead.

About 3:00 P.M. Saturday afternoon, Forrest's men attacked Trenton in two columns, initially being halted by sharpshooters stationed atop the buildings in the center of town surrounding the depot. Forrest apparently was in no mood for a dismounted, house-to-house engagement, for he immediately unlimbered Freeman's battery of six guns and from high ground on the edge of town began blasting away at the fortified depot. After a quick council of officers, punctuated by sixteen artillery rounds—one passing through the depot—Jacob Fry surrendered the approximately three hundred men defending Trenton (Fry 1887, 562; Forrest 1887, 593).

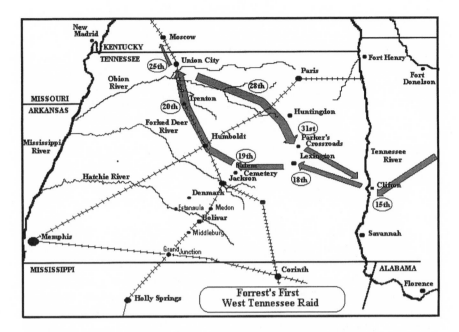

Map 8.1

During the surrender, Fry approached General Forrest with regard to his personal sword, indicating a desire to keep it, as it had been in his family for forty years. Forrest allowed Fry to keep the weapon, adding, "I hope, sir, when next it is worn, it will be in a better cause than in an attempt to subjugate your countrymen" (Morton 1992, 58). In another incident at Trenton, Forrest, learning that some of the captured Federals had set fire to a building full of supplies he had not yet inventoried for possible use, personally drew his sword and blocked the men's escape. He threatened to kill them if they didn't return to the building and extinguish the blaze, which they did with haste.

Throughout the remainder of the day, December 20, and into the morning, the Confederates busied themselves rearming and refitting with captured Union supplies. In addition to over four hundred Federal prisoners and three hundred Negroes assisting them, the garrison at Trenton had yielded one thousand mules and horses, thirteen wagons and ambulances, seven cassions, twenty thousand rounds of artillery, four hundred thousand small-arms rounds, one hundred thousand rations, and a tremendous amount of clothing, quartermaster stores, and the personal baggage of the Union soldiers. Many a previously cold and inadequately dressed Confederate cavalryman rode out of town the following day to face the freezing December weather in Federal-issue clothes—most likely *underneath* a gray or butternut outer garment—and a number of men now carried improved weapons. Young James Metcalfe, the nineteen-year old who had joined up with Freeman's artillery just prior to the fight with Ingersoll in Lexington, obtained a new pair of boots courtesy of the U.S. government. "His feeling of prowess in wresting them from the enemy was not lessened by the ill luck that one was a six and the other a seven" (Bond 1908, 108). Although Jordan and Pryor, nineteenth-century chroniclers of Forrest, are quick to liberally heap praise on the Confederate commander, they are unerringly accurate with reference to this observation: Forrest defeated and captured the garrison at Trenton by superior decision making and "dash," using only his escort company, Cox's untested battalion, and his artillery—a force numbering no more than two hundred seventy-five men (Jordan & Pryor 1977, 202).

As his force was preparing to leave Trenton, Forrest continued his campaign of disinformation. Assembling for parole the nearly thirteen hundred prisoners captured thus far during the raid, Forrest made sure they observed him sending out couriers to "different generals to bring up their commands" (Morton 1992, 59). The ruse appears to have been to use a selected set of riders who would individually arrive to take Forrest's "message" and then ride off to the supply depot, where they would change clothes and wait to be called up again for yet another communiqué to yet another field commander that did not exist. On the 21st, Forrest freed himself of the drag created by such a body of prisoners by issuing them paroles and sending them off in various directions, and with such theatrics played out right in front of them, it is little wonder that many of the parolees spread rumors of a huge invasion force as they passed back through Federal lines (Henry 1944, 113). Apparently the campaign of confusion was working, for the *Chicago Tribune* ran a December 22 report stating, "The capture of Trenton is confirmed by arrivals from there last night . . . the rebel force numbered about 4,000" ("The Rebel" 1862, 2).

December 21 and 22 were spent gobbling up detachments along the railroad north of Trenton. On Sunday the 21st, Forrest allowed his main body to rest several hours, then departed north out of Trenton with only his escort company, Freeman's artillery, and the freshly stocked wagon trains under Major G. V. Rambaut, chief commissary—in all not more than 125 effective cavalry (Morton 1992, 60; Henry 1944, 115; Jordan & Pryor 1977, 203). Nine miles north, Rutherford Station fell first, where a detachment of thirty Federals surrendered and watched in disgust as the trestles and bridges they were ordered to guard went up in flames. While the escort company was busy with the destruction effort, Rambaut proceeded up the railroad about five miles where, just south of the railstop at Kenton Station, he encountered enemy troops in line of battle. Forrest and his escort overtook Rambaut and found him halted before the deployed skirmish line, thus he initiated a sharp engagement that sent the Federals dashing back to the cover of their stockade. When the enemy refused his demand for surrender, Forrest wasted no time deploying six artillery pieces, and after a couple of volleys and a dismounted demonstration against the stockade, the defenders of the railstop surrendered (Morton 1992, 60).

Shortly after the surrender of Kenton Station, Forrest's main body closed from the south, with Colonel Dibrell remaining near Trenton as rear guard. Forrest realized the criticality of the fifteen-foot-high trestlework that spanned the Obion River bottoms just north of Kenton Station, thus he placed Colonel Starnes in charge of its destruction. All day Monday, December 22, and up until noon on Tuesday the 23rd, Starnes annihilated over eight miles of railroad that spanned the wide river bottoms much of the way between Kenton Station and Union City. The chore was made difficult by a recent freezing rain that left the trestlework encased in ice. By building fires atop the trestles, the Confederates were able to twist the track into useless bands of metal, and in spite of the melting ice, burn a large portion of the wooden trestlework. By the morning of the 23rd, a courier from Colonel Dibrell arrived from Trenton to inform Forrest that "a force of some ten thousand men had taken the field, and were moving rapidly northward, with the purpose of intercepting the return of the Confederates across the Tennessee" (Jordan & Pryor 1977, 204). At this point Forrest made an important decision that would impact upon the overall tenor of his mission. That the Federals had been slow to respond to his raid, slow to organize a force against him, and tardy in their pursuit, may or may not have surprised Forrest; but he had to realize he was running out of time. He had to have known that General Sullivan in Jackson, and especially Grant in Mississippi, could not and would not tolerate indefinitely the broad sweep of destruction he was bringing to the primary Federal supply route for the campaign against Vicksburg. How much longer could he reasonably expect the ruse of his inflated troop strength to hold sway over the Federal leadership before someone figured out he had less than three thousand men? Outnumbered at least five-to-one in total troop strength in west Tennessee, he must have recognized that it was only a matter of days, perhaps even hours, before the enemy would be in position to trap him. Yet despite Dibrell's early warning of the significant threat being mounted from Jackson, the Confederate commander chose not to abort his mission and begin his return east to the Tennessee River; instead, he left Starnes busily chewing up the railroad, and personally took Biffle's Regiment, Cox's Battalion, Capt. Jeffrey Forrest's Company, and a section of artillery and pushed on toward Union City.

9

The Treacherous Withdrawal

You will hear from me in another quarter . . .

—Gen. N. B. Forrest

On the afternoon of December 19, after Col. Adolph Engelmann had been driven back from Salem Cemetery, General Sullivan received into Jackson some six regiments of reinforcements that he immediately dispatched to the Cotton Grove Road to bolster Engelmann against an attack he believed imminent the following day. Sometime during the night, Sullivan must have determined that Forrest was slipping away, although he was unsure of which direction, since reports were trickling in of the railroad being severed both north and south of Jackson. But that same day, Col. Jacob Fry, in command at Trenton, actually knew Forrest's location and intent, telegraphing to General Davies in Columbus, Kentucky, that "the main force of the enemy was moving toward Trenton" (Fry 1887, 561). Unfortunately, he did not communicate this information, along with Forrest's location at Spring Creek, to General Sullivan in Jackson until the latter had started east after Forrest on Saturday morning the 20th. Finally taking to heart Grant's imperative to go after the enemy, Sullivan moved at daylight, leaving about two thousand men to guard Jackson, and declaring to Grant, "I need no more reinforcements, and can surely save all your rear communications this way" (Sullivan 1887, 552). Much to Sullivan's consternation, his sojourn out the Cotton Grove Road found Forrest gone, with only a shadow force casually engaging him as it delayed east. With Dengler's 43rd Illinois, veterans of the recent fight at Salem Cemetery, taking the advance, Sullivan moved his force to within ten miles of Lexington but still did not locate General Forrest's main body. Col. John W. Fuller, placed in command of a makeshift brigade consisting of the 39th and 27th Ohio Infantry Regiments, wrote regarding the expedition,

> I marched in the direction of Lexington, overtaking the main column about 10 miles east of Jackson. While halting here cannonading was heard in the direction of Humboldt. After an hour's halt we continued the march until about 19 miles distant from Jackson, where we bivouacked for the night. The next morning at 6 o'clock we returned over the same road, my command, which was in advance, reaching Jackson between 1 and 2 P.M. (Fuller 1887, 569)

Frustrated that he had missed Forrest, Sullivan determined to pursue him up the railroad line that was rapidly being destroyed between Jackson and Columbus. But upon his return to Jackson on the 21st, Sullivan received disastrous news from the south. Reports had come in during the night indicating an attack against the huge Federal advanced supply depot established by Grant at Holly Springs, Mississippi, to support his Vicksburg operation. Though early reports were sketchy, Sullivan was able to piece together that a large Confederate cavalry body under the command of Gen. Earl Van Dorn had dashed into Holly Springs and destroyed the better part of the supplies assembled there. But as bad as the report was for Grant's offensive, the uncertainty of Van Dorn's next move must have been particularly disconcerting to Sullivan. Would Van Dorn now turn north as some were predicting, dash up the railroad in a move reminiscent of Frank C. Armstrong's raid earlier that year? Would he attempt to link up with General Forrest and swell the Confederate numbers to beyond fifteen thousand? Van Dorn's whereabouts and intentions surely kept Sullivan glancing over his shoulder while he proceeded with the immediate task of locating, trapping, and defeating Forrest. What Sullivan did not know, but would learn over the next two days, was the combined effect on Grant's offensive created by Van Dorn's strike on Holly Springs and Forrest's rampage through west Tennessee. Maj. Gen. James B. McPherson, commanding the right wing of Grant's army in Mississippi, had telegraphed him on December 20 suggesting that he should "fall back to the north side of the Tallahatchie, hold that line," and use Federal cavalry to protect the railroads. "In view of the fact that . . . our long line of communication [is] interrupted and liable to be so again when reopened we cannot go well beyond Grenada . . ." (McPherson 1887, 446). While Grant was confident that he had assembled enough force to meet Forrest in west Tennessee (he indicated that "very few of them will get away"), he agreed with McPherson's suggestion, realizing even now that his Vicksburg campaign was in great jeopardy.

In his December 21 and 23 diary entries, Lieutenant O. C. Ayers of the inexperienced 39th Iowa notes the beginning of Sullivan's rigorous pursuit of Forrest.

> We started north on the Rail Road toward [Humboldt and Trenton]. About ten miles from here we found a bridge burned. [That night] we slept in the cars which is the first night since we came to Dixy [*sic*] that we have slept on anything harder than the ground unless sleeping on our arms could be called harder. Gracious knows it is hard enough for anybody. (Ayers 1984, 24).

Ayers described the charred devastation of the Federal camp at Humboldt and offers a revealing glimpse at a relatively new unit being thrown into the cauldron of battle against a particularly wary foe. Ordered to establish a picket line north of Humboldt on the night of the 21st, the inexperienced men of the 39th Iowa did not meet with great success.

> We were expected to keep a sharp look out. I was in command of the Company and kept awake, but so worn out were most of them that they lay down on the ground and were asleep in a very few minutes. Captain Elliot was Officer of the Day for the first time. He was required to Post a Picket Guard and a line had to be established. It was a very hard task even for a experienced officer and for one that never saw a Picket, it is still harder. So it is not surprising that Gen. Heaney [Haynie] was displeased with a part of the line. I think that Captain Elliot has but a very rare opinion of General Heaney.[1] (Ayers 1984, 24)

The General Haynie mentioned in the above diary account was in command of the pursuit forces in the vicinity of Humboldt until the evening of the 21st, when General Sullivan arrived to take over. The entire next day, while Forrest was resupplying with captured stores at Trenton, overpowering garrisons, and destroying the railroad at Rutherford and Kenton Station, Sullivan returned to Jackson apparently trying to decide how best to intercept Forrest and cut him off from the Tennessee River. Grant's prodding inquiries, for example, "What news from Jackson? Are the road and wires right north of you?" (Grant 1887, 458) did not elicit replies of "Rapidly pursuing the enemy," or other such preemptive actions. Instead, Sullivan replied, "Jackson, Humboldt, and Bolivar all right. The rebels are in strong force all around us—entirely cavalry. I am busy repairing the road north, and will use all my force to keep it open. Trenton was taken by Forrest . . . the wires are not in order above here" (Sullivan 1887, 456).

A destroyed telegraph line and uncertainty about enemy actions north of Jackson occupied most of Sullivan's attention, but these were not his only concerns. The telegraph south of town remained quite functional and buzzed with reports of General Van Dorn's cavalry operating virtually unimpeded along the Tennessee-Mississippi line in the vicinity of La Grange and Grand Junction. Isolated commanders in that section were now begging Sullivan to send help in their direction, as they feared Van Dorn would sweep north and "gobble up" the garrisons along the Mobile and Ohio Railroad between La Grange and Jackson. Meanwhile, General Grant had been successful in directing the recapture of a decimated Holly Springs, and he was rapidly repositioning forces in north Mississippi to counter Van Dorn and eliminate the threat against Sullivan from the south. Perhaps one of the reasons Sullivan hesitated to leave Jackson on the 21st or 22nd in pursuit of Forrest was a legitimate fear that Confederate General Van Dorn would slip in his back door and take a second, and possibly more critical, supply and transportation junction. A series of running fights on the 22nd and 23rd between detachments of Van Dorn's cavalry and Federal forces near Bolivar, Whiteville, and Sommerville did little to ease Sullivan's concern.

Whatever his reasoning, by December 23 Sullivan seems to have felt free to maneuver against Forrest. Since his return from the fruitless chase to Lexington on the 20th, Sullivan had been content to gradually push a small force up the Mobile Ohio Railroad line under the supervision of Brigadier General I. N. Haynie to discover what Forrest had wrought and, as he indicated in his reply to Grant, repair the railroad. That day, the 23rd, the illustrious Col. Robert G. Ingersoll, lately paroled by General Forrest, reported to Sullivan in Jackson. "The rebels have gone to Columbus and then to cross over and destroy Rosecrans' line of railroad [in middle Tennessee]," he told Sullivan. "They number at 7,500 men" (Sullivan 1887, 465). Everyone Sullivan communicated with seemed to confirm the exaggerated enemy strength report, and he must have surely given credence to the observations of a man who spent the past three days a captive in the midst of Forrest's army. But Ingersoll, like so many others, had been duped into the role of false prophet and sent out to spread an inflated gospel that Sullivan apparently believed. Sullivan reported to Grant on the 23rd that his forces under Haynie would "occupy Trenton tomorrow . . . with a force strong enough to open the [rail]road," and that he had dispatched a force south "toward Denmark and the north side of Hatchie [River]" (Sullivan 1887, 465).

Haynie, who was pushing north toward Trenton along the railroad in the wake of Forrest's destruction, sent a courier (the telegraph being a casualty of the Confederates) to General Davies at Columbus, Kentucky, on the 23rd requesting him to "move down this way and check Forrest so that we can drive him off of the railroad or whip him" (Haynie 1887, 467). But Davies at Columbus had his own troubles, many of them products of his own making. Having lost telegraph communication with General Sullivan in Jackson on December 21, he had been dependent upon his own scouts and couriers to learn Forrest's location and intent. Davies suspected for several days that his critical railroad junction, river port, and supply center at Columbus, Kentucky, would be a primary target of Forrest's movement. Unable to communicate with Sullivan, Davies directed his messages north to Maj. Gen. Henry W. Halleck, general-in-chief of the Army of the West.

General Sullivan has withdrawn force from Union City, Kenton, Trenton, etc., to Jackson. Trenton and the railroad to Union City in hands of enemy . . . shall push down and repair railroad and fight. Ordered boats below Fort Henry to be taken out of the river to prevent rebels crossing. . . . Think Columbus will be attacked, but am ready for any force they can bring. (Davies 1887, Part 1, 454)

The following day, as Forrest was driving toward Union City, Tennessee, Davies sent to Halleck the most accurate estimate in days of Forrest's troop strength. From a "paroled officer," one obviously not taken in by Forrest's ruse, Davies listed a nearly inclusive by-unit breakdown of the Confederate command, including the number of men in Forrest's bodyguard, arriving at a total of thirty-four hundred. While that was still an inflated figure, it was far closer to reality than any numbers driving the decisions of either Sullivan in Jackson or Grant in Oxford, Mississippi. Davies attempted to route his information to Grant via the telegraph in Memphis but appears to have had little success. What might Sullivan have done differently if he had received Davies' estimate of the enemy strength? Would he have departed Jackson sooner? Would he have been bolder in his pursuit? In the same dispatch Davies makes an interesting, albeit belated, recommendation that a mounted infantry force be raised to counter these raids.[2]

But if Halleck, Grant, Sullivan, or anyone else who received Davies' messages had begun to lend them credence, Christmas Eve of 1862 would have been a good day to stop such an indulgence. Davies sent a telegram to General Halleck at 8:00 A.M. that morning declaring that Confederate General Cheatham "has crossed the Tennessee with 40,000 men and is marching north. I cannot hold Columbus against that force. The information had reached me before that he had crossed but I did not credit it till now" (Davies 1887, Part 1, 470). Where Davies got such a report can only be surmised, but it sounds strangely like a product of the Nathan Bedford Forrest disinformation campaign. Perhaps an influential prisoner allowed to escape from Trenton or Union City came dashing into Davies headquarters at Columbus, or perhaps one of Davies' scouts mistook a locally raised command of Confederate cavalry enroute to join Forrest, that is, Napier's Battalion, as the vanguard of some advancing army. Either way, the news froze any effort by Davies to advance south, repair the railroad, or link up with General Haynie. His report spooked Halleck enough to elicit the orders, "Columbus must be held at all hazards," which Davies would, over the next two days, carry to an extreme. He began by gathering in all his detachments outside the town to consolidate a force of five thousand men, and he immediately went about loading U.S. government property on to boats.[3] But Davies' most significant act relative to Forrest was no action at all. Frozen by fear of forty thousand men, he presented no threat to Forrest from the north, despite his having five thousand troops with which to attack, and was content to wait within the defenses of Columbus for what he was certain would be a major battle. If Forrest and Van Dorn were not enough with which to contend, General Halleck, and consequently General Davies, learned that yet another cavalry raid was occurring in central Kentucky—this one under the command of Brig. Gen. John Hunt Morgan. Which way Morgan would turn must have also weighed upon Davies' mind as he waited within the fortifications of Columbus.

On Christmas Eve, Grant was still prodding Sullivan in Jackson for information, and more importantly, action. "What steps are you taking to drive out the enemy?" Grant asked. "Are you collecting forage and supplies?" (Grant 1887, 477). At last, the following day Sullivan left Jackson, Tennessee, with a division to attack Forrest, all the while protesting that he faced some "design of the rebels to weaken [Jackson] by making me send off my men, and then, marching rapidly to the rear, capture and destroy the stores" (Henry 1944, 115).

SPEED, MASS, AND THE THREAT OF FIREPOWER

At 4:00 P.M. on December 23, Forrest captured the Federal garrison at Union City without firing a shot. The pickets south of town had mistaken several hundred Federal parolees marching toward Columbus, Kentucky, as part of the Confederate attacking force, scampering back with reports of an impending massive attack. Although the commander of Federal troops, Capt. Samuel B. Logan of the 54th Illinois Infantry, claimed some impropriety over a flag of truce preceding the parolees, the simple truth is that the actual Confederate cavalry riding close behind overwhelmed him.

"General Forrest, I judge to the number of 1,500, surrounded my command in every direction but one, to within easy musket range. Their cannon were shotted and sighted upon us, three of which were in full view. From the time their forces first appeared in view *three minutes* [author's italics] did not transpire before we were thus surrounded" (Logan 1887, 567). Forrest's pattern remained unchanged—move fast, strike hard, envelop, display superior firepower and strength, and demand surrender. He had little reason to change a technique that had met with nothing but success for almost a week.

Using Forrest's technique on a smaller scale that very night, a detachment of only forty men was able to bluff the garrison defending Moscow, Kentucky, out of its barricade by calling aloud for nonexistent "artillery" to be brought "forward." This minor action marked the northern limit of Forrest's progress during the raid, only fueling the fires of panic among General Davies and the Federal defenders of Columbus, Kentucky, less than twenty miles away. Also that night, and all day on the 24th, Forrest's men labored to destroy (1) the railroad bridge over the bayou on the Tennessee-Kentucky line near Moscow, Kentucky, and (2) the bridges over the north and south fork of the Obion River. On Christmas Eve, Forrest at last took

the time to construct a report sent by courier to General Bragg, informing
him:

> We have made a clean sweep of the Federals and roads north of Jackson, and
> know of no Federals except at Fort Heiman, Paducah, and Columbus, north
> of Jackson and west of the Tennessee River. . . . My men have all behaved well
> in action and as soon as rested a little you will hear from me in another quarter.
> Our loss so far is 8 killed, 12 wounded, and 2 missing. The enemy's killed and
> wounded number over 100 men; prisoners over 1,200. . . . We have been so
> busy and kept so constantly moving that we have not had time to make out
> a report of our strength, and ask to be excused until the next courier comes
> over. We send by courier a list of prisoners paroled. (Forrest 1887, 595)

While Forrest most certainly underreported his losses, his enumeration
of the Federal losses seems reasonably accurate. After paroling some three
hundred additional prisoners collected at Trenton and Union City on
Christmas Day, Forrest allowed his men to rest and refit for the remainder
of the campaign. And while his command had suffered the usual attrition
due to illness, worn-out horses, and stragglers, Forrest actually increased
his strength at Union City with the arrival of Lieut. Col. Thomas Alonzo
Napier's Battalion of four hundred men. Napier's command, consisting of
five companies raised in middle Tennessee, had crossed the river at
Reynoldsburg the day after Forrest crossed at Clifton. Napier had enlisted
from Benton County, Tennessee, into the 49th Tennessee Infantry when he
was captured at Fort Donelson. He escaped from the Federals while being
transferred to Johnson's Island in April 1862 and returned to Tennessee to
raise his own cavalry force. As his battalion moved from Reynoldsburg to
link up with Forrest at Union City, they may well have been the force
spotted by General Davies' scouts and erroneously reported as part of
Cheatham's division. The arrival of Napier's Battalion did not go unnoticed
by the Federals, although they also inflated his strength to seven hundred
men and two pieces of artillery, and this particular command may have
prompted an observation in the December 24 *Chicago Tribune* that "the
Rebels are enforcing the conscript law as they pass along, and are received
with great rejoicing by nearly all the inhabitants" ("The War in Tennessee"
1862, 1).

On December 26, Forrest ascertained that he had accomplished the
mission General Bragg had assigned him, and amid a drenching, all-day
rain, he began a treacherous withdrawal toward the Tennessee River. The
command left Union City on a twenty-mile march to Dresden, destroying
enroute the Nashville and Northwestern Railroad and camping there that
evening. Pausing in Dresden for the better part of Saturday, the 27th, he
allowed his men and horses to rest while he sent scouts forward to find the
isolated Federal commands he knew to be converging upon him.

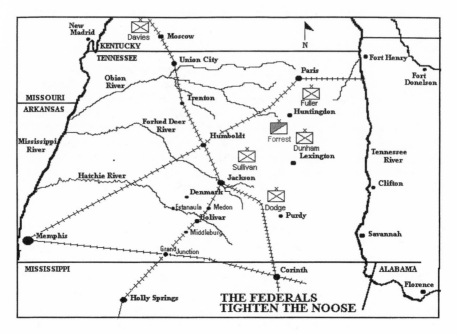

Map 9.1

Forrest learned that the force moving up the railroad from Jackson had turned east in an attempt to block his return to the Tennessee River. Scouts also told Forrest that a second Federal force was in the vicinity of Huntingdon, that all the river crossings were being guarded, and that gunboats were plying the river awaiting his attempt to cross (Mathes 1902, 88). The heavy rain was swelling the Obion River bottoms and guaranteeing that passage through them to the southeast would occur only over well-traveled roads—all of which the Federals were guarding. Forrest sent Russell's 4th Alabama in advance with orders to move toward Huntingdon and seize the crossing over the south fork of the Obion River; the remainder of the command proceeded to McKenzie Station and camped there on the 27th. When scouts informed him about 9:00 P.M. that evening that Russell had control of a crossing site after a contested struggle with a Federal detachment, Forrest sensed he must act cautiously, yet quickly. He dispatched Cox's Battalion to the Huntingdon-Paris Road to locate and check any Federal force in the vicinity, and then determined to cross the south fork of the Obion River further to the southwest, and out of reach of the enemy forces gathering about Huntingdon.

Given the destruction of bridges wrought by wary Federals in anticipation of Forrest's withdrawal, only one possible route remained open to the raiders. A little-used road wove through the swamps and bottoms of the Obion, across a "double-bridge" on a road leading to McLemoresville (Jordan & Pryor 1977, 207). The Federals had damaged the bridge and apparently believed it to be impassable, for they had neglected to place a guard upon it (Henry 1944, 115). Forrest immediately seized upon this weakness in the Federal noose and sent pioneer teams ahead of the main body to cut "timber-forks" and brace up the old bridge. A long, raised road, or causeway, built by slave labor many years before, led across the bottoms and up to and beyond the bridge that spanned the south fork of the Obion River. When Forrest arrived at the bridge, he found his men beneath a torchlight staring dejectedly at the dilapidated structure. But taking up an axe, he demonstrated what he expected to be done, and he "soon had the tired men working cheerily at the task, despite the mire and darkness" (Morton 1992, 62). Sensing this was likely the command's only way out of west Tennessee, Forrest became commander, site boss, and cheerleader all in one. Morton describes his commander as being "here, there, and every-where, directing, assisting, and encouraging. It must be admitted, too, that the great strain under which he was laboring found vent in frequent profanity, as was his custom in moments of great excitement" (Morton 1992, 62). Working by torchlight in the dark bottoms, the rickety old bridge was shorn up enough to allow some cavalry to pass over and secure the far side. The temperature was dropping fast, with a "sleety drizzle" falling, and Forrest, sensing the hesitation and fear among the wagon drivers, stepped forward himself to drive the first team across the precarious structure. As the wagon moved over the narrow, slippery bridge, the structure wobbled, creaked, and shuttered, but eventually Forrest reached the causeway on the opposite side.

Years of neglect and the heavy traffic of Forrest's command left huge ruts and holes in the causeway, which the Confederates were forced to fill with sacks of precious supplies such as coffee and flour only recently liberated from the Federal depots along the railroad. Bringing forward dismounts, he ordered twenty men to a wagon and fifty men to a gun to assist passage along the muddy road. Using only enough light to make the passage, yet avoiding detection by roaming patrols, Forrest's column must have made a haunting sight creeping along the narrow roadbed, the yellowish light from the lanterns tossing strange shadows off the swamp trees whose bare branches reached skyward into the darkness. All day on the 28th his command executed passage of the Obion River bottoms, camping that night in McLemoresville. So close were the Federal columns searching for For-rest's command, that once across the Obion, his lead regiment had to wait long enough for the trail of one such column to pass before emerging onto the road to McLemoresville. Russell's 4th Alabama rejoined the main body from his mission to the original, intended crossing site, and Cox's Battalion also linked up at McLemoresville (Jordan & Pryor 1977, 208). Although he intended on Monday, the 29th, to allow his men a brief rest from the difficult work of the previous night and day, his scouts informed Forrest that one of General Sullivan's brigades under the command of Colonel Fuller was in force only twelve miles northeast at Huntingdon. Forrest also learned that another of Sullivan's brigades, under the command of Col. Cyrus Dunham, had left Huntingdon en route to Lexington—the trail elements of this brigade being the unit he narrowly missed encountering as he emerged from the swamps the previous night. This would ultimately place the Federal force squarely across Forrest's route to the Tennessee River. So at 10:00 A.M. on the 29th, Forrest led his weary force toward Lexington, figuring a fight to be inevitable, and determining all the while how best to isolate and defeat in detail the various brigades. The road leading from McLemoresville to a community called Red Mound, or Parker's Cross-roads, was "rough, miry, and hilly," and proved yet another challenge for his artillery and wagons. Forrest had hoped to reach Lexington by nightfall, for he knew Dunham's force had not yet occupied the town. From there he would be poised to reach the Tennessee River in a day's march, but although he "ought to have reached Lexington that night," the condition of the roads slowed him so that he went into camp at Flake's Store, about four miles northwest of Parker's Crossroads, and twelve miles from Lexington (Forrest 1887, 595). Although Gen. Jeremiah Sullivan could not be certain of Forrest's exact location, he had finally closed off all avenues of escape, and at last he could wire General Grant, "I have Forrest in a tight place . . . my troops are moving on him in three directions" (Sullivan 1887, 569). Now, for General Sullivan, it was a matter of defeating him.

NOTES

1. The penalty for falling asleep on guard duty could be as severe as execution by firing squad. General I. N. Haynie obviously realized he was dealing with raw troops, and given that every man was critical, it would appear from the tone of Ayers' letter that Haynie used an old-fashioned "ass chewin'" to remind the Iowans of their duty in the face of the enemy.

2. Davies seems to have in mind a force similar to the "Jackass Cavalry" that operated so effectively against Frank C. Armstrong at Bolivar in August.

3. Even though he had the Confederate raiders outnumbered, General Davies seems to have been genuinely spooked by Forrest. Convinced that Columbus, Kentucky, would be attacked, Davies spiked artillery pieces and destroyed almost a million dollars' worth of U.S. government supplies and equipment to prevent them from falling into Forrest's hands. Other than a forty-man detachment that ran the Federals out of Moscow, Kentucky, Forrest did not even make a serious demonstration against Columbus.

10

Parker's Crossroads and Forrest's Escape

Charge both ways!

—Brig. Gen. Nathan B. Forrest

The old adage about cavalry raids declares that it is always easier to get in (behind enemy lines) than it is to get out, and that was never more true than with Brig. Gen. Nathan Bedford Forrest's cavalry force on the last day of 1862. Pursued from every direction by forces far outnumbering his own, Forrest pushed as rapidly toward the Tennessee River as the bad roads, bitterly cold weather, and swarming Federal patrols would allow. "To avoid the large Federal forces that were closing in on every side of his band of raiders," explained young artilleryman J. M. Metcalfe, "[Forrest] marched at night across country, through prohibitive swamps, and over almost impassable roads" (Bond 1908, 108). The common soldier's perception of being on the run and constantly dodging superior forces more closely represents the facts than the idea that Forrest was somehow pulling the strings on all the Federal movements around him. Some historians, such as Andrew Nelson Lytle, have argued that the events about to play out at Parker's Crossroads, eight miles north of Lexington, were the result of a gullible enemy falling into the jaws of Forrest's carefully laid trap. Lytle paints a picture of Forrest on December 30 and 31 that approximates hero worship, indicating that possessing nearly 100 percent accurate intelligence, and with "the situation completely in his hand," Forrest was somehow "deftly drawing the enemy into the very toils they had set for him" (Lytle 1931, 131). Lytle contends that Forrest planned all along to attack the last significant Federal supply depot in west Tennessee located at Bethel Station, southeast of Jackson. He argues that when Forrest emerged from the Obion County swamps on the 29th, he ascertained all the Federal positions, that is, Fuller, Dunham, and Sullivan driving toward Huntingdon to oppose his crossing the Tennessee River; and then realizing that he was now behind them, Forrest planned to "separate [Sullivan's] brigades and defeat them in detail on the thirty-first, fall on Bethel Station the second of January, then his work entirely done, and no obstructions in his rear, he could recross the river and return to his base" (Lytle 1931, 131). To support this contention, Lytle points to the fact that Forrest sent a company to cut wires and bridges and prepare forage twelve miles south of Jackson.

Lytle correctly observes that Forrest had considered attacking Bethel Station, for in his report to General Bragg dated January 3, the Confederate leader writes regarding December 27 and 28 that he was moving toward Lexington, "intending if possible to avoid the enemy and go on and attack the enemy at Bethel Station, on the Mobile and Ohio road, south of Jackson" (Forrest 1887, 595). But Forrest goes on in the report to indicate that because of the difficult time his command encountered "crossing the bottom" on the 28th, his timetable was disrupted, and there is no indication from the official report that Forrest maintained any intention of going to Bethel Station on the morning of December 31. As to the notion of preparing forage at distant locations, Forrest frequently sent companies off in various directions to prepare contingency forage—but such an act did not mean that Forrest would necessarily move in that direction. It appears relatively certain from the diary accounts of the troopers, as well as from the reports of Forrest himself, that Forrest recognized the fatigued condition of his men and horses and he was proceeding to Lexington to "either cross the Tennessee at Huntingdon or else . . . move northward" (Forrest 1887, 594). Forrest was manipulating no one at this point, for the noose was drawing tight, and to his credit, Forrest recognized his precarious situation and acted to relieve it.

The day that Forrest spent at Flake's Store (Tuesday, the 30th) not only allowed his men to rest, but it also allowed him to develop further the enemy situation. Starnes' Regiment conducted a reconnaissance north toward Huntingdon to find the brigade Forrest knew to be near the town, while Biffle's Regiment worked west toward Trenton to find and, if possible, fix any force still moving from that direction. Meanwhile, sixteen-year-old Capt. Bill Forrest, the general's brother, and his scouts moved east and encountered yet another brigade-sized force (Dunham's) near the town of Clarksburg, on the road from Huntingdon to Lexington. Any hopes the Confederate leader might have had of sweeping back toward Jackson to further the destruction of the Federal supply line must have instantly vanished. Realizing that he had a pinpoint location on two brigades, with one of them moving out of supporting distance of the other, he ordered Bill Forrest to delay southward against the force moving toward Lexington. If he could keep the road to Lexington open, Forrest knew he could occupy the town, use a rear guard to keep the nearest force at bay, and sprint the remainder of the command to a crossing on the Tennessee River.

A clue to the condition of Forrest's men can be found in the account of Dan Beard, a trooper in Starnes' Regiment, detached from the main body to observe a road intersection not far from Huntingdon. On the afternoon of the 30th, Beard had tied his horse to a tree and kicked the snow from a brush pile to make a hasty seat. Cradling his shotgun in his arms, the exhausted soldier fell asleep. Only the "infernal din of firearms, clattering of horses' feet, and yells," awoke him, and to his shock he watched as some eighty Federal cavalrymen galloped less than twenty feet past him to engage the remainder of his regiment perhaps a hundred yards down the road. Forced to retire by Starnes' stiff resistance, the Federals rode back past Beard who punctuated their retreat with a blast from both barrels of his shotgun. "I loaded and capped my gun with fingers so numb I could not feel the caps, mounted and set off in a gallop after the fleeing Yankees" (Beard 1909, 308).

So with a rear guard and flank security posted, and scouts to maintain contact with the enemy force most likely to oppose his roughly sixteen-mile march to Lexington, Forrest set out from Flake's Store at daylight on the 31st, marching southeast. Within four miles, he encountered Federal skirmishers, and the most significant fight of the entire raid—the Battle of Parker's Crossroads—had begun.

BLOCKING FORREST'S ROUTE

The force Gen. Jeremiah Sullivan led to block Forrest's crossing of the Tennessee and defeat him consisted of two brigades, one under the command of Col. John W. Fuller and the other under Col. Cyrus Dunham. Convinced that Forrest was heading east and would attempt to escape across the Tennessee River at Huntingdon, Sullivan marched his brigades directly to Huntingdon from Trenton and Jackson. The forced march did not endear Sullivan to the men in his hastily organized brigades. "Not an Officer has a horse nor have we a team with us. If this is not a fine plight in which to start out on a march I am no judge," wrote Lieutenant O. C. Ayers of the 39th Iowa. "Our Brigade Commander changed just before we left. It is now Col Dunum [Dunham] of Indiana. I don't believe there is a Commander in the whole expedition, who cares a pig what becomes of our Regiment. This night march gives us fits to start on" (Ayers 1984, 28). That soldiers will complain about marching is a given—that the Federals held so little faith in their leadership is significant and revealing, particularly when contrasted to the Confederate cavalryman's attitude toward General Forrest.

Dunham's Brigade arrived at Huntingdon in the early morning of the 29th, and Fuller's Brigade—having narrowly missed an encounter with Forrest's main body as it emerged from the bottoms—passed directly through McLemoresville and reached Huntingdon that same afternoon.

Sullivan set about establishing security around the town, convinced he had blocked Forrest's escape, and readied himself for the decisive battle to come. But while the general commanding the expedition felt comfortable with the situation, the soldiers in his regiments were anything but at ease.

Lieutenant O. C. Ayers, serving as regimental quartermaster, was dashing around Huntingdon that night trying to draw rations for his weary men. Locating General Sullivan's headquarters about 9:00 P.M., he "found the old fellow stretched out on the flore [sic]," and demonstrating his inexperience, the young lieutenant "woke him up to ascertain if the Trains had yet arrrived." If that were not bad enough, he again awoke Sullivan at midnight, and yet again at 2:00 A.M. It is little wonder that Sullivan "swore a little" at his adjutant and "abused [Ayers]," ordering him to find the quartermaster, feed his regiment, and, in effect, leave him alone (Ayers 1984, 28). Although Ayers' behavior was annoying to the general, he was, after all, trying to look after his men, who Ayers described as being "so abused that with their sore feet and sickness" that one hundred and thirty stragglers had fallen out of the march and "remained behind . . . with the intention of making their way back to Trenton." And though Ayers, in his December 29 diary entry, wondered, "Gracious knows what will become of them," Confederate regimental commander Biffle would answer that question the following day by capturing them on his security mission toward Trenton.

But for all of General Sullivan's confidence, his 50th Indiana reconnaissance elements west of Huntingdon, near the Obion River (south fork) bridge to Dresden, encountered not Forrest's main body proceeding to Huntingdon as Sullivan expected, but little more than pickets that gave way when pressed. Clearly, this was not the behavior of the vanguard of Forrest's command, and before long Sullivan confirmed that "cut off from passing through Huntingdon," Forrest had "moved south and westerly, intending, doubtless, to reach Lexington" ("The Battle of Parker's Crossroads" 1863, 1).

Sullivan ordered Dunham's Brigade to pursue Forrest in the direction of Lexington, so Dunham left Huntingdon at 2:00 P.M. on December 30 and arrived after dark in Clarksburg "weary and worn from toilsome marches and arduous duties" (Dunham 1887, 579). Dunham's brigade consisted of two companies of the 18th Illinois Mounted Infantry, the 50th Indiana Infantry, the 122nd Illinois Infantry, the 39th Iowa Infantry, and three pieces of artillery from the 7th Wisconsin Battery—in all, about sixteen hundred men. In Clarksburg, Dunham's advance guard of mounted infantry encountered Bill Forrest's scouts and pushed them out of town. After the remainder of the brigade settled in for the night, Dunham learned from his scouts that he had unknowingly camped within four miles of Forrest's command. Having produced the first solid information in days on the location of what must have begun to appear to the Federals as a ghost army, Dunham dispatched a courier to General Sullivan at 2:00 A.M. indicating not only Forrest's location, but yet another incorrect estimate of Forrest's strength at eight thousand men. Dunham added the prediction that the Confederates would move southeast to Parker's Crossroads "to escape by way of Lexington." He informed Sullivan that he would "try to coax or force a fight out of him" the next morning in hopes of delaying Forrest until Sullivan and Fuller could combine forces and overwhelm him (Dunham 1887, 580). How the Federals could have pursued Forrest for almost two weeks and still not realized he had no more than twenty-five hundred effectives challenges the imagination, but more importantly, the lack of accurate intelligence on the Confederate strength caused General Sullivan and his subordinates to continue to make inappropriate tactical responses to battlefield encounters with Forrest's main body, often giving way in the face of what they mistakenly believed were overwhelming numbers. But while Dunham overestimated Forrest's strength early on the morning of the 31st, there is evidence of even wilder reports that unfortunately combined the truth of Forrest's intentions with the myth of great strength. Lieutenant O. C. Ayers indicates in his diary account that a courier had arrived the previous afternoon reporting "12,000 rebels camped about 5 miles from here . . . on their way to the Tennessee [River] and trying to cross" (Ayers 1984, 29).

After a quick breakfast in the cold and darkness, Dunham marched from Clarksburg before daylight with Company A, 50th Indiana as advance guard. That unit engaged Confederate pickets at Parker's Crossroads, and as the remainder of Dunham's command closed up, the enemy pickets began a delay west from the crossroads, then northwest along a road leading to Flake's Store. Leaving the 122nd Illinois to block the intersection at Parker's Crossroads, and the 39th Iowa to guard the approach from the north, Dunham pressed the enemy with the 50th Indiana and two pieces of artillery. After steadily driving the Confederates' company-sized advance element northwest past a farm owned by a Dr. Williams, to and through Hicks' Field, a detachment of the 18th Illinois Mounted Infantry arrived at approximately 7:00 A.M. to form a line of battle with the 50th Indiana (Kennerly 1993, 25). The intermittent fire of skirmishers was drowned out by the eruption of a howitzer, first from the high ground on the Federal left, not more than four hundred yards away, and then from the Federal right. Realizing that the Confederate guns had but little dismounted cavalry protecting them, Dunham returned fire with his artillery and sent four companies of infantry advancing with the intent of defeating the light force opposing him and perhaps capturing the enemy guns. But the steady grape and cannister fire retarded Dunham's advance, and as the Federals attempted to regroup, "at least a full battery" opened fire on his men, dismounting one of his artillery pieces (Dunham 1887, 581). It was almost 9:00 A.M. by now, and as Dunham states in his report, "seeing that the enemy had put a heavy force in line along and just over the crest of the ridge, and

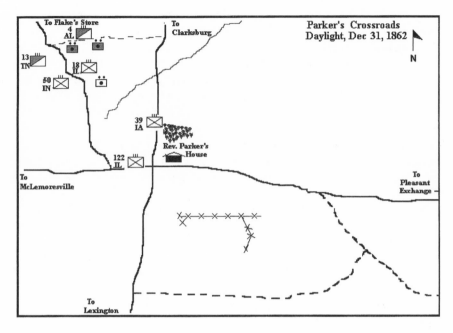

Map 10.1

having accomplished all I desired at that place and time, I ordered our fire to cease and the forces there to be withdrawn to the main column at the crossroads" (Dunham 1887, 581). Dunham had, in fact, accomplished two critical tasks: He had located and identified Forrest's main body, and he had interposed a blocking force between Forrest and the Tennessee River. All that remained for Dunham to do was to delay Forrest until the balance of General Sullivan's force could fall upon his flank or rear and destroy him. But that would prove to be a costly mission for Cyrus Dunham.

FIREPOWER WELL FORWARD

"Put a scare on the enemy and keep it on them," Forrest is often quoted as saying, and the tactics demonstrated thus far in his west Tennessee raid epitomized that philosophy. His pattern of leading with a light force of dismounted cavalry and his artillery well forward—within small-arms range of the enemy—ensured overwhelming shock and firepower sufficient enough to knock an opponent back on his heels. The situation developed congruently with Forrest's plan that morning against Colonel Dunham, and having seized the initiative, Forrest kept up the pressure, or the "scare," as Dunham fell back to Parker's Crossroads.

Prior to the initial engagement with Dunham at Hick's Field, Brigadier General Forrest had ordered Capt. William S. McLemore with his Company F, "The Williamson County Cavalry," and three other companies of Starnes' 4th Tennessee Cavalry (about one hundred men) on a reconnaissance to Clarksburg on the Huntingdon Road and north of Parker's Crossroads. Receiving his mission orders secondhand, Captain McLemore understood only that he was to conduct a reconnaissance and link up with Capt. Bill Forrest's independent scout company already at that location. Unfortunately, the message was somehow garbled when relayed to McLemore, proving to be "vague and inexpressive of the actual purposes of the movement" (Jordan 1887, 217), and McLemore assumed he should return to the main body once he had located the scouts. Thus, he departed east early that morning, covering the seven miles to Clarksburg by moving cross-country on narrow, wooded trails, only to discover Captain Forrest's scouts absent. Enroute, his detachment narrowly missed capturing Generals Sullivan and Haynie who were riding toward Clarksburg. The two Federal officers dashed into the woods to avoid McLemore's cavalry, emerging back on the main road once the Confederates had passed (Kennerly 1993, 28). A combination of events now led McLemore to a decision that would ultimately jeopardize Forrest's entire command. The young captain discovered that Bill Forrest's independent scout company had been forced out of Clarksburg by Dunham's advance earlier that morning, and he recognized the muddy evidence of infantry, cavalry, and artillery having moved south from Clarksburg during the night. Also, upon his arrival at Clarksburg, a detachment of Federal cavalry had retreated southward as well, and within minutes McLemore heard artillery from the south and southwest (Forrest engaging Dunham at Hick's Field). These indicators led McLemore to conclude that "having executed his orders, his presence was now needed as soon as possible with his regiment, evidently in conflict at the time with a superior force" (Jordan 1887, 218). Expecting a large enemy force to be on the road leading south out of Clarksburg toward Lexington, McLemore[1] swung to the west, retracing his route to avoid contact and rejoin the main body. Thus, as Forrest pressed the fight against Dunham at Parker's Crossroads, he was unaware he no longer had eyes on Fuller's avenue of approach from Huntingdon via Clarksburg.

Forrest found Dunham in line of battle running roughly north-south, positioned to block his advance toward Lexington. The 39th Iowa (Lieutenant O. C. Ayers' regiment) anchored the left, with the 122nd Illinois to the right, his three-gun battery next, and the 18th Illinois Mounted Infantry curling back to the right. Advanced slightly in front of the 18th Illinois was the 50th Indiana, positioned to cover the crossroads, with two companies thrown forward to the road itself. The brigade trains were tucked away in a draw some five hundred yards southeast of the 39th Iowa.

When the Confederates emerged near the crossroads, they began receiving artillery fire which had "but little effect" (Dunham 1987, 581). "Company G [50th Indiana] immediately moved up the road at double-quick, deployed in the lane, opened a galling fire and held his position until forced back by overwhelming numbers" (Dunham 1887, 581). Forrest's technique for maneuvering dismounted cavalry differed from the classic, set-piece motion of Napoleonic and European warfare so widely copied during the first two years of the war. Although describing specifically Starnes' men, cavalryman Dan Baird's explanation of fire and maneuver applied equally to the other regiments Forrest commanded.

> Starnes' men did not much fear to charge a line of Yankee infantry who fired by volley or command. It looked to be probable that everyone of our men would be killed or wounded, but these terrible volleys were often without effect, as the Confederate lines were open, and all the men who could were behind some obstacle, and when they could deliver their fire, it was effective. (Baird 1909, 367)

The technique described above successfully forced the Indiana companies out of the crossroads, allowing Forrest's main body to press east, through the crossroads, and threaten Dunham's flank. Thus Dunham, believing Forrest "desirous of escaping in that direction [east]," and fearing, as did

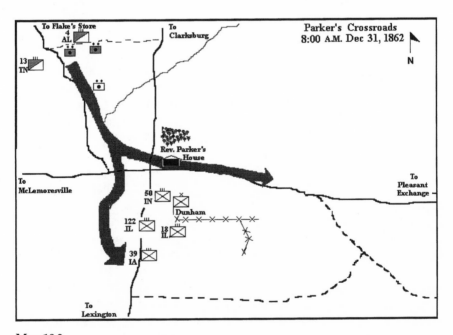

Map 10.2

Col. John I. Rinaker of the 122nd Illinois, that he would be flanked, changed front and reestablished his line a half mile north, running roughly west to east, and facing north, with the notion of enfilading Forrest as he moved. Rinaker's 122nd Illinois had fifteen or twenty men wounded in this facing move, and soon discovered that while they had successfully avoided being flanked, the Confederates had achieved yet another advantage.

> The rebels had obtained a ridge in the field in our new front, in shape of an arc of a great circle, behind the crest of which they had placed ten pieces of artillery at distances varying from 300 to 600 yards, and as we came into line, facing the north and in front of the rebels' guns, they opened on us most furiously with grape, cannister, shell, and solid shot. (Rinaker 1887, 586).

As the Confederate main body presented itself, Lieutenant O. C. Ayers of the 39th Iowa still believed he was facing eight thousand cavalry. "They covered over an emence [*sic*] tract of country. There was between them and us only an open field, a large Cotton field. Their guns and sabers gleamed in the sun [and] they evoked like an enormous host to move against our little force of about 1600" (Ayers 1984, 30). A correspondent with the *Chicago Tribune* rendered a strikingly accurate picture of Dunham's predicament when he wrote on January 9 after the battle,

> What was the surprise of Colonel Dunham to find his little brigade confronting, drawn up in a field of about a mile and quarter in length and one mile in width, supported in front by three batteries, on elevated points or hillocks, seemingly made expressly for the purpose, and rather encircling with cavalry and dismounted horsemen the road where he should pass, over 7,000 Confederates, all under the command of the redoubtable Forrest in person. There was no time to run, if he would—which was not his forte—and all he had before him was to fight it out. This he proceeded coolly to do. ("The Battle" 1863, 2).

Again Forrest turned to his artillery, and rushing it into position on the prominent terrain described by Rinaker, he began to pound Dunham's line. But this time there would be no return fire from the Federal artillery[2], as all the ammunition had been expended and not enough horses remained alive to pull the guns, thus they were pushed into a ravine and abandoned prior to Dunham's facing movement. All Federal commanders described the Confederate artillery concentration on their line as "murderous" and "terrible in its intensity," and realizing he could not long withstand such a barrage, Dunham ordered a charge at the batteries on his left front. Men of the 122nd Illinois and the 50th Indiana rushed toward the Confederate battery, which had been placed in advance of the dismounted cavalry that supported it by fire. But meeting a barrage of cannister and grape, and receiving a heavy fire from the dismounts behind, the Federals failed twice to take the guns, though coming within only a few yards the second time.

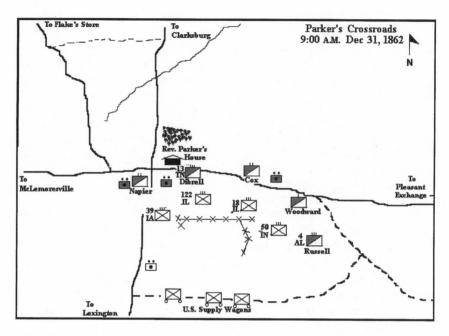

Map 10.3

Sensing his advantage, Forrest ordered an advance across the entire front, and Dunham's brigade gave way. The Confederates would roll the guns forward, following them on foot at "almost equal speed," stopping to fire, then continuing to the next available position (Morton 1992, 65). The line of dismounted cavalry in support of the artillery crept ever closer. Lieutenant A. L. Huggins of Freeman's Battery recalled the action of fellow lieutenant Nat Baxter. "The enemy were so close to us that Dibrell's men [dismounted in support of the artillery] were compelled to load and fire lying down. At this crisis, Lieut. Baxter did the loading of his gun of our battery himself, lying upon his back and ramming the charge home" (Huggins 1886, 796). When a Federal officer fell before the onslaught of Freeman's Battery, young J. M. Metcalfe picked up the officer's valise and proudly displayed it to a veteran, who issued an odd rebuke saying, "You may be in the same fix as that dead Yankee before night. Forrest is going to get the worst licking a soldier ever got" (Bond 1908, 108).

If Forrest was going to receive a "licking," there was certainly no evidence of it at this point in the battle, for Dunham's brigade had been driven to the cover of a split-rail fence that extended west to east, then curled south at the edge of some woods. It was about 11:30 A.M. now, and as the Confederates renewed their artillery fire, the Federals lay down behind the fence; but the exploding cannister shells began to shatter it, turning the rails into

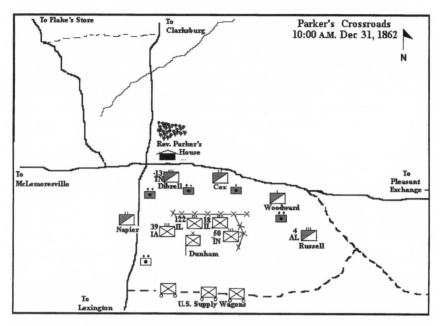

Map 10.4

splinters, and magnifying the guns' effect with deadly, wooden missiles. Moments later, Colonel Rinaker of the 122nd fell, the artery in his right leg severed just below the knee by cannister fire. Only quick application of a tourniquet by his second in command saved his life (Kennerly 1993, 33). The 50th Indiana suffered equally from the Confederate artillery, with "many a poor soldier [losing] his life and many [losing] arms and legs" (Kennerly 1993, 33).

At this point, though receiving no order from General Forrest to do so, Colonel T. A. Napier led his battalion in a dismounted charge against the 39th Iowa, occupying the extreme Federal left. Reaching the split-rail fence, he mounted it and was waving his sword and cursing his men to close quickly and follow him across when he received a mortal wound (Kennerly 1993, 49). The 39th gave ground, separating itself several hundred yards from the rest of the brigade before rallying. News of the death of Colonel Napier may have motivated Forrest to finish Dunham quickly, or the Confederate leader may have realized that the sound of this heavy engagement would soon bring Fuller's Brigade to the fight. Perhaps he had simply maneuvered Dunham into a tight position and felt he could now be easily surrounded, but for whatever reason, Forrest now ordered a double envelopment of the Federal position. He sent Woodward's two Kentucky companies and Russell's 4th Alabama on a sweep around Dunham's right, simultaneously ordering Starnes' Regiment, only recently having arrived from Huntingdon, to move parallel to the Huntingdon-Lexington Road and gain the Federal left. Upon this movement, Forrest began shifting his artillery and concentrating his batteries on the Federal left, southwest of the home of a Reverend Parker, for whom the crossroads was named. Dunham reports that "we were suddenly and furiously attacked from the rear by a heavy dismounted force [Woodward and Russell] which had, under the cover of the hills and woods beyond, turned our right flank" (Dunham 1887, 582).

Colonel Dunham issued an order to his brigade to about face and meet the new threat to their rear, but amid the roar of artillery and the steady small-arms fire, only about half his men responded to the command. The 50th Indiana, with bayonets fixed, and a portion of the 122nd Illinois, followed Dunham south to meet Forrest's envelopment. The Confederates under Woodward and Russell fell back before Dunham's counterattack, thus extending the distance between this force and the Federals still manning the fence line further north. Meanwhile, Colonel Biffle arrived from Trenton with his regiment and swept in behind Starnes as he flanked the Federal left. These dispositions, coupled with the steady artillery pounding, proved too much for the men of the 39th Iowa, who broke and fled in disorder almost a quarter mile to the southwest before they could be rallied. Their commander, Colonel H.J.B. Cummings, insisted in his report that his "raw . . . imperfectly drilled troops" had misunderstood an order, "rally to the rear," for instructions to retreat (Cummings 1889, 589) "Under this fire, so unexpected from both front and rear, . . . about half my regiment broke to the left of our line as formed behind the fence and crossed the road into the cornfield on the opposite side." Eventually Cummings rallied his men, and some stragglers from the other regiments, and returned to the main body, but in the meantime, the flight of the 39th left the remnants of the 122nd Illinois exposed to enfilading fire from the left.

Fearing that his supply wagons would be captured by the Confederate forces he was fighting back to the south, Colonel Dunham personally rode to the trains, and "curs[ing] the Brigade QM [quartermaster] in the most awful manor [sic]," relieved him on the spot and ordered the ranking quartermaster to take charge of the train and "get it out of there" (Ayers 1984, 30). Lieutenant O. C. Ayers took charge of the train and had moved it perhaps a hundred yards west when Freeman's artillery began to rake the column. "Rebel's shells began to drop among the teams thick and fast," Ayers wrote in his diary of the 31st of December. "These were the first shells I had heard and I must say I thought they made the most frightful screaming imaginable" (Ayers 1984, 30). Halting at revolver point an attempt to flee by the frightened wagon drivers, Ayers repositioned the wagons just in time to see Woodward's and Russell's dismounted cavalrymen approaching from the southeast. At this point, Ayers departed from the wagon trains to

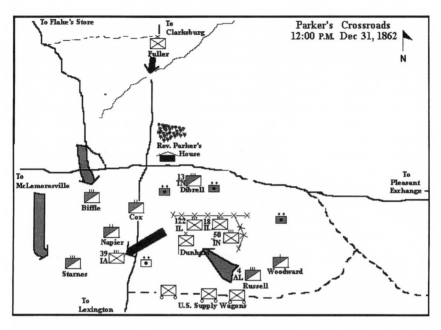

Map 10.5

rejoin his company, which was involved in a running fight with the rest of the 39th Iowa as the regiment attempted to rejoin the brigade line.

Returning to the southern half of his command, Dunham found them decisively engaged virtually from all sides, as Russell, Woodward, Biffle, and Starnes surrounded them. Forrest was pressing his thin line of troops remaining in the north—Dibrell, Cox, and Napier—toward the Federal elements still occupying the fence line, noting in his report, "we drove them through the woods with great slaughter and several white flags were raised in various portions of the woods and the killed and wounded were strewn over the ground" (Forrest 1887, 596).

From this point in the battle, about 12:30 P.M., two different versions have emerged as to the events leading to the finale of Parker's Crossroads. The Federal reports of Dunham and Rinaker read as though a great victory had been gained by Dunham's Brigade. When a general lull began to settle over the battlefield, Forrest sent his adjutant, Major Strange, to Colonel Dunham under a flag of truce, locating the Federal commander with his isolated band of troops south of the main line. Dunham claims he told Strange that he had "never thought of surrendering," and that if anyone had done so, "it was done without [his] authority or knowledge." Strange departed to inform Forrest and returned moments later demanding an "unconditional surrender." Dunham reports that he offered his compliments to Forrest, but assured the adjutant that "I never surrender," adding that "if [Forrest] thinks he can take me, he can come and try" (Dunham 1887, 583). In addition, Dunham claims that when he learned his supply wagons had been captured, he acquired a volunteer officer from the 39th Iowa who promptly recaptured the wagons and a number of Confederate soldiers, including Forrest's adjutant, Major Strange.

General Forrest's version of events differs considerably from Dunham's. By 1:00 P.M. Forrest believed that Dunham was soundly whipped, having his command split into pieces, each piece virtually surrounded, and his supply trains captured. Thus, he sent forth an emissary to demand surrender. His troopers also believed the Federals were surrendering, for artillery officer John Morton writes that "all firing ceased: and when the leaders met to arrange terms, the soldiers in both armies mingled freely, as was their custom" (Morton 1992, 67). Even Colonel E. F. Noyes, commanding the 39th Ohio Infantry in Fuller's Brigade, indicated that "a part, if not all, of Dunham's artillery, together with several hundred prisoners, had fallen into the hands of the enemy" (Noyes 1887, 576). Apparently, Dunham had suggested that if he might have permission to bury his dead, he would withdraw from the field. Whether or not he was making a serious request, or simply buying time for help to arrive, may never be known (Forrest 1887, 596). Colonel Dibrell reports, "we had captured about 300 prisoners, and we were parlaying about a surrender," when the unthinkable occurred. For the first time during the war, Forrest was taken by surprise. Firing erupted from the north behind the Confederate line in the direction of the Parker House near an orchard where horseholders had gathered about three hundred mounts of Dibrell's and Cox's dismounted men. In a strikingly straightforward admission, Forrest writes, "Thirty minutes more would have given us the day, when to *my surprise and astonishment* [author's italics] a fire was opened on us in our rear and the enemy in heavy force under General Sullivan [and Colonel Fuller] advanced on us. Knowing that I had four companies at Clarksburg, 7 miles from us on the Huntingdon Road, I could not believe that they were Federals until I rode up myself into their lines" (Forrest 1887, 596).

At long last Fuller's Brigade had arrived from Huntingdon. Marching on the double-quick for the past hour, Colonel Fuller knew from the sounds of battle to the south that Dunham was in trouble, but when he was within two miles of the Parker House, he was overtaken by a courier from General Sullivan, riding with the brigade's rear guard, indicating that Fuller should "halt until he [Sullivan] comes up." Fuller sent a courier to request Sullivan revoke the ridiculous order, and to his credit, Fuller recognized the need for immediate action and urged his men "forward as quickly as possible"—not waiting for an answer from Sullivan (Fuller 1887, 570)

The sudden attack by Fuller's men, consisting of the 27th, 63rd, and 39th Ohio, sent Dibrell's and Cox's horses in a wild stampede. Several cannon being held in the rear were immediately captured as the Federals pressed forward and the situation grew critical for Forrest. "It was he [Forrest] who was hemmed in," recalled one soldier. "The Trapper was trapped. To cut his way out seemed hopeless, but it must be done" (Bond 1908, 108). Morton says, "What had looked like a victory began to resemble a defeat."

Quite simply, a subordinate commander, Captain McLemore, whom Forrest had sent to Clarksburg with four companies to warn him of Fuller's approach, had let him down. Whether the failure was due to a misunderstanding of the relayed order or negligence on the part of McLemore, the result was the same. Fuller had been able to approach and engage Forrest's rear without warning, now having the opportunity to completely defeat him. In his report to General Bragg three days after the battle, one can read between the lines the seething temper of Nathan Bedford Forrest.

> The captains of the four companies sent to Clarksburg have not yet reached here with their commands. Had they done their duty by advising me of the approach of the enemy I could have terminated the fight by making it short and decisive, when without such advice I was whipping them badly with my artillery, and unless absolutely necessary was not pressing them with my cavalry. I had them entirely surrounded and was driving them before me, and was taking it leisurely and trying as much as possible to save my men. (Forrest 1887, 597)

Historians may argue the expediency of "taking it leisurely" against Dunham with Fuller's Brigade so nearby; and while one can make the case that to have pressed the battle to a rapid conclusion would have ultimately saved men from capture, the price in lives might have been equally as large. In either case, the failure of McLemore's detachment to warn of Fuller's approach would have guaranteed a meeting engagement at best, even if Forrest had been successful in finalizing the surrender of Dunham's Brigade earlier.

But now General Forrest stood on the brink of defeat, his command caught between Colonel Fuller's attack and Dunham's rather limbolike state of half-surrender, half-battle. By all laws of tactics, Forrest should have immediately been crushed between the two forces, but what occurred next simply added to the growing legend of Nathan Bedford Forrest's invincibility on the battlefield.

Colonel Fuller had advanced his artillery to the front yard of the Parker House and was positioning the weapons to rake Napier's, Cox's, and Dibrell's men. A correspondent for the *Chicago Tribune* writes,

> It was not until the artillery reached the top of the knoll in the lane, which was crowded with Confederate soldiers, had unlimbered, and was preparing to open upon them, the infantry had deployed at a double-quick, and was rushing upon them at charge bayonet, that the Confederate leaders seemed

to appreciate the fact that they were attacked ("The Battle of Parker's Cross-roads" 1863, 1)

Reverend John A. Parker, owner of the house at the crossroads, emerged to inform the Federal artillery officer that he, Parker, was a staunch Union man; but added in no uncertain terms that he did not want Federal artillery near his house.

> "Forrest will surely shoot back," Parker told the officer, "and he will destroy my house."
> "What is more important," the officer asked, "the Union or your house?"
> "I'm a Republican who voted for Abraham Lincoln," Parker told him, "but I still want those guns away from my house."

Reverend Parker lost the argument and developed a new view of seces-sionism.[3]

Instantly, Forrest realized he must act or lose his command, so he determined to fix Fuller's attacking force long enough to allow the men accepting Dunham's surrender to escape. Already, many of Napier's and Cox's men, having been dismounted for the fight, were being captured as they "scattered like a flock of sheep—a result of their mounts being stam-peded earlier ("The Battle" 1863, 1). So rallying the forces nearest him—about seventy-five men in his escort, perhaps fifty from Dibrell's Regiment nearby, and thirty or more artillerymen[4]—Forrest gathered a makeshift counterattack force about eight hundred yards east-southeast of the Parker House (Lytle 1931, 135; Kennerly 1993, 41).

At this point in the battle arises an anecdote referred to in Robert Selph Henry's and Dan Kennerly's work as "apocryphal." Lytle, in his book, *Bedford Forrest and His Critter Company*, relates the story as though it were fact, and while Jordan and Pryor make no mention of it in their seminal work of Forrest's campaigns, the alleged incident is indeed within the pattern and personality of Forrest as demonstrated throughout the war. According to legend, one of the general's staff officers, a Captain Carroll, rode up to Forrest in the height of the crisis.

> "General," Carroll shouted, "a heavy line of infantry is in our rear. We're between two lines of battle. What'll we do?"
> "Charge both ways!" Forrest replied.

In reality, that is precisely what occurred. From his position east of the Parker House, Forrest led a hasty counterattack against the Federal artillery position defended by the 29th Ohio, stinging them with such suddenness and ferocity as to check the advance of Fuller's entire brigade. When Woodward and Russell, in position to compel a surrender south of Dun-ham's command, heard the firing, they immediately sensed what was happening and launched a limited attack to occupy the lower half of Dunham's force. Between Forrest's plucky charge, and Woodward and Russell's suppression, many of the dismounted Confederates caught between the lines were able to find a mount and escape west to east across the front of the remnant of Dunham's command. Fuller was unable to prevent Forrest's escape, and as he lamented in his official report, "nor did the command of Colonel Dunham fire a shot at the enemy as he moved past their flanks to their rear" (Fuller 1887, 570).

Incredible as it may seem, the northern remnant of Colonel Dunham's Brigade did not engage Forrest's main body as it retreated across its front. A target of several hundred cavalrymen and six pieces of artillery, that only recently had been pounding the Federals into submission, seems far too irresistible for the average soldier. Even the Federal newspapers, notoriously generous in their treatment of Sullivan and his brigades, seemed at a loss to explain the inaction of Dunham's men. "Col. Dunham's men forgot to fire upon the enemy, and stood, apparently transfixed, until the 2nd brigade had actually scattered the intervening foe" ("The Battle" 1863, 1). Forrest carried off six of the nine pieces of artillery with which he entered the battle, the other three being captured, and three of Dunham's guns he had captured were abandoned for lack of teams to draw them (Henry 1944, 119). In the process, however, a number of artillerymen were captured, one

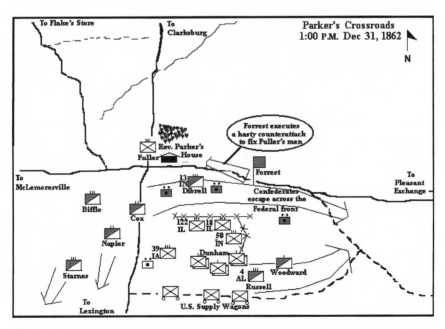

Map 10.6

of whom was J.M. Metcalfe—the young soldier who had discovered the wounded Federal officer's valise only hours earlier.

> The cannon on which Jim Metcalfe was a driver bounded forward to follow with the rest. But the gap closed in their faces, and at close range a volley was fired into the gunners. The two drivers in front of Metcalfe were shot down. He turned to ask the man behind him what he must do at the instant that that man also went down. The riderless horses plunged madly. (Bond 1908, 108)

Thrown from the team he was riding, Metcalfe was trampled, his ribs broken, and he was knocked semiconscious. When he came to, a Federal soldier stood over him declaring, "I have a notion to stamp the life out of you." A Federal officer intervened and gave Metcalfe a drink from his canteen. After acknowledging the artilleryman's youth, the officer said, "You ought to be home with your mother," then he departed, promising to see to him after the battle.[5]

While specific accounts may differ, one thing about the Battle of Parker's Crossroads is certain: The balance of Forrest's command escaped at about 2:30 P.M. from the very grasp of an overwhelming Federal force. Fuller, quite rightly, credits his command with having caught the Confederates by surprise, and there can be no question that had not Fuller arrived when he did, Colonel Dunham and his brigade were finished. Colonel Rinaker's (122nd Illinois) claim that "Forrest was unable to rally his men again, and was in full retreat *when the Second Brigade came in sight* [author's italics], is clearly false. His assertion, however, that "the 'Rebels' flight afforded our gallant Ohio friends no opportunity to participate in the rout of a force we could have destroyed had the Second Brigade arrived in time" contains an element of truth (Rinaker 1887, 587).

Referring back to the idea mentioned in the foreword that history is not as much about what happened as about what *might* have happened, consider for a moment the impact of timing on the resolution of Parker's Crossroads. If Fuller's Brigade had arrived one hour earlier when Forrest was decisively engaged with Dunham, the Federals might have, indeed, crushed his command between the two forces. Thus, Rinaker's curt observation that "but for the genius for tardiness exhibited by General Sullivan," the Federals would have defeated Forrest is not without merit. On the other hand, such a view demands that McLemore failed at his reconnaissance mission, else Forrest would have known of Fuller's approach and likely declined a full-scale, decisive engagement. Had McLemore not failed in his early warning of Fuller's approach, Forrest might well have pressed Dunham harder, obtained his surrender, and at the very least been able to turn his force to meet Fuller's attack. Unlike some historians who may argue that Forrest would have captured Dunham, engaging Fuller and defeating him as well, this author is convinced that Forrest's men were in no condition to conduct another battle after defeating Dunham. For in his report to Bragg,

General Forrest acknowledges that "considering our want of ammunition for small arms and artillery, and the worn-down condition of our men and horses I determined at once to recross the Tennessee River and fit up for a return" (Forrest 1887, 597). The combat status of his force, as described by Forrest himself, occurred as a result of the entire campaign, and was compounded by his decisive engagement with Dunham, thus his men were in no condition to take on Fuller's fresh brigade. And while Forrest may have mentioned wanting to continue to Bethel Station had he been successful in defeating Dunham, he also recognized that he was being "followed by Federals in heavy force" and that such a maneuver would make it easier for the enemy to cut him off from the Tennessee River and jeopardize the safety of his entire command.

Forrest's forces, having slipped from the grasp of two Federal brigades, drove on to Lexington and rested there the night of December 31. The fact that General Sullivan did not pursue the enemy is best illustrated by Lieutenant O. C. Ayers' biting commentary in his December 31 diary entry.

> the skired [scared] Rebels traveled about 20 miles before they stopped to get supper or camp but our forces did not persue [sic]. I cannot for the life of me tell why unless General Sullivan is drunk. He sent out a little cavalry, perhaps 100 men, who ran into the rear guard of the enemy and were badly cut up . . . Here we were camped and the enemy out making off carrying these things [wagon train, horses, and artillery] with them. (Ayers 1984, 32)

Ayers was particularly disgusted by the fact that Forrest's men had captured a supply wagon containing the 39th Iowa's knapsacks. "I am tonight without a blanket," he complained, and "I expect some infernal Rebel is enjoying mine." Ayers indicates that he considered the day's effort "a splendid victory," but that is based upon the ever present assumption that he was outnumbered five-to-one.

The Federal officers in their official reports made equally strong claims, Dunham calling the battle a "complete and overwhelming victory." General Sullivan telegraphed General U. S. Grant the next day: "We have achieved a glorious victory. We met Forrest 7,000 strong. After a contest of four hours, completely routed him with great slaughter. We have captured six guns, over 300 prisoners, over 350 horses, a large number of wagons and teams, and large quantity of small-arms. Colonel Napier killed; Colonel Cox and Major Strange, Forrest's adjutant, and one aide-de-camp, and a number of other officers captured" (Sullivan 1887, 552).

Forrest, in his initial report to Bragg, indicates a loss of "60 killed and wounded and 100 captured or missing" (Forrest 1887, 597), but that is most certainly underestimated. While the number of wounded may be accurate, a more realistic figure of the Confederate troopers captured at Parker's Crossroads would be closer to three hundred.

The official Federal casualty report for Parker's Crossroads, including both brigades, lists 27 killed, 140 wounded, and 69 captured or missing. But this report must also be considerably understated. And while Forrest's estimate that the enemy "must have lost in killed and wounded 800 to 1,000 men," is far too high, it is reasonable to assume the Federal loss was significantly higher than the figures listed in the official report. Within four days following the battle, initial newspaper reports placed the total Federal loss in killed, wounded, and captured, at six hundred; and while that, too, is elevated, it more closely approximates the truth than does Sullivan's report ("The War in West" 1863, 1). And in an obvious slap at what many Federal officers considered the crude, unlearned Forrest, the January 6 *Chicago Tribune* incorrectly reports that "Forrest himself was taken prisoner, but managed to escape, being so shabbily dressed he was mistaken for an inferior officer" ("The War in West" 1863, 1).

Inferior or not, Brig. Gen. Nathan Bedford Forrest's cavalry command was resting for the night in Lexington, less than twelve miles away from General Sullivan's combined force, while the men in Lieutenant O. C. Ayers' 39th Iowa shook their heads in amazement. That Dunham's Brigade was exhausted is understandable. "It is now twelve o'clock [midnight]," Ayers wrote, "and some of the men are up cooking. It is difficult to tell if they are most in want of sleep or food" (Ayers 1984, 33). Yet Fuller's Brigade was fresh, and still Sullivan's combined Federal force did not leave Parker's Crossroads in pursuit of Forrest until noon the following day. Lieutenant O. C. Ayers observed, "This looked but little like trying to catch the enemy. It does seem to me that our general is letting them get away purposely" (Ayers 1984, 33).

FORREST ESCAPES

While the Federal forces in west Tennessee were exchanging congratulatory telegrams on their "great victory," and generally taking their own sweet time in pursuing the Confederates, Forrest was driving toward the Tennessee River to recover the flatboats he had sunk at Clifton on his initial crossing. Having dispatched Captain Forrest ahead to Clifton with his independent company of scouts the night before, Forrest, after paroling some three hundred Federal prisoners, led his column out of Lexington on the morning of January 1, 1863. Within ten miles of the river Forrest encountered Lieut. Col. William K. M. Breckenridge's 6th Tennessee Cavalry (Union), the last remaining Federal force between himself and escape. In a movement reminiscent of several others during the raid, Forrest ordered Dibrell's Regiment to charge the enemy cavalry, while Starnes attempted to encircle the left and Biffle the right. When Freeman's Battery pressed quickly down the road behind Dibrell, the Federals withdrew to the southeast in a column of companies, opening the road to Clifton for the main body. Realizing he was outmanned and outgunned, Breckenridge "did not deem it prudent to follow farther," and remained content to "get in their rear and annoy him [Forrest] all we could." But Forrest's rear guard kept the Federal cavalry at a safe distance while the rest of the command began crossing the Tennessee River. The artillery crossed first, establishing a gun position to overwatch for Federal gunboats. Since the water was warmer than on their previous crossing, and the river was considerably lower, many of the horses were swum across as well as carried on the flatboats, and "the crossing was effected with great dispatch" (Morton 1992, 71). Forrest knew that Sullivan would eventually pursue him, and he also knew of other Federal columns marching from Corinth and Jackson to cut him off. Thus appeared "a spectacle full of life and movement; quite as many as 1000 animals were at one time in the river, which was about six hundred yards broad, with favorable banks" (Jordan 1887, 220). In eight hours, or by 8:00 P.M. on the night of January 1, Forrest's command of twenty-one hundred men and horses, less McLemore's four companies and some scattered parties that would cross elsewhere, "stood cheerfully once more in Middle Tennessee, with five pieces of artillery, six caissons with their horses, sixty wagons, and four ambulances with their teams" (Jordan 1887, 220; Mathes 1902, 93).

On January 2, the day *after* Forrest crossed the Tennessee River, General Jeremiah Sullivan had returned to Jackson, where he telegraphed Grant:

> Just arrived here from Lexington. Left Colonel Lawler with 3,000 men (old troops) and eight pieces of artillery to follow the retreating enemy to the river. Forrest's army is completely broken up. They are scattered over the country without ammunition. We need a good cavalry regiment to go through the country and pick them up (Sullivan 1887, 552).

"You have done a good job," General Grant replied, and promising to send him a "fine regiment of cavalry" told him to "clear out West Tennessee of all roving cavalry" (Grant 1887, 553). The next day Col. Michael K. Lawler, 18th Illinois Infantry, reached Clifton only to discover that the prey had vanished, their only evidence of having passed being the muddy ruts in the road and the tracks of a thousand horses. A section of Freeman's Battery had remained on the middle Tennessee side long enough to throw several shells at Lawler before disappearing to catch Forrest's main body.

Forrest's "broken up" command would not be policed up by Sullivan's cavalry, for it was moving to rearm and refit for further campaigns during the summer and fall of 1863. That Forrest had been checked at Parker's Crossroads is clear, but that check was a long time in coming, and only developed after a tremendous blow had been dealt to the Federal supply line and the overall Vicksburg Campaign. During his raid, Forrest averaged twenty miles per day, fighting almost everyday. He had destroyed fifty large and small bridges on the Mobile and Ohio Railroad and destroyed miles of trestlework that would be months in repair. Capturing and burning eighteen to twenty stockades, he had also killed or captured almost two thousand Federal soldiers. After capturing or disabling ten artillery pieces, capturing fifty wagons and ambulances, ten thousand stands of small-arms, and

1 million rounds of ammunition, he crossed the Tennessee River better armed and equipped than when he left. Many of the shotguns and muskets carried by Forrest's men on their entry into west Tennessee had been replaced with Enfield rifles, and where ragged, inadequate clothing had existed previously, soldiers now had new blankets and knapsacks. It is little wonder that even Gen. Braxton Bragg, a man modest in his opinion of Forrest, had to concede in his report that Forrest's efforts were an "entire success" and that his losses were "small in comparison with the results achieved and that of the enemy" (Bragg 1887, 592).

NOTES

1. Though the consequences of McLemore's misunderstanding of Forrest's order were severe, there is no evidence that Forrest held any animosity toward the young captain. Indeed, he assumed command of Starnes' regiment when the latter died of wounds on June 30, 1863, and served frequently under Forrest for the duration of the war.

2. In his report, Dunham issues a backhanded compliment about his artillery, saying that "for some cause our artillery was throughout strikingly inefficient, although both the officers and men with it exhibited the greatest bravery." Lieutenant O. C. Ayers of the 39th Iowa noted in his diary account of December 31 that many of the Federal shells "went wide of the mark," adding, "in fact, most of the Artillerymen are drunk and the one who trained the gun for the shell [that killed Napier] is the only one that was sober."

3. For the remainder of the war, Parker became a secessionist, and on his deathbed insisted that he be buried with his feet to the north and his head to the south, so that on Resurrection Day he could rise up and "kick the Yankees back up north." His is the only grave in the cemetery near Parker's Crossroads that is oriented north-south (Cupples 1985, 1).

4. Pvt. Nathan Bell Dozier was the sixteen-year-old bugler for Morton's section of Freeman's artillery. He had enlisted less than a month earlier from his home in Franklin, Tennessee. His father, Joseph, was bugler for Company G of Starnes' regiment. It may well have been young Private Dozier, the most proximate bugler with the artillery, whom Forrest turned to to sound first the assembly, then the charge (Miner 1988, 8).

5. True to his word, the Federal officer returned to J. M. Metcalfe, and taking him prisoner, removed him to a makeshift field hospital, where Metcalfe describes the tremendous suffering he observed as the Federal surgeons worked on the wounded. While one soldier was being placed on the table for a hasty operation, his revolver fell from its holster, hit the floor, and slid underneath a chest of drawers out of sight of the Federals. Recuperating over the next few days, he kept his eye on the weapon from across the room, until one day he asked a new medical attendant to "hand me my revolver from over there." The attendant casually handed Metcalfe the weapon and went on about his business. Though a southern woman attending him several days later discovered the revolver hidden in a blanket at the foot of his bed, she said nothing to the Federals. As soon as Metcalfe was able to walk, he retrieved his weapon and made his escape, returning to his home with enough physical disability to prevent any further service in the war.

PART III

BRIG. GEN. JOHN H. MORGAN'S CHRISTMAS RAID

December 22, 1862—January 5, 1863

11

General Situation

Vague rumors of my coming had preceded me.
—Brig. Gen. John H. Morgan

When President Jefferson Davis paid a December 1862 visit to Gen. Braxton Bragg's headquarters in middle Tennessee, these leaders spent several days planning the Confederate response to the two massive armies the Federals were raising in the western theater. General Grant was pushing south into Mississippi with the intention of taking Vicksburg, while Maj. Gen. William Rosecrans' Army of the Cumberland, presently occupying Nashville, was preparing to move on Chattanooga. Forrest's raid into west Tennessee, discussed in the previous chapter, was one part of the Confederate response. Gen. Earl Van Dorn's raid against the Federal supply base at Holly Springs was a second. The third counter to the growing Federal threat would be a raid into central Kentucky designed, much like Forrest's raid, to destroy the supply and communication lines that supported Rosecrans' growing depot at Nashville. Without an effective base of resupply, Rosecrans' southern advance would be stymied, buying valuable time for Bragg to reposition and strengthen his army.

In addition to the strategy session with Bragg, President Davis had the unexpected pleasure of observing a wedding—the wedding of Brig. Gen. John Hunt Morgan—the man who would lead the raid he and Bragg had planned into central Kentucky. But according to the December 17 issue of the *Chicago Tribune*, the Federals were well aware that something was brewing in Dixie, and apparently they were closer to the truth than they realized.

Jeff Davis declared in a speech, Saturday night [the 13th in Murfreesboro], that Tennessee must be held at all hazards. Polk and other rebels made violent speeches. The enemy say they will fight us between Tullahoma and Winchester. They will not attack. Their main body is about Murfreesboro . . . Morgan married Miss Mattie Ready at Murfreesboro, last night [the 14th], and will move with 5000 men tomorrow to cut the Louisville and Nashville Railroad. Several scouts confirmed this . . . Rebels are jubilating with Jeff Davis, who reviews by day and revels by night. ("The War in Tennessee" 1862, 1)

John Hunt Morgan, a veteran of Shiloh and numerous limited raids into and around central Kentucky, had received orders from General Bragg to do what he loved most in the place he loved best. Already recognized as a capable cavalry leader, Morgan had been instructed to depart middle Tennessee on December 22 and conduct a raid on the Louisville and Nashville Railroad with the ultimate military objective of destroying the two major trestles that spanned wide ravines just north of Elizabethtown, Kentucky.

Though born in Alabama, Morgan considered himself a Kentuckian, having been raised in Lexington and having long been a planter and businessman there before the war. A veteran of the Mexican War, Morgan had remained militarily active by raising the Lexington Rifles, a militia unit in his hometown. After a failed attempt at neutrality upon the outbreak of hostilities and the issue of a Federal arrest warrant for him in the fall of 1861, Morgan, along with the southern sympathizers who had served with him in the militia, escaped and evaded out of Lexington and reformed their unit in Bardstown. From there they moved to Bowling Green where Morgan, now with a commission as a captain, and two hundred of his men were sworn into the Confederacy. Because his men were "picked riders—Kentuckians—born and trained horsemen, and accustomed to weary hours in the saddle," Morgan's command[1] soon gained recognition for rapid dashes on exposed outposts, for example, irregular service (Hardin 1963, 3). His success in these short raids and scouting forays eventually led to a commission as a colonel, and it was as such he and his men participated at the battle of Shiloh as an independent command. Over the next year, Morgan's command grew, a result of his effective raids into Kentucky where he not only stirred up the Federal detachments guarding towns from Lexington to Cynthianna, but he also successfully recruited men and gathered horses. But while Morgan's success had established him as a valuable raider, neither Bragg nor Davis believed that Morgan was a viable, field-grade, maneuver commander on the traditional battlefield—an opinion they also held of Forrest. Both General Bragg and President Davis considered Morgan and Forrest "partisans," that is, commanders whose men were best suited to independent, unconventional operations. Many historians have faulted Bragg and Davis for this attitude, citing later achievements of both men, particularly Forrest at Brice's Crossroads. While a solid case can be made that, having been given the opportunity to command perhaps a corps in a traditional battlefield maneuver, both leaders would have been effective,

Brig. Gen. John Hunt Morgan. Photo courtesy of the Kentucky Historical Society.

the Confederate high command drew their conclusions about Forrest, and particularly about Morgan, from two unavoidable truths. The discipline within Morgan's command was decidedly more loose than that of a line unit, and the fact that General Bragg was a stickler for discipline did not tend to endear Morgan's command. Secondly, men like Morgan and Forrest did not feel the weight of military tradition when it came to respecting the authority of their superiors. Of course, Morgan rendered the proper courtesies, but neither he nor Forrest were likely to suffer a fool gladly. Morgan might not get face-to-face and threaten Bragg like Forrest did, but the Kentuckian would be just as likely to ignore what he believed to be a foolish order, or one that was inappropriately expensive in terms of the lives of his men. Notwithstanding the labels Bragg may have placed upon Morgan and his men, they were clearly the right choice when it came to the mission against Rosecrans' supply line in December 1862.

That Morgan and his men had previously been able to move so frequently and effectively into and out of Kentucky should be no surprise. Ninety percent of his troops were from Kentucky, and the state itself, though attempting to remain neutral, contained numerous citizens loyal to the southern cause. A true border state, Kentucky's divided loyalties made it a natural battleground. In 1860, Kentucky had about 225,000 slaves, from seven in Jackson County to 10,000 in Jefferson County. The people voted against Lincoln that year, seemingly wanting to maintain the institution of slavery, yet holding fast to "their Henry Clay legacy"—an abiding belief in the Union. Numerous slaveholders were among the approximately 75,000 to 100,000 Kentucky men who fought for the Union army; but the Commonwealth also sent over 35,000 men into the Confederacy (Hall 1995, D1). It was from this base that John Hunt Morgan drew his command, and between their knowledge of the geography, and their families and friends remaining in the state after Federal occupation, Morgan was able to tailor his routes and his objectives to take advantage of southern sympathies.

Like Forrest's raid, which had already begun when Morgan finalized preparations on December 20 and 21, Morgan had a classic cavalry mission: harass the enemy, interdict its supply line, destroy the bridges and trestles at Muldraugh Hill north of Elizabethtown, and *do not become decisively engaged*. The headstrong breed of western cavalrymen he would lead—men who often chafed from strict military discipline—were about to embark on the most ambitious mission of their short military careers. It would be a long, arduous march, with mobility and firepower remaining the primary requirements for success. Thus as Morgan prepared his command, he urged his men to leave behind the cavalryman's classic saber, declaring that it simply added weight and offered limited utility, opting instead for the revolver and short-barreled Enfield rifle. Some men were armed with sawed-off, double-barreled shotguns, perhaps supplemented with one or two Colt army revolvers. Morgan, like Forrest, had about four hundred men without weapons, condemned to duty as horseholders until armament could be captured from the Federals.

At his inspection prior to departure, Morgan and his staff insured that the troopers, most of whom were between eighteen and thirty-five years of age, had prepared three days' worth of cooked rations. Each man was to carry two extra horseshoes, twelve nails, one blanket, and an oilcloth or overcoat. No ammunition wagon stood inspection that day, as Morgan believed it would slow his march; instead, each man carried forty rounds. Only the artillery would travel on wheels during this raid. And so, at approximately 9:00 A.M. on a bright, clear, December 22, 1862, some four thousand cavalrymen and seven pieces of artillery, organized into two brigades under the command of Col. Basil Wilson Duke and William Breckinridge,[2] rode out of Alexandria, Tennessee, to begin what would later be called Morgan's Christmas Raid.[3] According to Lieut. James McCreary, "As company after company moved forward into line with horses prancing, firearms glistening, bugles blowing, and flags waving, and with our artillery on the right flank and finally halted in a beautiful valley with bright eyes and lovely faces gaping at us, it formed a grand and imposing scene" (Brown 1975, 13).

Leading the main body out of Alexandria was Tom Quirk's sixty-man Independent Scout Company, many of whom had been with Morgan since

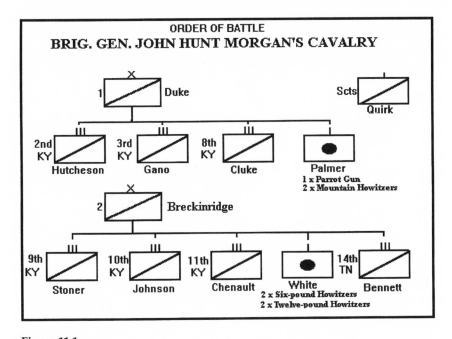

Figure 11.1

the early days in Lexington. Quirk, an Irish-born candy-store owner before the war, would be Morgan's eyes and ears for the next two weeks. Morgan soon rode along the column, described as moving with a "splendid staff, magnificently mounted, superbly dressed, riding like a centaur, bare-headed, with plumed hat in right hand, waving salutations to his applauding followers" (Brown 1975, 13).

NOTES

1. Not every man in Morgan's Lexington unit was a native Kentuckian. Men like John Hibble Carter—Connecticut-born and New York-educated—lived in Lexington at the beginning of the war. Carter joined the charismatic Morgan and served the cause of the south. He enlisted in Company D, 2nd Kentucky Cavalry, and though captured three times during the war, Carter escaped each time and rejoined his unit. He served throughout the war, eventually escorting President Jefferson Davis until his capture at Washington, Georgia, in May of 1865 (Ertzgaard 1986, 8).

2. The command of this brigade would have normally, by virtue of rank, gone to Col. Adam R. Johnson of the 10th Kentucky Cavalry. Although Morgan had offered the command to Johnson, the latter deferred it to Breckinridge, as he had the "understanding that General Morgan would divide his battery with me and allow me to return to my old department of Western Kentucky during the raid." Morgan did not relinquish any of his artillery, however, and Johnson remained with him throughout the raid (Davis 1904, 133).

3. Whether or not Morgan knew of Van Dorn's successful raid against Holly Springs before he departed is uncertain. He almost certainly knew that Forrest had successfully reached west Tennessee and was wreaking havoc with Grant's supply line. If Morgan did know of Van Dorn's and Forrest's success, he must have surely felt additional pressure to make his own raid as bold and effective, less he lose face among the premier cavalry leaders in the west.

12

Glasgow, Bacon Creek, and Nolin

He didn't know how to quit and retire gracefully.
—Pvt. John A. Wyeth

For almost a year John H. Morgan had been trafficking in and out of Kentucky, harassing the occupation Federal army almost at will; thus, for there to be a rumor afloat among both the citizens and the Union soldiers that Morgan was coming presented nothing unusual. Whether or not the ongoing talk in December 1862 was based upon real intelligence of his impending raid or simply another rumor, the encounter between Morgan's advance guard and two companies of Michigan cavalry in Glasgow, Kentucky, on Christmas Eve vanquished any doubts in the minds of either the locals or the Federals.

On their approach to Glasgow on the afternoon of December 24, Morgan's men had overtaken a huge Union sutler wagon drawn by twenty Percheron horses and loaded with a wide variey of Christmas delicacies en route to the Federal soldiers in the vicinity. Liberating the sutler of his goods, Morgan's men spread the food and drink among the command as they went into camp in the late afternoon about five miles south of Glasgow. Describing the spirit of Morgan's jubilant command, trooper James McCreary wrote, "'Tis Christmas Eve [and] I am sitting with many friends—around a glorious campfire. Shouting, singing and speechifying make the welkin ring, for the boys have a superabundance of whisky and are celebrating Christmas Eve very merrily. We have not seen an enemy yet" (Brown 1959, 14). But not everyone was content to sit around the campfire. Tom Quirk, ever to the forefront of the march, moved a makeshift quartering into Glasgow party consisting of his own company of independent scouts, and some representatives of the 9th and 2nd Kentucky. According to John Wyeth, Forrest biographer and boy trooper in Quirk's scouts, the move was motivated from more than a desire to search the town for the enemy. "One great advantage of this position [being in the scout company] was that by being first on the ground we got the choice of the fat of the land; and when we struck a town at night and could stop, we took possession of the livery stables for our horses and the hotel beds for ourselves before the main column swarmed in" (Wyeth 1911, 119).

Representatives from the other commands accompanying Quirk's Scouts probably sought accommodations on behalf of their commander and staff officers. The Confederates had been in town for several minutes, and had dismounted and entered a saloon for "Oh Be Joyful," when men from the 2nd Michigan Cavalry rode into the center of town unaware of the Confederates' presence. In the exchange of gunfire, one Federal was killed and two wounded, and the Confederates had three wounded (two mortally) and a half-dozen men captured. "Not knowing in what force the enemy might be," Quirk and his men withdrew to the south toward the main body and the Federals dashed out of town in the direction of Munfordville (Wyeth 1911, 119; Morgan 1887, 154).

On Christmas Day the main body pressed to and through Glasgow moving toward Munfordville along the Bear Wallow turnpike. But by now the rumors of Morgan's approach had been confirmed and the Federals in central Kentucky began orchestrating an effort to stop him. Capt. Frank W. Dickey, in command of the 2nd Michigan Cavalry that had encountered the Confederates that previous evening in Glasgow, had already telegraphed General Rosecrans about his engagement, reporting, "Rebels supposed to be strong—have two batteries" (Dickey 1887, 150). Thus the first major players in the effort to thwart Morgan would be a battalion of cavalry comprised of two companies each from the 4th and 5th Indiana Cavalry. This Federal command, under Col. Issac P. Gray, encountered Quirk's Scouts in advance of Morgan's main body approximately ten miles southeast of the Green River. In a move reminiscent of Forrest's troops at Salem Cemetery, Gray ordered the fences thrown on both sides of the pike and his cavalry moved into line of battle right and left. Company C of the 5th Indiana succeeded in secreting itself in a draw just as the Confederates mounted a hasty charge. Here Capt. Tom Quirk demonstrated a personality trait that made him at once respected by his men, yet reckless in a fight. "His bravery was unquestioned," wrote John Wyeth, "but he did not possess other qualities which make a capable and successful leader" (Wyeth 1911, 118). Wyeth was referring to Quirk's tendency to launch into an attack "without regard to anything or anybody," and such was precisely his action against Colonel Gray that morning. Seeing the Federals "thick as hell" up ahead, Quirk yelled out, "Charge 'em, damn em'," and led his sixty-man company galloping down the road. But upon closing to within two hundred yards of the Federals, now deployed on both sides of the road in line of battle, Quirk reconsidered. Ordering his men to halt, he had them dismount and form a skirmish line on both sides of the road; but the Federal line, extending almost two hundred yards wide, began to converge fire on Quirk's men now less than one hundred yards away. "We crouched as low as we could," Wyeth wrote, "[and] took refuge in the fence corners and began firing." Suddenly, Company C of the 5th Indiana burst forth from the gully where they were hiding and rode up to within a few yards of the Confederates, firing a volley and sending them running. Though Gray's men killed and wounded several, capturing six of Quirk's men, Morgan's advance guard arrived to support Quirk, and after assisting them in securing their horses, joined the scouts in a hasty attack that forced the Federals to retreat. "I had scarcely got my command reorganized before the main force of the enemy, 4,500 strong, came on at full speed, flanking at both sides for the purpose of surrounding my command, but were not fast enough to effect this object" (Gray 1887, 151). The impetuous Tom Quirk, though suffering two scalp wounds that rendered his head and face a bloody mess, participated in the Confederate charge and "got close enough to one of the hindmost Hoosiers and killed him with his pistol" (Gray 1887, 151; Wyeth 1911, 120). In a comment of subtle criticism, Wyeth said of Quirk, "this wild Irishman never let anyone get ahead of him in going into a fight, and he didn't know how to quit and retire gracefully" (Wyeth 1911, 118). Following this rather inauspicious beginning, Morgan's command pressed north across the Green River and reached the Louisville and Nashville Railroad, where they camped Christmas night between Hammondsville and Upton Station. Again they feasted on liberated turkeys and abundant Federal libation.

But while Morgan's men were bedding down after their Christmas dinner along the Louisville and Nashville Railroad, Col. John Marshall Harlan, commander of the 10th Kentucky Infantry (Union), and now commanding a brigade stationed at Gallatin, Tennessee, received a message from Brig. Gen. Jeremiah T. Boyle, commander of the District of Western Kentucky in Louisville. Boyle gave Harlan the mission of moving his brigade—five regiments of infantry and a battery of artillery—by rail, through Bowling Green and Cave City, to "drive from the line of the Louisville and Nashville Railroad the rebel cavalry of Morgan" (Harlan 1887, 137). Boyle also sent Brigadier General J. J. Reynolds with elements of the 12th Division toward Glasgow to trap Morgan in the event he was repulsed by forces along the railroad. Morgan's raid was no longer a secret, if it had ever been, and Brigadier General Boyle had begun the process of surrounding and defeating the enemy cavalry. Morgan was loose in Kentucky and the race was on to catch him.

BACON CREEK

On the morning of December 26, amid a road-softening drizzle, Morgan's column began moving along the Louisville and Nashville Railroad north toward its primary objective: the twin railroad trestlework at Muldraugh Hill north of Elizabethtown. As stated earlier, his command was divided into two brigades. One brigade, led by Col. William Breckinridge, was composed of Stoner's 9th Kentucky Cavalry, Johnson's 10th Kentucky Cavalry, Chenault's 11th Kentucky Cavalry, Bennett's 13th Tennessee Cavalry, and White's Battery.

The other brigade, lead by Col. Basil Wilson Duke, consisted of the following regiments: John B. Hutcheson's 2nd Kentucky Cavalry, R. M. Gano's 3rd Kentucky Cavalry, Leroy Cluke's 8th Kentucky Cavalry, and Palmer's Battery. Basil Duke, though a native Kentuckian, was a lawyer practicing in St. Louis, Missouri, before the war. As the nation drew closer to hostilities, Duke, an ardent states'-rights man, was involved in all manner of intrigue and near-espionage activities on behalf of the south in the pivotal border state of Missouri. When the secessionist movement appeared doomed within the state, Duke returned to Kentucky and joined Morgan's Lexington Rifles, and when that unit later became part of the 2nd Kentucky Cavalry, Duke rose to the rank of lieutenant colonel, and with Morgan's eventual promotion, Duke became colonel of the unit. While Duke proved his value as an officer, his popularity was in no way hindered by the fact that he was John Hunt Morgan's brother-in-law, having married Morgan's sister, Henrietta Hunt Morgan in June 1861.

The previous evening Morgan had sent two companies from Breckinridge's Brigade to threaten Woodsonville, and two companies from Duke's Brigade toward Munfordville to drive in the enemy's pickets. He hoped to "induce the enemy to believe that I intended to attack the fortifications at Green River, and by so threatening him, to divert his attention from the combined attack which I intended to make . . . on the stockades at Bacon Creek and Nolin" (Morgan 1882, 155). Thus, that Friday morning, the 26th, Morgan sent Gano's 7th Kentucky, Hutcheson's 2nd Kentucky, and a section of Palmer's Battery to attack the Bacon Creek stockade (present-day Bonnieville), while he moved north with the main body to attack the Federals at Upton Station.

No Federal garrison occupied Upton to offer Morgan resistance, and upon arriving there he immediately began a deceptive campaign against Brigadier General Boyle in Louisville and the other enemy commanders conspiring to catch him. In one of the earliest recorded uses of electronic warfare, Morgan turned to a fidgety, small-framed man by the name of Charles "Lightnin'" Ellsworth. A Canadian-born telegrapher, Ellsworth worked in Texas before the war and eventually made his way to join Morgan, whom he had come to know in previous years. Ellsworth's value had been proven to the Confederate commander on his July raid into Kentucky during which Ellsworth was put to work monitoring Federal telegraph communications and, on occasion, creating false messages to distract and confuse the enemy ("The Last Roll" 1900, 35). Just such an effort

Col. Basil Wilson Duke. Photo courtesy of the Library of Congress.

was what Morgan wanted from Ellsworth at Upton Station on December 26, and the wiry, mustached Ellsworth set to work.

Eavesdropping on telegraph communication was common on both sides during the war, for with the use of a portable telegraph key, almost anyone could tap into a line without revealing himself to either station on the end of the line. And while both Union and Confederate armies developed ciphers, or encryption techniques, the Federal forces were apparently making no attempt to shield their messages along the Louisville and Nashville Railroad during the winter of 1862 (Antonucci 1995, 49). But while eavesdropping was relatively easy, Charles Ellsworth brought a special skill to Brigadier General Morgan's Raiders that few could match. Ellsworth had the ability to monitor a telegraph line for only a few minutes before learning an operator's unique rhythm on the key, or his personal "Morse fist," that, almost like an individual's voice, distinguised his traffic from that of any other telegrapher. Having memorized the fist, or pattern, of a given station attendant, Ellsworth would then originate his own traffic as though it had come from that station, mimicking the sender's individual technique. On one of Morgan's previous forays, a respondent had become suspicious of the traffic and asked, "Who are you, and what's the matter with your office?" Apparently, Ellsworth's handheld key had created a "wobbling and uncertain 'tick' " in the line. The Canadian quickly replied, "O.K. Lightning," indicating that a storm was interfering with the telegraph line. The listener fell for the ruse and continued to provide the requested information, and Charles "Lightnin'" Ellsworth got his nickname (Wyeth 1911, 121).

John Allan Wyeth describes the scene at Upton Station as one of Morgan's troopers shimmied up the telegraph pole, planted two strands of wire on each side of the telegraph line insulator and tied Ellsworth's portable key into the Federal army's line of communication.

> I sat on the end of a crosstie within a few feet of General Morgan and heard him dictate messages to [Ellsworth] to be sent to General Boyle in Louisville and to other places, making inquiries as to the disposition of the Federal forces in Kentucky and telling some awful stories in regard to the large size of his own command and its movements. (Wyeth 1911, 121)

Apparently Ellsworth used his extensive associations before the war to determine the name of a telegrapher known as "Aud" who recently left the Louisville office. He then wired General Boyle that Morgan was in the vicinity of Bowling Green where an attack was imminent. "Aud" requested not only aid from Boyle, but the disposition of any Federal forces in the vicinity that might come to his aid. "Gen. Boyle told him the force and position of his troops, spoke of their efficiency, etc., and gave all the information in regard to them that Morgan wanted" ("The Third" 1863, 1). Having received critical intelligence on enemy dispositions, Morgan then had Ellsworth send a message calling Boyle "a bright youth and smart boy, ending with characteristic vulgarity." Ellsworth closed with "a love-letter to his sweetheart in Lexington" ("The Third" 1863, 1).

Where Forrest had used paroled prisoners, phantom regimental drum and bugle commands, and fleeting glimpses of staged troop movements as the vehicles for his campaign of disinformation, Morgan used the telegraph and the skills of Ellsworth to misdirect the enemy. "I cut the telegraph wire, and my operator was soon in communication with Louisville, Cincinnati, and other points," Morgan indicated in his report (Morgan 1887, 155). During this session Ellsworth learned of an approaching train which Morgan ordered Quirk's Scouts to intercept, and but for the quick thinking of the engineer, who saw the trap coming and reversed his engine, Morgan would have captured "ammunition, small-arms, and two pieces of rifled cannon" just north of Upton Station.

Sometime after 2:00 P.M., Morgan dispatched most of the main body under Col. Basil Duke to take Nolin, keeping only Johnson's Regiment and a section of Palmer's Battery with him. The Confederate commander had become concerned when by 3:00 P.M. he was still hearing cannon fire at Bacon Creek. Morgan feared that what should have been a quick affair had turned into a major fight, perhaps with Federal reinforcements arriving from Munfordville. So Morgan took Johnson's Regiment and the section of Palmer's Battery and went to Bacon Creek to support Hutcheson. The icy rain increased in intensity causing the artillery to bog down, slowing both his progress and Duke's movement to Nolin (Morgan 1887, 155).

The force under Hutcheson had reached Bacon Creek that morning and began shelling the stockade at 11:00 A.M. Since this particular bridge had been destroyed at least three times previously during the war, the Federals had constructed a strong stockade that allowed the soldiers inside to cover the length of the bridge with protected rifle fire. Hutcheson's men made several attempts during the afternoon to set fire to the bridge, under the support of well-aimed Parrot guns, only to have the torches shot away by marksmen from inside the stockade.

"On my arrival there, I immediately sent in a flag of truce, and demanded an unconditional surrender," Morgan reports, and the Federal officer in charge, a Captain James, acquiesced, surrendering some ninety-three Illinois infantrymen. Only three or four men were wounded on both sides in this affair, and soon after the surrender the Confederates had the Bacon Creek Bridge once again in flames. But something happened that day between Lieutenant Colonel Hutcheson, his men, and the Federals in the stockade that resulted in a Lieutenant Colonel Huffman being brought up on charges before Morgan. Perhaps Morgan was angry at having to personally come to Bacon Creek and institute the surrender, or perhaps, as Duke suggests in his book *History of Morgan's Cavalry*, the incident had something to do with the surrender terms afforded the Federals. Whatever the reason, and to this date no one has discovered the actual charge against Huffman, Morgan deferred the court-martial to a more opportune time, and headed north to link up with Colonel Duke at Nolin.

The three officers and seventy-three privates of the 91st Illinois Infantry guarding the railroad trestle at Nolin were no match for Morgan's main body, and they surrendered to Colonel Duke without opposition. Duke promptly had the stockade and the bridge burned, and as they had done at Upton, destroyed the telegraph poles and wires, and built large fires "all along the track for some 3 or 4 miles in order to warp and destroy the rails," creating with the twisted steel rails what became known as a "Confederate necktie" (Morgan 1887, 155).

Overtaking the main body after Duke had compelled the surrender at Nolin, and having satisfied himself that the railroad and the telegraph line between Louisville and Nashville had been thoroughly cut, Morgan took his entire command north. The weather began to clear as they went into camp within five miles of Elizabethtown, and less than ten miles from their primary objective: the trestles at Muldraugh Hill. Whether his false telegraph messages had frozen the Federal response, or whether his enemy was simply slow in organizing a force to pursue him, Morgan could not have been certain; but he must have been pleased to have penetrated this deep into occupied Kentucky without having any serious resistance. Again his men got a good night's rest before the heavy work of destruction began in earnest.

Members of the 2nd Kentucky Cavalry. During Morgan's Raid into Ohio in July 1863, these men of the 2nd Kentucky were captured and photographed on their way to prison. They would have been part of Basil Duke's Brigade, serving under Colonel Hutcheson during Morgan's Christmas Raid of 1862. From the names and addresses recorded on the back of this old photograph, one can easily see that Morgan drew recruits from throughout Kentucky, providing him with a thorough knowledge of the terrain. 1. J. W. Friddle, Louisville; 2. S. G. Adams, Nelson County; 3. O. B. Norvelle, Lynchburg, VA; 4. I. F. Davis, Bowling Green; 5. T W. Bibb, Cave City; 6. R. R. Simmons, Nelson County; 7. H. H. Barlow, Cave City; 8. Chas. Haddox, Logan County; 9. Wood Longmore, Covington; 10. Wm. Lewis, Warren Co. Photo courtesy of Scott E. Sallee.

13

Harlan's Pursuit and the Battle of Elizabethtown

Sublimely audacious

—Col. Basil Duke

Col. John Marshall Harlan was a native Kentuckian who, like his friend Basil Duke, graduated from Centre College and studied law at Transylvania University in Lexington. He was a slaveholder and an ardent conservative, but unlike Duke, his sympathies, and thus his military service, went to the Union. After the political attempts of Harlan and others like him to avoid war and peacefully preserve the status quo had failed, Harlan recruited the 10th Kentucky Volunteer Infantry for the Union, serving as its colonel. Thus far in the war his service had carried him into Tennessee and Alabama, but now Harlan would have the primary responsibility of pursuing and defeating Brig. Gen. John Hunt Morgan's cavalry already loose in his native state.

The trains that Brigadier General Boyle had authorized for Harlan's use arrived in Gallatin on the 26th, so his men loaded up and launched forth after Morgan. From the outset, Harlan had difficulty, complaining that "the cars were barely sufficient to contain the men, horses, and guns of the brigade" (Harlan 1887, 137), the single engines barely able to pull the load. In fact, at South Tunnel en route to Bowling Green, one engine failed entirely, causing the 4th Kentucky Infantry under Colonel Croxton to fall behind. When Croxton attempted to impress a civilian passenger train, "the conductor refused to permit his engine to be used" in spite of the Federal officer's insistence on the "great importance of the expedition" (Harlan 1887, 137).

Colonel Harlan, ever the litigator and judge, from the outset of his mission began to couch his reports in language only a lawyer could love. Claiming "no personal knowledge of the facts" surrounding Croxton's rebuff, Harlan delivers the first of what would be several indictments against the railroad personnel ordered to ferry him toward Morgan.

> Whether the conductor is to be blamed for refusing to permit his engine to be detached for the purpose indicated, I do not pretend to say; that is for others to judge; my duty is simply to state the facts. It may be proper also to state that the track of the railroad was, when I left Gallatin, in bad condition, from recent rain, though that difficulty might have been obviated had more engines been furnished. (Harlan 1887, 137).

Harlan's full brigade did not reach Bowling Green until 10:00 P.M. that evening (the 26th), a fact for which Harlan was careful in his report to state "I am not in any wise responsible." Having provided "full information as to the number of men, horses, and guns" in need of transport, he clearly held the railroad and transportation department responsible for what he perceived as a tardy arrival.

From Bowling Green, Harlan immediately wired Col. Edward Hobson, commander of the 13th Kentucky Infantry and a small brigade located at Munfordville, to learn of Morgan's progress. Tom Quirk's Scouts had encountered part of Hobson's Brigade under the command of Col. Issac Gray on Christmas Day, thus Hobson was able to accurately indicate Morgan's route of march to Harlan. Other of Hobson's men had been skirmishing with Morgan on the 25th and 26th, but apparently Morgan's demonstration toward Munfordville had been effective enough to fix Colonel Hobson and compel him to draw in his troops and prepare to defend the town. "I kept the Twelfth Kentucky Cavalry in line of battle between Bacon Creek and Munfordville until after dark on the 26th," writes Hobson, and in an insulting comment that reveals a complete misunderstanding of Morgan's purpose, adds, "the gallant hero of inferior numbers did not attack me" (Hobson 1887, 150).

That the "gallant hero of inferior numbers" had no intention of attacking Munfordville seems to have gone unrecognized by Hobson, but he did manage to inform Colonel Harlan that Morgan had destroyed the Bacon Creek stockade and two miles of railroad that day, and that all the Confederate forces appeared to be north of the Green River. Based primarily upon Hobson's information, Harlan secured one day's rations at Bowling Green and departed by train the following morning for Munfordville—"to push forward and save as much of the railroad as it was possible to do" (Harlan 1887, 138). After only ten miles' progress, he again suffered an engine breakdown, the replacement of which created a "second unfortunate delay" such that his command did not reach Munfordville until 10:00 P.M. on the 27th. Tired and frustrated, Harlan's men detrained at Munfordville, their battery horses having been "forty hours, without a drop of water or a pound of forage." Harlan writes that his men, "wearied and fatigued by loss of sleep and the crowded condition of the cars . . . lay down upon the damp ground, without tents to shelter them, to rest as best they could" (Harlan 1887, 138).[1]

Harlan's original orders had been to proceed to Munfordville and drive the enemy from the vicinity, but he showed initiative by recognizing that the situation had changed. He realized that "Morgan, if unchecked, would destroy every bridge and structure on the entire road." Having received reports upon arrival at Munfordville that the garrison at Nolin had been captured that afternoon and the bridge destroyed, Harlan accurately assessed the situation and determined that his "only hope was to save the immense trestle-work at Muldraugh Hill, and failing in that, to save the bridges over Rolling Fork, near Lebanon Junction, and over Salt River, at Shepherdsville." To supplement his brigade, Harlan received from Colonel Hobson the 13th Kentucky Infantry and Shanks' 12th Kentucky Cavalry bringing his total force to twenty-nine hundred. Harlan rested a few hours and, forsaking the railroad transportation, marched his brigade from Munfordville at 3:00 A.M. on the morning of December 28.

Col. John M. Harlan. Photo courtesy of the Library of Congress.

BRACING FOR AN ATTACK

While John M. Harlan wrestled the railroad between Bowling Green and Munfordville, and fell farther behind Morgan's cavalry force, Lieut. Col. Harry S. Smith in Elizabethtown, commander of the 91st Illinois Infantry, sorted through reports of the Confederate approach up the Louisville and Nashville Railroad. Smith had received bad news upon arriving at 8:00 A.M. on the morning of the 27th with five companies from the lower trestle fortifications. This force joined a company already in Elizabethtown. Thus far, he had lost three of his companies stationed at Bacon Creek and Nolin, and now he had to determine how best to defend Elizabethtown and the two critical trestles that spanned wide ravines about five miles northeast of town. Approximately five hundred men remained in the fortifications overwatching the trestles. Smith may have felt obliged to hold Elizabethtown against the possibility that Morgan might bypass the town, thus placing Smith in position to attack the Confederates' rear before they could destroy the trestlework.

Lieutenant Colonel Smith must have been angry at having this crisis of command thrust upon him. The 91st Illinois had arrived in Elizabethtown on December 10, and sometime around the middle of the month, the commander, a Colonel Day, had gone on furlough. Smith had set up headquarters in the depot where he and the other staff officers "endeared themselves to the citizens of [Elizabethtown] by their gentlemanly deportment," according to a pro-Union report in the *Louisville Journal* (Moore 1866, 302). The secessionist citizens of Elizabethtown would most likely have disagreed with this *Louisville Journal* observation about Lieutenant Colonel Smith and the 91st Illinois.

> We were never visited by a better behaved set of men. There was not a solitary complaint of any outrage or depredations committed by them, even to the burning of a fence-rail, or the killing of a pig or chicken; nor did they offer any insult to a citizen or tamper with a negro, but were busily engaged in endeavoring to complete the stockade. . . . I am certain the statement would be indorsed [*sic*] by every citizen of the town, without distinction of party. (Moore 1866, 303)

Angry that the fortifications scheduled to be built at Elizabethtown were uncompleted, and aware that Morgan's force far outnumbered his 650 men with the town, Smith realized he could not meet Morgan in the open. His only chance would be to defend from the town itself, so he set about loopholing the buildings in and around the town square, and occupying them with his infantry. He posted one company about a mile south of town as skirmishers and to provide early warning of Morgan's approach, and basically hunkered down for the impending confrontation. He did not have long to wait, as sporadic firing erupted from the skirmish line south of town on the morning of December 27.

THE BATTLE AT ELIZABETHTOWN

As John Hunt Morgan approached Elizabethtown from the southwest on the morning of December 27, he entertained no doubts about attacking and capturing the town. Unlike Frank C. Armstrong, who probed Bolivar but chose to bypass the town in favor of avoiding decisive engagement, and unlike Forrest, who threatened Jackson only to sweep north and destroy the railroad supplying Grant's army, Morgan methodically set out to take Elizabethtown. Some have suggested, such as Dee Brown in *The Bold Cavaliers*, that Morgan "thought it would be wiser to capture the town's garrison rather than risk being caught between the forces there and those at the trestles" (Brown 1959, 149–50). But Morgan could have used a single regiment to fix any force that tried to march from Elizabethtown while he assaulted the trestles. Others have indicated that Morgan wanted to loot the town, perhaps offering some bounty for his men's hard riding and sacrifice. It might even be interesting to speculate about how much Morgan knew of Forrest and Van Dorn's success, and the degree to which that might have influenced his own desire to capture Federal garrisons and "liberate" the citizens of Elizabethtown. But Morgan's action was subject to one simple military reality: He possessed an overwhelming force and could likely pound the city into submission with artillery, resulting in relatively little loss of his personnel; he was within five miles and probably no more than twenty-four hours of accomplishing his primary objective (destroying the trestles at Muldraugh Hill), with no significant Federal force threatening his success or likely to block his escape; and lastly, Morgan had known since the night before that the town was garrisoned with only "some seven or eight companies of United States troops" (Morgan 1887, 155). Those facts, combined with elements of the other factors mentioned above, provided to Morgan's satisfaction adequate reason to risk a decisive engagement.

About a half mile southwest of town, Morgan's men saw the Federals across a hill in an open field. Although Lieutenant Colonel H. S. Smith attempted with his advance company to execute the Forrestesque trick of parading "in double file across the brow of the hill" in an attempt to fool the Confederates into believing he had a larger force, Morgan was not buying the ruse. Yet as they began to drive the Federal skirmish line back into Elizabethtown, during which time the impetuous Tom Quirk almost managed to get himself killed once again, the Confederates received a strange communiqué (Wyeth 1911, 121). A Union corporal galloped down the road, splashing mud and carrying a flag of truce. In a thick, Dutch accent he demanded to see General Morgan, and upon being delivered to him, rendered a stiff hand salute, and gave him this message "scrawled in pencil on the back of an envelope" (Morgan 1887, 156; Brown 1959, 150):

> To the Commander of the Confederate Forces:
> Sir: I demand an unconditional surrender of all your forces. I have you surrounded, and will compel you to surrender.
> I am, sir, your obedient servant,
>
> > H. S. Smith
> > Commanding U.S. Forces

Morgan and his staff received the message with considerable humor, Col. Basil Duke declaring the correspondence "the most sublimely audacious I ever knew to emanate from a Federal officer" (Duke 1960, 332). Wasting no time, Morgan replied to Smith that he "had the positions reversed; that it was his forces, and not mine, which were surrounded, and called upon him to surrender" (Morgan 1887, 156).

With the obligatory declaration that it was a United States officer's duty to fight, not surrender, Smith refused, and Morgan at once deployed for an attack. Sending Duke's brigade to the right of the railroad, and Breckinridge to the left, Morgan also positioned his artillery on a cemetery hill that commanded the town from the south. He kept one regiment back to guard the wagon trains he had collected thus far on his raid, and sent a small force under command of Captain C. C. Corbett, with one mountain howitzer, to the east of Elizabethtown. Duke and Breckinridge dismounted most of Roy S. Cluke's 8th and Robert Stoner's 9th Kentucky, and began advancing on the center of town where the Federals had occupied brick buildings to make what Morgan called "a street fight of it." Using several mounted companies to surround the town and cut off any Federals who might try to escape, Morgan ordered Capt. Baylor Palmer's battery to open fire from cemetery hill. For the next half hour, Palmer shelled Elizabethtown, his "rapid and accurate fire (nearly every shot striking the houses occupied by the enemy)" responsible for the "quick reduction of the place" (Morgan 1887, 156; Bearss 1964, 178; Duke 1960a, 333).

Pinned inside the buildings by the Confederate artillery, Lieutenant Colonel H. S. Smith's men attempted to fire on the approaching enemy through loopholes and from the attics[2] and windows of the buildings. The nature of their dispositions made it impossible for them to concentrate their fire, having to settle for isolated pockets of resistance that might be able to counter enemy movement along one street or the other. On occasion, taking advantage of a brief lull in the artillery fire, the Federals would dash into the streets and attempt to deliver a coordinated volley at Cluke's and Stoner's men as they worked their way into town. In one such instance, they were successful in driving the gunners away from the howitzer Captain Corbett commanded on the east end of town. Corbett had positioned the gun where the road into town crossed over the railroad embankment, offering it a broad field of fire into town, yet also making it vulnerable to enemy fire. The weapon was protected by a company of dismounts lying behind the embankment. Whenever the Federals dashed into the streets to fire at the gun crew, "the company lying behind the embankment would retaliate on the enemy in a style which took away their appetite for the game" (Duke 1960, 334). Only when a staff officer mistakenly ordered the men forward, did the Confederates receive any significant, coordinated fire, and they quickly returned to the embankment. In the process, however, the gunners were driven away from the howitzer, leaving only Captain Corbett "seated on the carriage, while the bullets were actually hopping from the . . . piece" (Duke 1960, 333). But the Federal advantage was localized and temporary, for the gunners soon returned, the howitzer went back into action, and Morgan cited Corbett for gallantry in his official report.

Whether or not Brigadier General Morgan gave the civilians in Elizabethtown the opportunity to leave before the shelling began is a matter of some dispute. Historian Dee Brown states that he did allow "the defenders time to remove women and children," however the pro-Union *Louisville Journal* tells a different story (Brown 1975, 16). According to a December 31 account of the fight at Elizabethtown, Smith's men attempted to defend the stockade and railroad embankment initially with skirmishers, but as previously stated, he drew his force into town and "placed men in the second story of the houses around the public square." Palmer's Battery on Cemetery Hill stood not more than five hundred yards from the courthouse.

> His firing commenced without any warning to the non-combatants, including women and children, to leave. Some of Morgan's friends contend that he did send warning for women and children to leave in forty-five minutes; but if there was such a respite offered, it is certain that no man, woman, or child, heard of it; and none could leave, for some attempted to leave town on the west and north side, but were fired on, and driven back by Morgan's men. And before half the time pretended to be given had elapsed, the artillery was banging away and fired one hundred and seven shots of shell and ball into the town, which lay at his mercy—almost under his feet—and, the only wonder is, that the town was not battered down. (Moore 1866, 303)

The *Louisville Journal* lists several buildings damaged by artillery, that is, numerous homes,[3] the Baptist and Catholic churches, and the Masonic lodge. Two Elizabethtown boys, James Poston and Harry Wintersmith, showed the attitude of invincibility so ever-present in youth by casually observing the steady shelling from atop a fence behind the Alfred M. Brown home. To their surprise and horror an artillery round passed through the front door of the Brown house, rolled through, and came bounding out the back door, stopping at the feet of the two boys (Jones 1995, 32). John Allen Wyeth indicates in his postwar writings that Morgan gave the citizens a half-hour notice to get out of town before the shelling started. Whatever the case, taking cover in the buildings of Elizabethtown may well have been Lieutenant Colonel Smith's only military option in opposing Morgan; but that decision having been made, the *Louisville Journal*'s intimation that the destruction in the town was purely at the whim of Brigadier General Morgan overlooks the fact that Smith *chose not to surrender*.

Smith himself was wounded in the shelling, as one of Palmer's rounds "passed through the room where [he] was posted, killing a man and striking [Smith] with a splinter in the face, nearly felling him" (Moore 1866, 303). The building Smith used as his headquarters drew heavy fire since the U.S. flag flew above it, and as Duke writes, "the enemy seemed thickest" there (Duke 1960, 238). Wyeth offers a unique description of Palmer's men servicing the battery from cemetery hill. He writes,

> I was just behind our battery and was fascinated by the regularity with which the pieces were manned and the accuracy of aim. It was more astonishing to be able to see a cannonball in flight . . . being right behind the gun as it fired and looking in the line of projection, it was easy to recognize a hazy, bluish streak or tail which seemed to be chasing the missile. I could plainly see great holes knocked in the walls, and soon a soldier here and there would run out of the houses, evidently looking for a safer place (Wyeth 1911, 122)

While Palmer battered the town, Cluke's and Stoner's men advanced, the rounds passing over their heads. A soldier from the 9th Kentucky, Robert L. Thompson, described forming in line of battle below the cemetery hill and advancing on foot across a waist-deep, flooded creek, weapon held high above his head, then hugging the buildings for cover as he advanced through the streets. Capturing three Federals by himself, he sent them to the rear and entered the hotel they had emerged from, only to find their breakfast on the table. Joined by other Confederates, Thompson and the group paused and ate breakfast, during which time "the little battery on the hill was being worked to its full capacity. When we had finished our breakfast and went out on the street again, we saw white handkerchiefs tied to ramrods hanging out the courthouse windows" (Thompson 1905, 571).

Not every Confederate soldier attacking Elizabethtown that morning had such a leisurely stroll with a free breakfast included, for isolated pockets of Federal resistance made the streets hot in several locations for the dismounts attempting to invest the town. Stoner's men often battered open the doors of buildings with their rifle butts, entered and compelled the Federals inside to surrender (Duke 1960, 338). Cluke's men approached town more slowly, having first to determine that the unfinished stockades were not manned, and then pushing forward. But the steady advance of Stoner's and Cluke's men, coupled with the mounted men surrounding the town, and more importantly, the continued battering by Palmer's artillery, proved too much for the Federals. The handkerchiefs Thompson saw were mirrored all over town as the defenders, seeing other soldiers surrendering, believed Smith had issued a general order to that effect. The *Chicago Tribune* reported that the initial capitulation was begun by a Lieutenant Seilbock "without the knowledge of the commanding officer." In a differing account, the initial surrender was precipitated by the actions of a Captain Fouchey ("The Morgan Raid" 1862, 2; Moore 1866, 304). With white flags emerging from windows and doorways all over town, Major D. H. Llewellyn, Morgan's quartermaster, followed immediately by Tom Quirk's Scouts, galloped into town bearing a white handkerchief to negotiate the surrender. Wyeth writes, "I distinctly recall the loopholed walls on either side as we galloped by, and hoped the men inside knew the surrender had been made. Otherwise, they could have riddled us" (Wyeth 1911, 122). Learning of the unauthorized surrender, Smith was irate, but he had little choice but to see it through. "Smith was not ready to surrender," Duke writes, "but his men did not wait on him and poured out of the houses and threw down their arms" (Duke 1960, 334). Seilbock probably saved numerous Federal and civilian lives (not a single citizen was killed or wounded) that would have resulted from the continued shelling of the town. And with his forces isolated in buildings, and no resultant unity of command, Smith should not have been surprised that individual, company-level commanders in his 91st Illinois made a determination about the viability of resistance from their immediate perspective.

Morgan captured 652 prisoners, among them 25 officers, and 600 altered flintlock muskets with which he promptly equipped the remaining unarmed troopers in his force (Morgan 1887, 156; Bearss 1964, 182). By late that afternoon, the Federals had been paroled and started in their march toward Louisville, and Morgan began destroying the railroad, burning the depot and the unfinished stockade. In a stinging indictment, the *Louisville Journal* records that "nearly three thousand five hundred bushels of wheat were consumed in the depot, all belonging to Southern rights men. Then every horse in town worth picking up, indeed, the horse-taking extended many miles round" (Moore 1866, 303). Morgan's men did not limit their resupply to horseflesh, for after confiscating the overcoats and boots from many of the captured Federals,[4] most of the stores in town were opened with or without the owners' permission. The *Louisville Journal* details the outrages attributed to Morgan's men that night in Elizabethtown, listing by name merchants who were "liberated" of thousands of dollars worth of goods. Some store owners appealed directly to Brigadier General Morgan, but the merchants, particularly those who openly admitted to being Union men, received little sympathy from the Confederate commander. According to the pro-Union news account,

> Morgan himself went into the store of B. Stadaker & Co., and in a very polite way said he wanted goods and would pay for them in good money; made free to open drawers and boxes and helped himself, all in a very polite way,

except now and then charging the merchant with lying, and wound up with a bill of upward of one thousand two hundred dollars in silks and costly merchandise, had them boxed up, and launched down the pay in confederate trash, not worth, as Stadaker says, a continental cent. (Moore 1866, 304)

The same newspaper that indicted the behavior of Morgan and his men among the stores in Elizabethtown admitted that private residences were respected. "The soldiers entered nearly all the houses for something to eat, but in all cases behaved civilly, and seemed thankful for the fare" (Moore 1866, 304). Lieutenant McCreary describes one such visit, whereupon entering the home at the bequest of some "very handsome young ladies," he immediately noted where an artillery round had crashed through the window and exploded in the house, killing three Federal soldiers and wounding a number of others. The men of the 91st Illinois lay "weltering in their blood on the floor, while the ladies, like proud Spartans walked contemptuously through the blood of those who had insulted them" and offered McCreary wine and holiday food. "I did justice to Christmas, and a hungry stomach," writes McCreary, "and ample justice, I hope to the dear fair ones . . . these so dear Kentucky ladies have a charm which no others possess" (Brown 1959, 151). McCreary's account is supported by Wyeth, who writes, "there seemed to be a strong Southern sentiment in Elizabethtown, and we were royally entertained in private houses" (Wyeth 1911, 122). Many of the Confederates slept in feather beds that night, Morgan himself staying in what is today known as the Brown-Pusey House, less than a hundred yards from the courthouse square. No more than five miles north lay the Muldraugh Hill trestles, so with no significant Federal opposition within thirty miles, Morgan's men spent a relaxing evening celebrating their victory with whiskey and Christmas goodies.

NOTES

1. Compare the tone of this message to Harlan's report when his men encountered General Armstrong during his Courtland, Alabama, raid in August.

2. As recently as 1990, the town square buildings in Elizabethtown that survived the war have yielded remnants of this fight, for example, a perfectly preserved, paper-encased Minie ball found in an attic.

3. Many Confederate cannon rounds still remain in the yards of Elizabethtown. At one historic home, the residents collected the expended solid shot and dropped it down a cistern after the battle, where the rounds remain today. One of the rounds of solid shot has been left in the wall of a building in the Elizbethtown square in the approximate position it landed over 130 years ago. A historical sign identifies it.

4. Rosecrans and Bragg were already in a "paper war" over what Rosecrans deemed the excesses of guerrilla warfare. He complained bitterly to Bragg about Morgan's men taking the captured Federals' overcoats, and accused them of not

always wearing recognizable Confederate uniforms—this, in Rosecrans' mind, made them guerrillas.

14

The Muldraugh Trestles and
the Battle at the Rolling
Fork River

Morgan is at liberty to do as he pleases.

—Chicago Tribune

The Louisville and Nashville Railroad covered some 187 miles from Louisville to Nashville, the first track being laid in 1855 and the last link, the Green River Bridge, completed in 1859 to create through service. The architect of the Green River Bridge, then considered one of the "triumphs of man's intelligence," was a 6-foot 7-inch German immigrant named Albert Fink. Fink, whose reputation as a bridge builder preceded him, developed a style of bridge and trestle support called the "Fink Truss"; and it was Fink who also designed and supervised the construction of the primary target of John Hunt Morgan's Christmas Raid—the two enormous railroad trestles four miles northeast of Elizabethtown (Herr 1943, 21).

With grade specifications requiring no steeper grade than seventy feet per mile, trestlework was the only solution to routing the railroad over Broad Run and Sulfur Fork Creek beneath Muldraugh Hill.[1] The northernmost trestle over Broad Run was 500 feet long and 90 feet high, and since late 1861 had been covered from the hilltop above by the initial construction of what would become Fort Boyle, named for the Federal military commander of Kentucky. The lower trestle over Sulfur Fork Creek was 500 feet long and 80 feet high, and was covered from above by earthworks that would eventually become Fort Sands, named after Alexander Sands, the U.S. marshall from southern Ohio, and from a stockade located adjacent to the tracks (Jones 1955, 34; Walden 1995, 43).

In command of the 560 Federal troops of the 71st Indiana Infantry occupying Fort Boyle and Fort Sands was Lieut. Col. Courtland S. Matson. The troops listed above, including in their total Companies B and C of the

78th Illinois on detached service from New Haven, were all that stood between Morgan and mission success. Up until the past week, life had been tedious for the troops stationed at Forts Boyle and Sands. James Theaher, a soldier in Company F, 50th Ohio Volunteer Infantry, who occupied Fort Sands just after Morgan's raid, offers this description of the site and his duties.

> We . . . have a pretty good camp after you get to it, but have to carry everything up a steep hill. No wagons can reach us much nearer than a quarter mile. Scarcely a horse can reach us . . . I don't like the situation at all, don't like guarding RRs. We have not got sufficient force here to protect our position against any very large force. (Rieger 1989, 37, 39)

Although the forts had emplacements for artillery, guns believed "suitable" had not yet been procured, thus Matson was left to defend the two trestles with small-arms fire alone. Apparently, his superiors were willing to accept that degradation, for Gen. Charles C. Gilbert, after inspecting the forts prior to Morgan's attack, "hoped . . . they could make good their hold on the place for one day" to allow purusing forces, for example, Harlan's Brigade, to overtake Morgan (Bearss 1964, 187). With news of the defeat and capture of Smith and the 91st Illinois in Elizabethtown, Matson concentrated his defense at Fort Sands above the lower trestle, kept approximately two hundred of his men posted at Fort Boyle to cover the trestle over Broad Run, and waited for the inevitable.

Bugle calls awakened the Confederate troops sleeping in and around Elizabethtown on the morning of December 28, and after breakfast and a leisurely weapons inspection, the force moved east along the railroad toward Bardstown. About four miles from town, where the Louisville and Nashville Railroad broke to the north, Morgan sent Breckinridge's Brigade to the left to attack the lower trestle at Sulphur Fork while he accompanied Duke's Brigade to the upper trestle at Broad Run. His forces arrived at both trestles around noon, and Morgan immediately sent to Matson a demand for unconditional surrender of Forts Boyle and Sands; but as Smith had before him in Elizabethtown, Lieutenant Colonel Matson refused to surrender. Occupying hilltops above the trestles, and, in the case of the lower fort, having a partially completed stockade near the tracks, Fort Boyle and Fort Sands offered excellent fields of fire down to the trestles, thus preventing Morgan's men from burning the structure without sustaining heavy casualties. Consequently, after positioning their brigades to effectively surround both forts, both Breckinridge and Duke opened up with artillery sometime around 2:00 or 3:00 P.M. With little significant overhead cover, no artillery to answer the Confederates, and their small arms out of stand-off range of the artillery, Matson determined after almost two hours of shelling that his position was hopeless and negotiated for surrender. This must have been particularly bitter to Matson as his unit had only been returned for duty a short time since being previously captured and paroled at Richmond, Kentucky ("The Third" 1863, 1)

Most of the men defending Fort Boyle were positioned in the stockade, and Wyeth writes that prior to the official surrender, "when our shells had made it too hot for the Hoosiers to stay inside the stockade, . . . some of them, hoping to escape, ran out and hid behind logs and in the underbrush of the near-by woods." He describes how he and Quirk's Scouts scoured the woods for the enemy, where at one point, Wyeth literally slid down the hill and between the legs of Brigadier General Morgan, almost tripping him. Upon finding a Federal soldier attempting to hide behind a tree, Wyeth, only a young boy himself, made his first capture.

> He seemed no older than myself, a good-looking lad with "peachdown cheeks" which had tears trickling over them. His crying quickly aroused my sympathy, and I tried to reassure him by saying: "Don't be afraid. Nobody shall harm you. You'll be paroled now and can go home." At this he sobbed out: "I've got a good mother at home; and if I ever get back, I'll never leave her again." By this time my own feelings were getting the best of me; and when he mentioned his mother, the thought of my own . . . never long out of my mind, overwhelmed me, and I began to cry too, telling him that I had a good mother too and doing my best to comfort the poor fellow. (Wyeth 1911, 161).

While Wyeth was escorting his prisoner to join the others, Morgan's men were accepting the surrender of the two forts under the command of Lieutenant Colonel Matson, and busily preparing to destroy the immense trestlework. One of a handful of Morgan's men who came from Indiana had occasion to encounter an old friend among the surrendered Federals. Sgt. Henry L. Stone recognized his friend Lieut. Col. Billy Brown during the surrender meeting with Morgan, and after "call[ing] him aside to take a heavy horn of good old Cogniac [sic] brandy," prevailed upon the captured Federal to take a letter home to Stone's mother. In his letter Stone confessed to his mother, "It is true that I take a little spirits occasionally, for these cold mornings it is beneficial. I've seen almost the infernal regions on earth since I left home but have endured it all and today rejoice that I'm a Confederate soldier" (Brown 1959, 152).

In his official report Morgan indicates that he captured seven hundred prisoners and destroyed "a large and valuable amount of medical, quarter-master's and commissary stores" (Morgan 1887, 156). His men gathered wood, fence rails, and even the lumber from the temporary barracks that had housed the defenders of Fort Boyle and Fort Sands, and burned the trestles.

> The destruction of this immense network of timber made the most brilliant display of fireworks I have ever seen. . . . The flames climbed swiftly along the timbers, until every upright and crosspiece was blazing in outline, more

vividly defined than if it had been strung with Chinese lanterns. When at last they were burned through, the flaming beams began to fall, and as the whole structure came down the heavens were brilliant with the column of sparks which shot skyward. (Wyeth 1911, 161)

After paroling Matson's men and starting them north toward Louisville, Morgan instructed "Lightnin'" Ellsworth to attach his telegraph key to the line that ran along the railroad, and had him wire Governor Morton of Indiana saying he would like to "thank you to send the oilcloths and overcoats next time and save him the trouble of making out paroles" (Wyeth 1911, 161). Morgan explains in his report, "At 7 o'clock that evening I had the satisfaction of knowing that the object of the expedition was attained," thus he led his command approximately six miles east-southeast, arriving late that night at a campsite where the Elizabethtown-Bardstown Road crosses the Rolling Fork River. A reporter for the *Chicago Tribune* would, while describing the capture of Elizabethtown and the destruction of the trestles, bitterly declare the following day that "the advent of Morgan into Kentucky has been attended with the usual consequences. It finds those who have the railroad to guard unprepared to meet him. Generals Boyle and Gilbert have never yet been in condition to repulse him from the road, and are not now. Morgan is at liberty to do as he pleases" ("From Kentucky" 1862, 2).

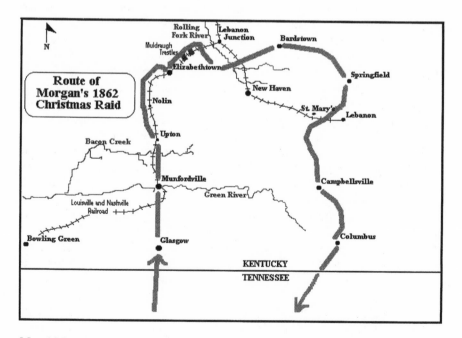

Map 14.1

Arriving at their campsite on the west bank of the Rolling Fork River that Sunday night, Wyeth recalled the weary, yet upbeat mood of Morgan's men. "Up to this time we had had a picnic, and sang with feeling and faith that gay chant of the mounted man, 'If You Want to Have a Good Time, Jine the Cavalry,' but in more senses than one the clouds were gathering" (Wyeth 1911, 161).

THE BATTLE AT ROLLING FORK RIVER

When Col. John M. Harlan's Brigade reached Elizabethtown on Monday morning, December 29, he discovered he had arrived too late to save the trestlework at Muldraugh Hill, but he also learned that Morgan's command had encamped only ten miles east of Elizabethtown on the Rolling Fork River. At long last, after frustrating railroad delays and uncertain information as to his enemy's location, Harlan's force had closed within striking range of Morgan's command. Harlan knew he must act quickly to seize what might be his only opportunity to defeat Morgan, for once across the Rolling Fork, the mounted Confederates would again quickly out-distance his infantry. Despite the day and night forced march that had allowed his troops to reach Elizabethtown that morning, Harlan pressed his men to continue and "marched immediately in [Morgan's] direction, ordering [Shanks' 12th Kentucky] cavalry to go far in advance" (Harlan 1887, 139). When the main body had traveled less than five miles east of Elizabethtown, Shanks returned with confirmation that Morgan's men were indeed still on the west side of the Rolling Fork, but would likely cross within the hour.

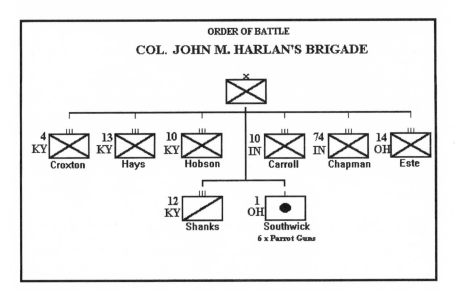

Figure 14.1

Colonel Harlan sent forward a section of Southwick's Battery to join the cavalry and lay down a suppressive fire that would "detain the rebels at the crossing" until he could arrive with his infantry. While the infantry advanced east at the double-quick along what is present-day Highway 62, Shanks returned with the artillery to the high ground overlooking the Rolling Fork River basin where he observed "in the plain below, a body of rebel cavalry, upon whom he ordered the artillery to open," causing them to rapidly disperse. Once the artillery erupted up ahead, Harlan himself rode forward and confirmed "a very large body of cavalry, formed in line of battle near the river. Their officers were riding along their line, apparently preparing to give us battle" (Harlan 1887, 139).

From this point, until the end of the battle to come, Harlan seems never to have realized the size of the enemy force he encountered that morning along the river. Why his cavalry did not or could not confirm for him how many men he opposed, is a matter of serious concern. Had Harlan known that from the first moment Shanks' Cavalry spotted Morgan's men, he had them outnumbered, the resulting engagement might have ended more favorably for the Union. Harlan, however, even after personally viewing the enemy force in the plain below him, determined that Morgan must outnumber him, and "proceeded cautiously, and yet as expeditiously as the nature of the ground and the circumstances admitted" (Harlan 1887, 139). Southwick's Battery had accurately ranged the ford within minutes, and throwing shells vigorously, the artillerymen slowed, and in some cases, halted all together the Confederate river crossing. Over the next half hour, Harlan's infantry regiments began arriving, and after extending a skirmish line, he placed them in line of battle as follows: On the extreme right, and supporting a section of Southwick's Battery occupying a small hill, was the 10th Kentucky under Lieutenant Colonel Hays. To Hays' left was the 10th Indiana under Colonel Carroll, then Croxton's 4th Kentucky, Este's 14th Ohio, Chapman's 74th Indiana, the other section of Southwick's Battery, and the 13th Kentucky under Hobson in support on the extreme left. The Confederates appeared to be pinned between the bursting canister that rained over their river crossing site, and a gradually increasing Federal line. Sporadic firing began on Harlan's left and spread along the line, and the Confederates seemed to be orienting themselves for an attack to silence his rightmost gun section; but for all the positioning and shelling, Harlan made no attack.

DUKE'S REARGUARD ACTION

The late Albert Harned, longtime Hardin County resident and respected member of the Younger's Creek community, entertained the author in his living room one cold, February day in 1980. Mr. Harned had grown up on the farm his grandfather maintained along the Rolling Fork River near the community of Younger's Creek. The author was researching the fight between Colonel Harlan and Morgan's men and had been led by other community members to speak with the elder Mr. Harned. Harned's father was a boy of eight that Monday morning, December 29, 1862, when Brig. Gen. John Hunt Morgan's men prepared their breakfast along the Rolling Fork. The boy's father (and Mr. Albert's grandfather), Wilford Lee Harned, of Company H, 6th Kentucky Infantry (Orphan Brigade), had been wounded at Shiloh in April 1862 and died eight days later at Burnsville, Mississippi. Thus Albert Harned's father was being raised alone by his mother when Morgan's men arrived in the valley. It was just after daylight, and the young Harned boy was riding in a wagon with his mother when the first of Harlan's Parrot gun rounds whistled overhead and exploded over the river. According to Albert Harned, the Confederate soldiers near the river had been caught completely by surprise, and immediately began trying to gather their force and effect a rapid crossing (Harned 1980, 1).

   Contrary to what Colonel Harlan believed, most of Morgan's command had already crossed the river when Shanks' Cavalry spotted them that morning. According to Basil Duke, "the bulk of the troops and the artillery were crossed at a ford a mile or two above" the evening's campsite where the Elizabethtown-Bardstown Road intersects the river. This site where the main body crossed was known as Hamilton's Ford. This alternate crossing was chosen due to the high water level and swift current of the Rolling Fork that time of year. "The pickets, rear-guard, and some detachments, left in the rear for various purposes, in all about three hundred men," had been gathering just after daylight that morning to cross at two fords further downriver—a very deliberate effort being required since the fords were "deep and difficult to approach and emerge from" (Duke 1960, 336). Albert Harned confirms this account, indicating that the "Confederates had to cut down the banks with shovels at the fording points in order to get the cannons across the river" (Harned 1980, 1).

   That morning most of Cluke's 8th Kentucky, supported by a section of Palmer's guns and Tom Quirk's Scouts, had been ordered northwest to destroy the bridge over the Rolling Fork at Lebanon Junction. Simultaneously, a portion of Stoner's 9th Kentucky, along with a gun section, crossed with the main body, then rode southeast to attack the garrison at New Haven. Moving in advance of the main body, Chenault's 11th Kentucky rode for Boston to destroy the railroad and seize the tiny town. Remaining on the west side of the Rolling Fork, at the Hamilton House,[2] some six hundred yards from the ford used by the main body, both of Morgan's brigade commanders and three regimental commanders (Cluke, Hutcheson, and Stoner), sat on a court-martial hearing that had been ongoing for several days. On trial was a Lieutenant Colonel Huffman, accused of violating the surrender terms Morgan had established for the Federals at Bacon Creek. The hearing had just adjourned, resulting in

The Hamilton-Hall House. Photo by the author.

Huffman's acquittal, and the officers were departing the Hamilton House, when the sound of artillery to the northwest grabbed their attention. Shortly, one of the rear guard's pickets rode up and declared that the enemy was approaching. "We knew that a force of infantry and cavalry was cautiously following us," Duke writes, "but did not know that it was so near" (Duke 1960, 336). Duke, who places the time of this initial firing at 11:00 A.M. (it was most likely earlier, perhaps 9:30 or 10:00 A.M.), rode immediately north to take charge of the rear guard and "throw into line the men who had not yet crossed, and hold the fords, if possible." Holding the fords was critical not only so that the rear guard might escape, but to provide a route for that separated portion of Cluke's Regiment under Major Bullock to cross the river upon his return from Lebanon Junction—a return surely to be expedited when he heard Harlan's artillery in his rear.

Basil Duke chose a wide field, framed by woods on both ends, through which a natural depression ran that provided protection "as if they had been behind an earthwork" (Duke 1960, 337). Deploying the two stay-be-hind companies of Cluke's 8th Kentucky on his left, and Stoner's 9th Kentucky on the right, he placed approximately two companies of Gano's 3rd Kentucky in the center and prepared to hold the crossing. Horseholders attempted to shelter the horses in the only covered spot—a stand of trees on the Confederate left. Using the terrain to shield his force from view of the Federals, Duke had his men move about so as to pop up from behind the depression and create the illusion of greater numbers. The ruse must have been successful, for Colonel Harlan hesitated in his advance; in fact, he conducted no advance whatsoever. A surprised Colonel Duke wrote that Harlan's force, "if handled vigorously and skillfully, if its march had even been steadily kept up, would have, in spite of every effort we could have made, swept us into the turbid river at our backs" (Duke 1960, 337).

The same Colonel Harlan who chose to seize the moment and conduct a forced march from Elizabethtown to overtake Morgan, now elected to be deliberate, slowly extending his forces such that "their long line tediously crept upon us and all around us, [such that] I would almost have preferred, after an hour of it had elapsed, that Harlan had made a fierce attack" (Duke 1960, 338). The hour that Harlan spent positioning his forces bought Major Bullock time to return from Lebanon Junction and rejoin Duke with five companies of Cluke's Regiment and a section of six-pounders. To his credit, Harlan kept up the shelling, his guns cited by Duke as "the best served of any, I think, that I ever saw in action," thus rendering crossing the ford itself "out of the question" (Harlan 1887, 139; Duke 1960, 338).

Even with Cluke's men and Quirk's Scouts bringing the total Confederate strength to almost eight hundred men, Duke knew he was in a precarious position. Harlan appeared to be advancing to attack, and Duke wrote,

> his infantry deployed in a long line, strongly supported, with a skirmish line in front, all coming on with bayonets glistening, the guns redoubling their fire, and the cavalry column on the right flank (of their line) apparently ready to pounce on us too, and then the river surging at our backs, my blood, I confess, ran cold. (Duke 1960, 338)

The Confederates prepared to repulse the attack, perhaps to the last man, but suddenly, for some inexplicable reason, as soon as it came under fire the Federal advance halted. Sensing uncertainty, hesitation, and perhaps even fear on the part of the Federals, Duke determined to exploit Harlan's indecision by launching a limited counterattack. He ordered Captain Pendleton to lead three companies of the 8th Kentucky against the Federal right to seize the devastating battery occupying a small hill. While Pendleton fixed the Federals with his counterattack, Duke would attempt to lead the remainder of the rear guard across the river. Pendleton's counterattack was described by Harlan as a "demonstration to occupy an eminence upon my right," and he responded by maneuvering the 10th Indiana to support the guns on the hill, then attempting to clear the nearby woods of the Confederates. But Pendleton's attack succeeded in driving the Federal gunners away and silencing the right section of Southwick's Battery for approximately fifteen minutes before the 10th Indiana could regain control of the hill. Pendleton himself was wounded in the hand when a minie ball struck his revolver handle and shattered it, sending wooden shards into his palm and lacerating his hand.

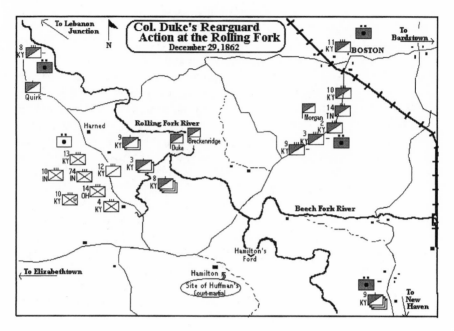

Map 14.2

While Harlan's line wavered and Pendleton occupied the Federals on their right flank, Duke positioned himself by the ford and began directing his troops across the Rolling Fork. A third fording point had been discovered only moments before behind Cluke's position, and concentrating the crossing effort there meant that the half of Harlan's guns still in operation would have to acquire a new aiming point. The lull in firing accounted for the majority of the Confederate cavalry being "thrown into columns and dashed across the river, leaving the army on the other side cheated of its prey" (Duke 1960, 339).

Not all the Confederates made it over the Rolling Fork unscathed. "They had a tough time of it crossing that river," Albert Harned explained, struggling particularly to pull the artillery through the swift water.[3] As Basil Duke directed the withdrawal from near the riverbank, Southwick's Battery on Harlan's left accurately ranged the Confederate horseholders stationed near Duke, killing ten horses within a twenty-foot circle near one of the ford sites. A fragment from one of these shrapnel rounds struck Duke in the head, knocking him unconscious, and yet another fragment killed the horse of his aide-de-camp. "I had no doubt that [Duke] had been instantly killed," writes John Wyeth, who describes how his commander, Capt. Tom Quirk, rode up to the wounded Colonel Duke and, with the help of some of his men, had Duke placed astride the pommel of Quirk's saddle. With one arm around Duke's chest, Quirk urged his powerful, large bay into the raging water of the Rolling Fork, running about saddle skirt deep, and carried Duke to safety across the river. Command fell to Colonel Breckinridge, and within minutes the skirmishers and a handful of Pendleton's men came rushing back from the Federal line, mounted their horses, and dashed across the river.

Morgan's rear guard had, in the very grasp of a force three times its size, escaped without a single man being killed and only three men wounded. On the Federal side, Colonel Harlan suffered an officer killed, Captain Pollis of Southwick's artillery, and two privates, Louis Finney of the 10th Indiana and Thomas J. Burton of the 4th Kentucky. One other soldier was reported as wounded. What Harlan describes in his report as the enemy "[breaking] and [fleeing] precipitately in every direction," was, in effect, Duke and Breckinridge leading their men to safety. Harlan writes, "Some struck out into the woods; some went up the river as far as New Haven; some swam the river with their horses," then citing the "exhausted state" of his men, the Federal commander declared that "further pursuit that evening was impracticable" (Harlan 1882, 139). In the latter observation, Harlan was correct. He had no chance of overtaking the Confederates once he let them cross the river; but for all the inferences that the enemy broke and ran in all directions, his report fails to list a single prisoner; and the *Chicago Tribune*'s subsequent claim that Harlan captured a captain and six privates would appear to be erroneous.

Harlan's command had planned to spend the evening on the battle site, but when a courier sent to inspect damage to the Rolling Fork Bridge (the aborted target of Cluke's Regiment), returned to indicate the bridge intact, Harlan marched his weary command at midnight, not stopping until he reached the bridge at daylight the following morning. He would position his forces to protect the Rolling Fork Bridge in case Morgan's men attempted to double back. Brig. Gen. Speed S. Fry, commanding the division from which Harlan launched his force at Galatin, Tennessee, would write some two weeks later that "Colonel Harlan, for the energy, promptness, and success in pursuing and driving rebel forces from [the] railroad, is entitled to the gratitude not only of the people of Kentucky, but of the whole Army of the Cumberland" (Fry 1887, 141).

NOTES

1. Muldraugh Hill actually refers to a much larger terrain feature than the steep hill between Elizabethtown and Louisville. Although the localized name came from a man named Muldraugh who was given a patent for a hugh tract of land from the present site to the Salt River, central Kentuckians often use Muldraugh['s] Hill to refer to a long, twisting, escarpment ("hogback") that leads from the Salt River, past Bardstown, in the general direction of Springfield. Thus, other nineteenth-century references to movements on "Muldraugh['s] Hill" may or may not refer to the area near Elizabethtown.

2. This historic home, one of the oldest in Hardin County, Kentucky, still stands today. It is sometimes called the Hance Hamilton House or the Hamilton-Hall House for its most recent owners. The author spoke with the late Ben Hall in 1980 while researching the battle at the Rolling Fork. Mr. Hall explained how in 1828 President-elect Andrew Jackson spent the night in this house on the way to his inauguration in Washington. The home, albeit in need of some repair, stands as a fascinating work of architecture representing the early nineteenth-century "frontier" home.

3. The author sat in Albert Harned's living room in the winter of 1980 drinking coffee and listening as Mr. Harned related his grandfather's story of the Battle of the Rolling Fork. Harned explained that the third fording site the Confederates found—the one that eventually allowed them to push Cluke's two artillery pieces across the swift river—was near Slate Run, not far from his grandfather's home. "The Elizabethtown Road was just a wagon trail then," Harned explained, "and when [the Confederates] found this other ford, it pretty much saved the day for them. After they got across, the Yankees came. My grandfather said they drove off sixteen head of mules and sixty cattle from his farm, but the Confederates had already taken any horses worth having." Harned went on to explain that a couple of days after the battle, his grandfather went down to the ford site where the carcasses of several horses lay stewn about. He noticed something sticking out of a large beech tree, some six to eight feet high. Climbing up the tree, the young Harned boy removed a Confederate cavalry officer's saber.

Pausing in his relating of the story, Albert Harned disappeared into a back room of his home and returned within a minute or so with the saber his grandfather had found. The author asked Mr. Harned what he'd done with the saber all these years, and the elderly gentleman explained, "Oh, we just used it to kill rats in the barn." Upon returning to the Elizabethtown area in 1984 to renew my research on Morgan's Raid, one of my first stops was to the home of Albert Harned, but I was saddened to learn that "Mr. Albert" had passed away only months before. I was also disappointed to discover that the sword he said he "was keeping for his grandchildren" was rumored to have been sold at public auction along with much of his other property.

15

Lebanon and Home

This roving, predatory warfare
—Indiana Governor O. P. Morton

Once Brig. Gen. John Hunt Morgan outdistanced Colonel Harlan's pursuit, the Federal telegraph wires—at least those Morgan had not disabled—began to buzz with interrogatives regarding the raider's location. Maj. Gen. Horatio Wright, commander of the Military Department of the Ohio, and headquartered in Cincinnati, had for the past four days been trying to determine Morgan's true strength and intentions. Already Wright had underestimated Morgan's combat power, for on the 27th—the same day Morgan captured Elizabethtown—he assured his subordinate, General Boyle in Louisville, that Morgan only had three regiments constituting a fighting force of no more than twelve hundred—a force Boyle "should whip at important points" (Wright 1882, 250).

General Rosecrans saw his major Federal offensive against Murphrees-boro compromised by a destroyed supply line, a mounted threat in his rear, and a telegraph line that was alternately being torn down or monitored by the enemy. He revealed his frustration over Morgan to Gen. Mahlon D. Manson in command at Bowling Green. "If General Wright, with 20,000 men, cannot take care of Morgan, I shall not send any more troops [to Kentucky]" (Rosecrans 1887, 272). This was quite a turnaround in attitude on Rosecrans' part, for only two days before he had confidently declared Morgan to be "in the toils, and being rapidly hemmed in. He will find it so difficult to escape," Rosecrans had observed, "that he will have little leisure to think of offensive operation." By the following evening, Morgan had destroyed the trestles at Muldraugh Hill.

On the other hand, General Wright, while underestimating Morgan's strength, had never taken the enemy threat lightly. To his credit, once he had determined that Morgan moved east from the trestles, he began orchestrating forces to converge on Lebanon in enough strength to compel Morgan into a decisive engagement and perhaps defeat him.

Harlan's artillery fire at Duke and the Confederate rear guard along the Rolling Fork River on the morning of the 29th had not only pressed the enemy into a rapid flight, but it had also alerted Col. William A. Hoskins, commander of Federal troops at Lebanon, that Morgan was moving in his direction. Having just that morning received at Lebanon a reinforcing infantry brigade, Hoskins sent forward a twenty-five man scouting party, and a "citizen-scout" in the direction of Bardstown and New Haven to find Morgan.

AVOIDING DECISIVE ENGAGEMENT

Morgan's command rallied in Bardstown on the night of December 30. Chenault's Regiment arrived from successfully destroying the bridge and stockade at Boston. Having made a narrow escape from Colonel Harlan, Colonel Breckinridge and the rear guard closed upon the town, with Colonel Duke still unconscious and riding in a makeshift ambulance. Cluke's Regiment came in with the rear guard, having been prevented by Harlan's sudden attack from achieving its mission of destroying the Rolling Fork Bridge. A detachment from Stoner's Regiment remained in the vicinity of New Haven where they had encamped for the night with the intent of attacking and capturing the stockade there the following morning. Tom Quirk's Scouts had ridden the length of the column to arrive in Bardstown first, quartering themselves and their horses in the best livery stables before the main body arrived. Finding a store still open for business, some of Quirk's men used Confederate money to purchase boots, riding gauntlets, and other items scarce in the deep south. The owner, upset at being forced to take what he deemed worthless currency, quickly closed his store and disappeared. The following morning a crowd of Morgan's men, annoyed at the proprietor's inconsiderate action of leaving town and taking the key to his store with him, broke down the door and began a wholesale looting of his business. "Within a short half hour nothing was left inside but the shelves and counters," writes John Wyeth, "for in the riot of this uncontrolled desire to plunder these men took piles of stuff they could not possibly use." Wyeth indicates this was the "first act of plunder" he had witnessed, and though it shocked his Presbyterian sense of values, he admits to joining in, "charging it up in my conscience to necessity, since the government could not provide for us." And in the hindsight brought on with age, Wyeth notes how "much in war is en-nobling, but much more tends to degradation" (Wyeth 1911, 162).

"About dark Morgan's men began to throng the streets," noted Bardstown circuit preacher J. W. Cunningham. He described how some of the troopers carried the wounded Col. Basil Duke into the upstairs bedroom home of a Dr. Cox. "I was invited to examine a cannon's work," recorded Cunningham. "A piece of skin and bone behind the ear was gone." Cunningham says that as he bent over to observe the wound, Duke opened his eyes and commented, "That was a pretty close call" (Brown 1975, 13).

Quirk's Scouts led the main body out of Bardstown early the following morning, Tuesday the 30th, enroute to Springfield. Morgan was described as a "splendid-looking man, dressed in a fitted jacket and green woolen trousers. He wore a black low-crowned soft hat with a broad brim" (Brown 1975, 13). When Quirk's men reached Fredericksburg, one of the locals they breakfasted with that morning was Colonel Hoskins' "citizen-scout," who promptly rode back to Lebanon and informed Hoskins of Morgan's approach. Hoskins responded by ordering strong detachments from the 6th and 9th Kentucky Cavalry (Union), under command of Colonel Halisy and Lieutenant Colonel Boyle, on a reconnaissance-in-force to determine if Morgan was moving directly upon Lebanon or by way of Springfield. Hoskins learned that advanced elements of Morgan's command had already reached Springfield, thus he determined to use Halisy's force to block the road to Lebanon and buy time to prepare his defense of the town. "With the force at my command I did not think that I would be justifiable in attacking Morgan," Hoskins reported, "particularly when I had no definite idea of his real strength, which was variously estimated at from 3,000 to 11,000." If any Federal commander with more than fifteen hundred men had drawn Morgan into a decisive engagement, precious time for an escape might well have withered away, allowing the Federals pursuing the Confederate raider from every direction to converge and defeat him. But Morgan's electronic war of disinformation had once again worked to his advantage, and Hoskins, in command of a force almost double that of Morgan's, was intimidated into the defense. Unlike H. S. Smith in Elizabethtown, Colonel Hoskins determined to meet Morgan *outside* of town, a plan strengthened, no doubt, by the fact that he possessed at least a section of artillery. He reasoned that to give up defensible terrain north of town would allow Morgan to "shell us in the town," with the Confederate dismounts advancing under cover of timber, while his own troops would be "exposed" and "entirely open" (Hoskins 1887, 144). The position Hoskins chose for his artillery section "commanded the Springfield road for one and one-half miles" and would certainly have challenged any approach Morgan made to attack Lebanon.

The only problem with Hoskins' defense of Lebanon was that Morgan was not coming to Lebanon. Upon arriving in Springfield on Tuesday night, Morgan "learned that the enemy had withdrawn all his forces from the southern portion of the State, and had concentrated them at Lebanon.

Troops from Danville, Burkesville, Campbellsville, and Columbia had been collected there to the number of nearly 8,000 and several pieces of artillery" (Morgan 1887, 157). Morgan also knew that a force of ten thousand men was moving from Glasgow to Burkesville to intercept him, leading him to rightly discern "my position was now sufficiently hazardous." The mission that had gone so smoothly since departing Alexandria, Tennessee, on the 22nd seemed to be gradually unraveling. Stoner's detachment sent to destroy the stockade at New Haven had arrived in Springfield that evening, having been repulsed in their attack. The close call with Harlan had diverted Cluke's Regiment from destroying the Rolling Fork Bridge near Lebanon Junction, and now Morgan had solid intelligence that the Federals were finally mobilizing enough force to threaten his return to Tennessee. Realizing there was no time to rest his command, Morgan determined that evening to press on and bypass Lebanon "by a night march, to conceal my movements from the enemy," and avoid a decisive engagement that would almost certainly have allowed the Federals to converge upon him. He hoped to reach and cross the Cumberland River before the force marching from Glasgow could stop him. By 11:00 P.M. the entire command was in motion.

To divert the Federals' attention from his bypass, and to reinforce his deception, Morgan used the technique Forrest had applied at Salem Cemetery. He had Quirk's Scouts and detachments from other regiments to build numerous fires north of town to deceive the Federals into thinking he was encamped on the Springfield-Lebanon Road, "only waiting for daylight to attack" (Morgan 1887, 157). Col. Adam Johnson's 10th Kentucky demonstrated that night against Hoskins' force at Lebanon, dividing his command into three equal sections of one hundred men each, and engaging pickets on three different roads. Temperatures were dropping fast, and a "fine, slow-falling rain" was turning into sleet and snow, as Quirk's Scouts approached Hoskins' defense north of Lebanon on the evening of the 30th. John Wyeth writes, "We were kept busy piling fence rails and making fires late in the night, but were not allowed to stay long enough by any one fire to warm ourselves." Morgan, in the meantime, had scoured the countryside to find a suitable guide that could lead them on a narrow, little-used country road that circuited Lebanon to the west. "The night was dark and stormy and the road rough and intricate," noted Morgan, and John Wyeth vividly describes the "bitter, penetrating cold, the fatigue, the overwhelming desire to sleep." Frequently the artillery became mired, and in a scene reminiscent of Forrest's torchlit drive through the Obion River bottoms in west Tennessee only a day earlier, Morgan's cavalrymen had to dismount and "put their shoulders to the wheels" during what many would call "a night of misery never to be forgotten" (Wyeth 1911, 163).

> I remember passing a small cabin near the roadside and seeing the gleam of the fire from the hearth through the crack under the door, and I felt then as if I would give everything I had in this world or any hope for another just for the privilege of lying down in front of that blaze and going to sleep. . . . The sleet pelted us unmercifully and covered our oilcloths with a coating of ice. Finally I became so numb that I could not hold my gun, and somewhere in the darkness it dropped from my hands and was lost. (Wyeth 1911, 163)

But while these southern cavalrymen suffered greatly at the hands of what many called a "blizzard," the intensity of the storm may have been their salvation, keeping Federal troops close to their fires rather than searching the roads around Lebanon for them. Col. Adam Johnson called this the "most disagreeable night of the war," and when he was satisfied that the main body had reached St. Mary's, he led his command away to link up with Morgan in Burkesville. "It was a weird sight when day dawned; all the men were sheeted in ice and looked like a ghostly army, as they moved silently through the woods" (Davis 1904, 134).

By noon the following day, Morgan's command had completed its bypass of Lebanon, and the Confederate general gazed down on the town from some high ground to the south. He had avoided decisive engagement, but he had not slipped by completely unnoticed. Hoskins must have suspected something when the enemy had not probed his position by daylight, so at 7:00 A.M. on the 31st he sent another reconnaissance-in-force under Colonel Halisy in the direction of Morgan's camp. Halisy immediately sent a courier back to Hoskins when he discovered the Confederate camp abandoned, indicating he was pursuing them south toward Muldraugh Hill (again, this refers to a long escarpment that runs through central Kentucky, not a singular location). Hoskins directed Halisy to "hang upon their rear, and if possible, harass them to a stand" in the event he discovered they had bypassed either side of Lebanon. By noon reports were reaching Lebanon that Morgan's force had passed in the vicinity of St. Mary's, and fearing an attack from that direction, Hoskins drew his regiments into line of battle on the west and southwest of town. No attack was forthcoming, and eventually Hoskins learned that the entire Confederate main body had cleared St. Mary's and was moving rapidly south. Immediately he gathered his command—some eight infantry regiments and the equivalent of a regiment and one half of cavalry—and pursued Morgan south toward Muldraugh Hill in the direction of Campbellsville.

Infantry chasing cavalry is seldom successful, and despite his best efforts, Morgan's command simply outran Hoskins. On New Year's Eve the raiders reached Campbellsville where they found much needed forage and food. From Campbellsville they moved to Columbia where they arrived at 3:00 P.M. on January 1, still with no significant opposition. But Morgan was concerned that the force thought to be marching toward Burkesville might intercept them if they delayed, thus he led his men on yet another night march. "Stops were seldom made," writes Robert Thompson. "It might be that the guide had lost his way, when we would stop to establish the right direction, etc. At such times we would snatch a moment's sweetest sleep, either leaning over on our horses' necks or dropping down on the cold earth, holding the horse by the bridle" (Thompson 1905, 572). Reaching Burkesville on January 2, he "halted the command for a few hours to rest and feed, and then crossed the Cumberland without molestation"[1] (Morgan 1887, 158). Over the next three days Morgan's command slowed the pace, convinced he was well beyond the range of any Federal pursuit, and made it to Smithville, Tennessee, on January 5. Three days later, Morgan prepared his report to General Bragg in which he claimed massive destruction of the Louisville and Nashville Railroad between Munfordville and Shepherdsville, the capture of 1,877 prisoners, and the destruction of $2 million in U.S. government property. As to casualties, he noted the loss of two men killed, twenty-four wounded, and sixty-four missing.

The damage that Morgan did to Rosecrans' supply line is indisputable. Indiana Governor O. P. Morton in a message to Secretary of War Stanton on December 29 urged that "bridge-builders from Cincinnati, Pittsburgh, and other cities" be immediately sent to rebuild the trestles at Muldraugh Hill. "The presevation of Rosecrans' army may depend upon it," he wrote. Then, after urging Stanton to authorize new units of mounted infantry to protect against such raids, Governor Morton made an insightful observation not only about Morgan's raid, but about the effect of southern cavalry raids in general. "Unless this is done speedily, this roving, predatory warfare will instantly destroy our communications and wear out our armies" (Morgan 1887, 956).

The Federals would be rebuilding the trestles at Muldraugh Hill until the end of February; and few, if any, among the Federal high command would doubt their vulnerability to the type of raids Governor Morton describes. General C. C. Gilbert, commander of troops along the Louisville and Nashville Railroad, would continue to argue for the stockade as a critical element in the defense of the railroad, but he would demand "well-seasoned" troops to garrison them. "Of the stockades attacked," Gilbert writes, "only two were finished. Of these, one held out five hours and required two or more changes of position before the guns brought to bear on it effected the reduction" (Gilbert 1887, 56). He pointed out that the New Haven Stockade had repulsed Morgan's attack, and he decried the transfer to a "distant field" of the "two cavalry regiments fitted out with light guns" for the "special service" of guarding the railroads. But in spite of the indignation at their vulnerability, and the rhetoric about how to oppose such a enemy expedition, the next time Morgan would raid into Kentucky—July 1863—the Federals would be only slightly better prepared to meet him. And while Morgan's 1863 raid ended in the capture or scattering of most of his command, the result was decidedly a factor of

Morgan overextending his force into Ohio rather than any efforts on the part of the Federals along the Louisville and Nashville Railroad.

These men who followed Morgan were mostly Kentuckians, with a handful of Texans (Gano's Regiment) and some Tennesseans as well. Their ideas of discipline did not conform to that of the regular cavalry, and particularly that of Gen. Braxton Bragg. They were young, and for many of them, this was their first serious contact with the enemy. "Gen. Morgan was only thirty-eight," writes Robert L. Thompson of Breckinridge's 9th Kentucky. "My colonel was twenty-six, and there was not an officer in the regiment whose age exceeded thirty, except one, and he was not over forty . . . [and] there was little John Kemper, aged thirteen, who rode a pony and carried a carbine. I was sixteen, and the youngest soldier in my company" (Thompson 1905, 571). "The men prided themselves on moving rapidly for hours without food or sleep, erect and eager for unheralded combat at any time" (Hardin 1963, 3). But Morgan had shown on this raid, and would show on subsequent missions, a more effective use of cavalry than his Federal opponents. Adapting techniques used to fight Indians, rather than the set-piece movements of European cavalry, Morgan operated primarily as mounted infantry, his preference for the pistol and carbine over the saber being evidence of his varied approach. His horses were *vehicles* rather than battle-mounts, in that the animals carried his troops from place to place, yet the men dismounted to engage in anything greater than a skirmish. Some researchers attribute Morgan's tactics more to Col. Basil Duke than to the general himself. And while it is true that Duke supervised much of the training and was often the man Morgan turned to at the most decisive moment of a battle, the influence and tactical thought process of Morgan himself must not be discounted. According to historian Bayless Hardin, "Scouting parties [i.e., Quirk] were organized to spy on the enemy forces miles distant, and Morgan himself often gained admittance to Federal Camps and interviewed opposing officers in various disguises, securing much valuable information" (Hardin 1963, 3). While this infiltration was not a factor in the Christmas Raid, it demonstrates the irregular attitude of both Morgan and his men. This attitude, though often producing success, kept General Bragg, as well as his nemesis, Rosecrans, in the mindset of viewing Morgan as fundamentally a guerrilla leader—a man not quite dependable in more regular operations.

During Morgan's absence on the Christmas Raid, the Battle of Murphreesboro would be fought in Tennessee, with Braxton Bragg's resultant withdrawal to Tullahoma. While the destruction Morgan wreaked upon the Federal supply line had contributed to the difficulty with which General Rosecrans operated, it had not been significant enough to change the outcome at Stones River. Yet buoyed by their success, and encouraged by the gratitude of a Confederacy desperately in search of something to claim as a victory, Morgan's men rested and readied themselves for yet another campaign.

NOTE

1. The only exception to an uneventful escape was a brief encounter with a half-dozen bushwackers firing from a mountain opposite the ford at Burkesville. A squad from Johnson's 10th Kentucky flushed the enemy from their hideout, shot three of them, and drove the others into a cave. Piling wood and brush at the entrance to the cave, they set a fire that would "last long enough to keep the skulkers imprisoned till the command had passed" (Davis 1904, 134).

Closing Thoughts

We have examined three of the most tactically revealing and strategically important Confederate cavalry raids conducted in the western theater during 1862. Within each of the three commands there were some regiments better trained and more experienced than others, but overall, the quality of the soldiers in each raid was relatively equal. The same can be said for the Federal troops that opposed each raid, for example, the quality of Union soldiers defending the Louisville and Nashville Railroad against Morgan was neither significantly better nor significantly worse than that of those who fought against Armstrong at Medon or Forrest at Parker's Crossroads. The individual companies or regiments parsed along the various railroad stations were defeated not because they lacked training or the will to fight, but due to their isolation and distance from mutually supporting units. Instances where the Federals had the greatest success against the raiders occurred in those situations in which troops could be massed; and in every raid, at least at some point, the Federals managed to draw the Confederate cavalry into a decisive engagement. The results of those decisive engagements, for example, Britton's Lane, Parker's Crossroads, and Elizabethtown or the Rolling Fork River, varied because of the tactics, terrain, and leadership present at that particular fight, and have been discussed in detail within the corresponding chapters. However, the effectiveness of the overall raid and the degree of strategic success obtained by each commander was a function of the following considerations: (1) the role of the railroad, (2) habitual tactics, (3) reconnaissance, (4) the role of artillery, (5) the role of the weather, (6) deception, and (7) commander's leadership style.

THE ROLE OF THE RAILROAD

In the introduction the railroad was discussed as a primary target for all the raids, but while each Confederate commander's goal was to interdict the railroads, the path they chose to reach the rail line became a function of the resistance they encountered. For example, Armstrong conducted his raid primarily *along the path* of the railroad, striking the line at Grand Junction, Tennessee, and traveling along the tracks for three days until he reached Medon Station. That choice had two important consequences: (1) Armstrong was able to destroy the railroad and bridges *as he went*, providing efficiency and speed in accomplishing that phase of his mission; and (2) the railroad he followed gave the enemy a means of rapid reinforcement to oppose his advance.

At Middleburg, it is the arrival of the 2nd Illinois Cavalry, under Col. Harvey Hogg, that effectively stifles the Confederate advance on Bolivar. Without the 2nd Illinois' timely appearance, what ended up in a bypass movement might well have given way to a deliberate attack and occupation of the town of Bolivar. Without Hogg's reinforcement, perhaps Armstrong chooses to fight his way through the handful of infantry companies opposing him, and once past them, he may have been able to defeat Leggett's entire force.

At Medon Station, it is the timely arrival of Federal reinforcements *by rail* that saves the garrison at Medon from an overwhelming Confederate attack. Without those reinforcements, perhaps Armstrong drives due north to Jackson and attacks the ill-prepared defenses of one of the Union's most critical supply hubs. Because of his repulse at Medon, Armstrong sweeps west to bypass the resistance and encounters Colonel E. S. Dennis at Britton's Lane. With no railroad present to reinforce the Federals, Armstrong now accepts decisive engagement, a decision that may have led to the undoing of the raid.

Nathan Bedford Forrest has the destruction of the railroad as his mission as well, however his raid is not conducted along the axis of the railroad, per se, though he does move along the rails from Trenton to Moscow, Kentucky. Because Forrest approaches the Mobile and Ohio Railroad from the east, and does not travel along a rail line initially, Colonel Ingersoll receives no reinforcement and is easily defeated. After Forrest demonstrates against Jackson and fixes Gen. Jeremiah Sullivan, he does strike the railroad and move along it for some five days before turning cross-country for his withdrawal. Because he beat Sullivan to the railroad and began to destroy it as he went, Sullivan (even allowing for his perpetual tardiness) could not ferry troops into direct contact against Forrest as Colonel Lawler and General Ross did against Armstrong.

Brig. Gen. John Hunt Morgan's route more closely resembled Armstrong's in that he entered Kentucky and struck the railroad at Bacon Creek, then continued along the line for four days before turning cross-country for his escape. The Federals attempted to rush troops to counter Morgan, for example, Colonel Harlan's Brigade, but the destruction of the track south of Morgan's route continually delayed Harlan. Why did not the Federal commander in Louisville rush reinforcements to Elizabethtown to counter Morgan as did General Ross against Armstrong at Medon Station? The reason may be found in the electronic warfare campaign of deception that Morgan instituted against General Boyle in Louisville. Where, exactly, does Boyle send reinforcements if he has a dozen different reports of Morgan's location?

HABITUAL TACTICS

Each of the Confederate cavalry commanders we examined found a particular tactical solution and attempted to apply it on a repetitive basis, in other words, they reinforced success. When Frank C. Armstrong is stung by the ambush at Courtland, Alabama, he is successful in overcoming the enemy by flanking the two isolated companies. So, at Middleburg he again attempts to fix Col. Manning Force on the Van Buren Road and uses a flanking action along the Middleburg Road. Only Colonel Leggett's quick response with the "Jackass Cavalry" prevents Force's men from being defeated, and the way opened to Bolivar. At Medon Station, Armstrong attempts to bring the 2nd Tennessee Cavalry against the depot from the east, and only upon failing to reduce the position with that maneuver does he order Colonel Jackson to charge down the main street in a column of four. At Britton's Lane, Armstrong meets resistance in his initial assaults and again attempts a flanking action that is ultimately successful in capturing E. S. Dennis' wagon trains. The difficulty that Armstrong faced in applying habitual tactics at Britton's Lane rests in the fact that in all of the previous cases, he was facing a few companies at the most. He had never committed his full combat power, yet had managed to roll up several blockhouse detachments, bypass Bolivar, and even disengage at Medon Station. At Britton's Lane, that tactic of piecemealing the force into the fight did not work as it had before.

Forrest's habitual tactic was to find the enemy, fix him with one or two regimental-sized forces, pound—or threaten to pound—the enemy with artillery, execute a flanking action, and then either demand surrender or fight it out. This approach seems to have governed virtually every engagement during the raid, whether the entire force was united or, as at Union City, Forrest, his escort, and one regiment constituted the attacking force. One consistent, reoccurring factor in all of Forrest's engagements was the absence of stand-around forces. Unlike Armstrong, and to a lesser extent, Morgan, Forrest always seemed to bring maximum combat power to bear upon the enemy. Forrest's use of artillery in the direct assault will be discussed under the role of artillery.

Morgan's employment of his cavalry as mounted infantry, for example, the horse as transportation rather than as battle-mount, has already been discussed in Part III, but perhaps a word about Morgan's subdivision of his force is in order. Given his understanding of Federal troop movements around him, Morgan never hesitated to subdivide his command and attack various targets simultaneously, for example, Bacon Creek and Nolin, New Haven and Lebanon Junction. The age-old prohibition of dividing one's force in the face of the enemy found little support in the mind of Morgan, primarily because the enemy was not organized and mobile enough to trap one of his isolated detachments and defeat it in detail. The very fact that the Federals were receiving reports of attacks at simultaneous locations only fed their fervor to inflate Morgan's numbers. The same was true of Forrest as he approached Jackson. By sending assault forces of two or three regiments on both sides of the city, he effectively froze Sullivan's response. In the case of Brigadier General Armstrong, except for Pinson's and Adams' regiments that he detached to Estanaula, later rejoining the force at Medon, Armstrong made no use of smaller task forces to strike specific targets. Perhaps that lack of simultaneous attack contributed to the Federals seemingly constant awareness of Armstrong's location.

RECONNAISSANCE

At Medon Station, Armstrong failed to push his "eyes" well beyond the point of attack. By not cutting off the rail line north of Medon, or at least positioning an observation post to warn of approaching trains, Armstrong allowed the Federals to rush reinforcements almost directly into the fight, for example, Oliver's 7th Missouri. A commander must see not only the battlefield, but also what is *beyond* the battlefield, to accurately anticipate the enemy's next move and to *get into the enemy's decision cycle*. A lack of quality reconnaissance on the road from Medon to Denmark forced Armstrong to recon by battle, or accept decisive engagement to determine the size of the force blocking the road to Denmark, and perhaps ultimately to Jackson. From the very beginning, and at least until the loss of his artillery, Col. Elias S. Dennis had the initiative at Britton's Lane, a product of the early warning he received from Lieutenant O'Connell's cavalry platoon.

Forrest kept his scouts, supported by at least a regimental-sized force, almost a day's march in front of his main body, allowing him to seize road networks, bridges, forage, and so forth, in anticipation of the arrival of the full force. This organization parallels the Forward Security Element used by many modern armies to precede the main body. In the one instance in which Forrest's reconnaissance failed, he was nearly defeated at Parker's Crossroads. The failure to communicate his true intent to McLemore's reconnaissance force, that is, to watch for Colonel Fuller's approach from

Huntingdon, resulted in his entire command being surprised and compelled to fight its way out of trouble.

Within Morgan's command, Capt. Tom Quirk epitomized the quintessential scout leader with his daring, brashness, and anticipatory actions. Morgan's success can be directly attributed to the quality of intelligence that Quirk provided in advance of the main body attacking a given objective. Wherever Morgan was unsuccessful, for example, Lebanon Junction and New Haven, Quirk is conspicuously absent. Unlike Forrest, Morgan did not generally push forward a regiment in direct support of his scouts, and the absence of this force led to some close calls for the impetuous Quirk. Morgan's reconnaissance failure came at the Rolling Fork River. From the fact that Quirk's Scouts remained on the west side of the river with Colonel Duke's rear guard, it may be surmised that Quirk's men has some responsibility to offer early warning of Harlan's approaching force. If that is the case, Quirk's men clearly failed in their duties by allowing Duke to be overtaken and defeated before crossing the river.

THE ROLE OF ARTILLERY

Both Morgan and Forrest recognized the shock and firepower that artillery brought to the battlefield, but it was Forrest who employed that artillery as a forward element of his attack, that is, in the direct assault, rather than as a long-range supporting weapon. Once he had seized the initiative, he followed his artillery prep with a swift, mounted attack, or in some cases, a dismounted attack.

By habitually presenting artillery forward in the direct assault, Forrest frequently managed to elicit a surrender without risking troops. Though occasionally detaching guns with a regiment to achieve a limited objective, Forrest tended to keep his artillery massed and traveling just in advance of, or with, the main body.

Morgan softened Elizabethtown with over one hundred artillery rounds, and used his guns to overcome the resistance at Fort Sands and Fort Boyle above the Muldraugh Hill trestles. While he did not fight an open-field battle with his full force, as did Forrest at Parker's Crossroads, nothing in Morgan's maneuver pattern indicates that he would have used his artillery in the direct assault as did Forrest. To a greater extent than Forrest, Morgan broke his guns into sections and sent them to accompany regimental-sized forces operating against a limited objective.

Regarding Armstrong's Raid, the *absence* of artillery may have been the single most important factor in the outcome of the mission. Yes, Armstrong was successful in accomplishing much that would interdict Federal operations in west Tennessee and north Mississippi; but what might he have been able to do had he possessed a battery that could have routed Colonel Force at Bolivar, reduced the depot defenders at Medon Station, and countered

Lieutenant Dengel's battery at Britton's Lane? Forrest and Morgan demonstrated what the mere *threat* of artillery could do to an otherwise determined Federal unit. Armstrong could offer no such threat, indeed, his enemy made him conduct either a direct assault or bypass the objective entirely. For Armstrong, there was no middle ground, and that led to accepting decisive engagement without the combat multiplier necessary to bring about victory.

THE ROLE OF THE WEATHER

For all the discussion about tactics, reconnaissance, and artillery, the weather may have been one of the most influential factors in the success of each raid. The fact that the ground was frozen during Forrest's and Morgan's December raids precluded dust trails that would have betrayed their maneuvers. Also, the harsh winter weather worked to convince the Federals that certain tactical options, for example, moving through the Obion River bottoms, or conducting a forced march around Lebanon through freezing rain, were impracticable and thus not to be expected.

The dry August weather meant that Frank C. Armstrong's column could not move a mile east or west of the primary direction of march without producing a dust signature visible for miles. Flanking actions and maneuvers to bypass enemy forces were revealed immediately to the enemy commander, thus eliminating the element of surprise. And in what would appear almost a contradiction, the cold weather may have been less detrimental to the troops and their mounts than was the August heat Armstrong had to handle, that is, when it is cold you can always build a fire and warm up, but stifling, summer heat lends itself to little respite. Animals likely gave out more quickly in the heat than in the cold, thus creating for Armstrong either attrition in the ranks or the distraction of foraging for fresh mounts.

Also attendant to the weather was the reverse effect of cover and concealment. With the leaves off the trees in December, the Federals were able to observe Morgan and Forrest at greater ranges and over longer periods of time than they would have been able to see Armstrong in August. This would lead, at least in theory, to more accurate assessment of the enemy strength. But Forrest employed a deception plan that turned this disadvantage into an advantage by parading troops within sight of the enemy to achieve false strength reports. The thick undergrowth and tree obscuration of late summer worked to hide Armstrong's force, but any advantage gained by concealment was likely negated by the constant dust trail discussed previously.

DECEPTION

Forrest employed an extensive deception plan to mislead the enemy as to his true troop strength, using both verbal disinformation as well as visual and audio tricks. Morgan employed electronic warfare with Charles "Lightnin'" Ellsworth's eavesdropping and imitative deception on the telegraph. Armstrong had no deception plan, so consequently the Federals tracked his movements and successfully repositioned forces to counter him.

COMMANDER'S LEADERSHIP STYLE

Of the three cavalry leaders examined in this book, only two—Morgan and Forrest—emerge from the war with a larger-than-life persona. While Frank C. Armstrong served until the end of the war as an effective commander, largely under Forrest, he never seemed to develop the closeness with his men that the other two leaders possessed. Unfortunately, no biography of Frank C. Armstrong or detailed study of his war record currently exist, and the only discussions of his generalship occur as a sidebar to works on other leaders. Despite his solid record of performance, he seems to have inspired no one to delve deeper into his battlefield presence. But an examination of this raid, and subsequent operations, indicates that Armstrong was a competent field commander. He differed from Forrest in that when the two men encountered an enemy, Forrest fought to win, committing maximum force at the decisive point, while Armstrong fought to avoid defeat, usually holding back a significant part of his force, thus frequently missing opportunities to rapidly overwhelm and destroy the enemy.

John Hunt Morgan made his reputation during the war as a raider, and seldom did he engage in a protracted battle that involved maneuver of his entire force. Would he have committed his full command with violent execution as did Forrest at Brice's or Parker's Crossroads, or would he have been more conservative as was Armstrong at Britton's Lane? Morgan's capture during the Ohio Raid in July 1863 may offer a clue, for his determination to cross the Ohio River and raid through Indiana and Ohio was not based on any order from his commander to proceed so far north. Some argue it was to grab headlines. Others say Morgan simply wanted to carry the war to the heartland of the enemy. In either case, by overextending himself he saw his command captured and scattered. Morgan's death in 1864 occurred before he had the opportunity, if men like Bragg would ever have extended such, to command a force in a conventional battlefield scenario.

This book has attempted to focus upon the cavalry raid as an integral military mission during the War Between the States by examining the operations of three of the south's more prominent cavalry leaders. The pivotal year of 1862 saw the momentum of the war shift from the early Confederate victories of 1861 that shocked the Union and inspired the south, to the Federal occupation of the Tennessee River and Mississippi River valleys, the march on Vicksburg, and the subsequent Union successes of 1863. There would be other raids in the western theater before the war ended, many of them quite spectacular. Forrest would dash through west Tennessee on two more occasions in 1863 and 1864, wreaking havoc with the Federal supply and communication lines. Morgan would sweep into central Kentucky again in July 1863 and terrorize the north by crossing the Ohio River into states thought previously to be insulated from the horrors of the war. But at no subsequent time during the war would the ascendency of Confederate cavalry be as great, or the military successes be as thorough, as that demonstrated by the Raiders of 1862.

Appendix: "Whatever Happened to . . .?"

Numerous characters have strolled across the military stage during our examination of the Raiders of 1862. The following is a partial list of what became of those soldiers.

ARMSTRONG'S RAID

Brig. Gen. Frank C. Armstrong—In the remaining years of the War Between the States, Frank C. Armstrong went on to become an impressive southern cavalry leader, playing a significant role in numerous critical battles and campaigns under Joe Wheeler, Stephen D. Lee, Benjamin Chalmers, and Nathan Bedford Forrest. It was while fighting with Forrest, who considered Armstrong one of his most dependable subordinate commanders, that Armstrong surrendered following the battle of Selma, Alabama, in May 1865. Armstrong's strength may well have been his ability to serve in a subordinate role, for he seems to have been at his best while acting under the orders of a Forrest or a Wheeler, and somewhat less successful when operating independently. After the war, Armstrong worked in the overland mail service, served as a United States Indian Inspector from 1885 to 1889, and an Assistant Commissioner of Indian Affairs from 1893 to 1895. He died in Bar Harbor, Maine, in 1909 (Warner 1959, 13).

Col. Elias S. Dennis—Promoted to brigadier general on November 29, 1862, largely because of his performance against Armstrong at Britton's Lane, Dennis was active in the Vicksburg Campaign and breveted major general for gallantry and meritorious service at the capture of Mobile, Alabama. His last assignment during the war was a brief tour as Military Governor of Shreveport, Louisiana; however, his record of justice and fairness in the position made him welcome enough among the southerners that he remained in Madison Parish, Louisiana, after the war and married a local woman. Dennis was elected sheriff of Madison Parish in 1880, but moved back to Carlyle, Illinois, where he died in 1894 (Warner 1964, 118).

Col. Wirt Adams—Rising to the rank of brigadier general during the Vicksburg Campaign, he, like Armstrong, served with Nathan Bedford Forrest at the close of the war. Returning to civilian life, Adams was a Mississippi state revenue agent and a postmaster at Jackson, Mississippi, through 1885. Adams was killed in a street fight with a Jackson newspaperman in 1888.

Col. William H. "Red" Jackson—Jackson was the only West Point officer (class of 1856) involved in Armstrong's Raid. After the raid, Jackson was promoted to brigadier general for gallantry in action at Holly Springs, Mississippi (a major contributor to the success of Van Dorn's Raid). Jackson was active in the Vicksburg Campaign, commanded Leonidas K. Polk's cavalry during the Meridian Expedition, and commanded the cavalry corps of the Army of the Mississippi during the Atlanta Campaign. Jackson, like Armstrong and Adams, finished the war commanding a cavalry force under Nathan Bedford Forrest. After the war, Jackson established Belle Meade Plantation near Nashville (still a popular tourist attraction) and became a leading breeder of thoroughbred horses. He died at his home in 1903 (Warner 1964, 153).

Col. Mortimer Leggett—After being transferred to the eastern theater, Leggett rendered important service on General U. S. Grant's staff during the Wilderness and Appomattox Campaigns. Following the war he founded one of the most successful and well-known companies to emerge from the technological explosion of the late nineteenth century: General Electric Corporation.

Col. Manning Force—This officer won the Congressional Medal of Honor later in the war. His disabling wounds that resulted from his gallantry led him to establish numerous veterans' groups whose model created the foundation for the present day Veterans Administration.

Col. William F. Slemons—Later in the war, Slemons became embroiled in a controversy with W. H. Jackson, the hearing officer in Slemons' court-martial for misappropriating horses from Federal prisoners. Though Slemons was acquitted of the charges, he bore a lifelong grudge against Jackson, calling him a "villainous coward and scoundrel" (Richards 1990, 90). Operating with his 2nd Arkansas cavalry in a guerrilla role, Slemons plagued Federal shipping along the Mississippi on several occasions and finished out the war as a prisoner following his capture in Arkansas. Slemons later served as a U.S. congressman for the state of Arkansas.

Capt. Orton Frisbee—Though initially considered for promotion to major for his gallant leadership of the 20th Illinois at Britton's Lane, Frisbee was court-martialed and drummed out of the service for dereliction of duty within three months of the battle. The same fate befell Major S. D. Puterbaugh, whose "jackass cavalry" had been so instrumental in preventing the destruction of Mortimer Leggett's force outside of Bolivar, Tennessee.

Pvt. Charles Prindle—As the man who fired the first shot at the Battle of Britton's Lane, Prindle was killed within a year of the fight. Ironically, he was the *only* member of Company H, 12th Illinois Cavalry, to be killed during the war.

Lieut. William Dengel—Passed over for promotion, Dengel resigned his commission a year after Armstrong's Raid and returned to civilian life.

FORREST'S RAID

Brig. Gen. Nathan Bedford Forrest—For the next thirty-six months of the war, Forrest conducted numerous other successful raids behind Federal lines. With an impressive victory over a larger Federal force at Brice's Crossroads, Mississippi, in 1864, he finally got the attention of Jefferson Davis and the Confederate high command, who came to realize Forrest's value as more than just a partisan raider. After the war, Forrest engaged in several business ventures, including railroad building, but he struggled with debt and suffered from a lingering illness brought on by his service during the war. He died October 29, 1877, in Memphis, Tennessee.

Col. Robert Green Ingersoll—Receiving a discharge from Federal service in July 1863, Ingersoll returned to the legal profession and became a premier litigator. A self-declared "agnostic," Ingersoll became one of the most eloquent orators of the nineteenth century, frequently speaking and writing treatises such as "The Mistakes of Moses." A clever debater who often infuriated the Christian world by his sharp, yet thought-provoking rhetoric, he lived in Washington, D.C., for a period, and later died of complications of the heart at Dobbs Ferry, New York, in 1899 (Malone 1961, 470).

Gen. Jeremiah Cutler Sullivan—After Forrest's Raid, Sullivan was transferred to the eastern theater where he commanded a division in the Department of West Virginia and fought at New Market. Having been involved in several engagements that amounted to debacles for the Union, Sullivan seemed unable to find a commander that wanted him as a subordinate. Thus without a command, he resigned on May 11, 1865. Sullivan held a series of clerical positions after the war and died in 1890 (Sifakis 1988, 634).

Col. George Dibrell—Being assigned to Gen. Joe Johnston in 1864, he fought in the Atlanta Campaign and through the Carolinas. Following the war, Dibrell was a successful merchant, railroad executive, and mining financier. He also served in the United States Congress. Dibrell died in 1888 (Boatner 1987, 239).

Bugler Nathan Bell Dozier—Continuing to serve with Colonel Dibrell, young Dozier was wounded at Saltville, Virginia, in 1864, and after recovering in a hospital in Augusta, Georgia, accompanied his commander on the escort of President Jefferson Davis in his flight through the Carolinas and into Georgia. After the war he was instrumental in creating a National Battlefield Park at the battlesite of Franklin, Tennessee.

Col. John W. Fuller—Eventually promoted to brigadier general, Fuller served in the Atlanta Campaign, Sherman's March to the Sea, and through the Carolinas. He entered the footwear business after the war and held public office until his death in 1891 (Sifakis 1988, 232).

Brig. Gen. I. N. Haynie—His commission expiring in April 1863, Haynie returned to Illinois and resumed the practice of law, serving the state as adjutant general for several years. He died in 1868 (Sifakis 1988, 298).

Brig. Gen. Thomas A. Davies—Suffering considerable embarrassment over his premature destruction of millions of dollars worth of Federal supplies at Columbus, Kentucky, during Forrest's Raid, Davies was transferred to district commands in Missouri, Kansas, and Wisconsin until the end of the war. He became a writer of prose and died in 1899 (Sifakis 1988, 169).

Colonel A. A. Russell—Commanding one of the most trusted and often used elements of Forrest's command, Russell eventually rose to brigade command in Wheeler's cavalry corps. After serving with the Army of the Tennessee during the Atlanta Campaign, he became instrumental in opposing Stoneman's Raid into east Tennessee and western North Carolina, as well as Wilson's Raid into Alabama and Georgia (Sifakis 1988, 562).

Lieut. O. C. Ayers—After Parker's Crossroads, Ayers served with the 39th Iowa guarding railroads in northern Mississippi and Alabama. He participated in Sherman's Campaign for Atlanta and was killed in action in October 1864 defending the Federal supply depot at Allatoona, Georgia (Ayers 1984, 33).

Captain W. S. McLemore—This young officer, who failed to warn Forrest of Fuller's approach at Parker's Crossroads, led his detachment of some two hundred men to escape and evasion of Federal forces in west Tennessee and rejoined Forrest's main body approximately one week after the force crossed back into middle Tennessee. He seems to have suffered no damage to his career as a result of Forrest's surprise, in fact, he assumed command of Starnes' Regiment upon the latter's promotion to brigade command.

MORGAN'S RAID

Brig. Gen. John Hunt Morgan—During his most extensive raid, Morgan was captured July 26, 1863, near New Lisbon, Ohio, but he and several others escaped from the Ohio State Penitentiary in Columbus in November of that year. By the spring of 1864 he was again in command within the Department of Southwest Virginia, and on September 4, 1864, Morgan was surprised and killed by Federal troops at Greenville, Tennessee.

Col. Basil Wilson Duke—Following his exchange from prison after Morgan's Ohio Raid, Duke rose to brigadier general, commanding in eastern Kentucky and western Virginia. He accompanied Jefferson Davis on the ill-fated retreat into Georgia after the fall of Richmond. After the war he had a varied career as a lawyer (for the Louisville and Nashville Railroad he sought so diligently to destroy during the war), educator, author, and editor. One of his lasting legacies was his contribution as commissioner of the Shiloh National Military Park from 1895 until his death in New York City in 1916 (Warner 1959, 77).

Col. John Marshall Harlan—Resigning his commission in 1863, Harlan became Kentucky's attorney general following the war. He ran twice for governor of Kentucky but was defeated both times; however, his greatest success came as a justice on the United States Supreme Court where he served for over thirty-three years. He became known as "the great dissenter" for his thoughtfully written opinions, and he was highly respected by his fellow judges. A close friend once wrote, "He retires at eight with one hand on the Constitution and the other on the Bible, safe and happy in a perfect faith in justice and righteousness." Harlan died October 14, 1911 (Malone 1961, 272).

Charles "Lightin'" Ellsworth—Captured along with Morgan during the Ohio Raid, Ellsworth escaped to his native Canada, where he assisted in the ill-fated attempt to liberate Confederate prisoners of war from Camp Douglas, Illinois. Imprisoned again, he escaped yet again and returned to Canada, and eventually made his way back into the south aboard a blockade runner. Ellsworth served for a time on the staff of Gen. Simon Buckner, being wounded at Chickamauga. Constantly running afoul of the law, Ellsworth found work as a telegrapher in the United States after the war, dying in 1899 "with his finger on the key" (*The Last Roll* 1900, 35).

John Hibble Carter—This Connecticut-born, New York–educated southerner in Morgan's original company out of Lexington, Kentucky, survived imprisonment at Camp Douglas, a bout with smallpox, and a two-week walk back to join his command after escaping from Federal prison. After the war Carter became a farmer and insurance agent, being active in many Confederate veteran reunions.

Works Cited

Alexander, Harbert L. "The Armstrong Raid Including the Battles of Bolivar, Medon Station, and Britton Lane." *Tennessee Historical Quarterly* 21 (March 1962).

Antonucci, Michael. "Code-Crackers." *Civil War Times Illustrated* (July/August 1995).

Armstrong, Frank C. Report. *U.S. War Department, The War of the Rebellion: A Compilation of the Official Records of the Union and Confederate Armies*. Vol. 28. Part 2. Washington, D.C.: 1887.

Ayers, Oliver C. "Pursuing General Forrest: This Looked But Little Like Trying to Catch the Enemy." *Civil War Times Illustrated* (September 1984).

Baird, Dan W. "With Forrest in West Tennessee." *Southern Historical Society Papers* 37. Richmond: Southern Historical Society, 1909.

"The Battle of Parker's Crossroads." *Chicago Tribune*, January 9, 1863.

Bearss, Edwin C. "General John Hunt Morgan's Second Kentucky Raid." *Register of the Kentucky Historical Society* 71. Frankfort, Ky.: 1964.

Bedford, Wimer. "Memoirs of Some Generals of the Civil War." *Lippincott's Magazine* (January 1877).

Blanchard, Ira. *I Marched With Sherman: Civil War Memoirs of the 20th Illinois Volunteer Infanty*. San Francisco: J. D. Huff & Company, 1992.

Boatner, Mark M. *The Civil War Dictionary*. New York: David McKay Company, Inc., 1987.

Bond, Octavia Zollicoffer. "The Fortunes of a Boy Under Forrest." *Confederate Veteran* 16 (1908).

Bragg, Braxton. Report. *U.S. War Department, The War of the Rebellion: A Compilation of the Official Records of the Union and Confederate Armies*. Vol. 17. Part 1. Washington, D.C.: 1887.

Brooksher, William and Snider, David. *Glory at a Gallop: Tales of the Confederate Cavalry*. New York: Brassey's, 1993.

Brown, Dee. "Morgan's Christmas Raid." *Civil War Times Illustrated* (January 1975).

Brown, Dee Alexander. *The Bold Cavaliers: Morgan's 2nd Kentucky Cavalry Raiders.*
    Philadelphia: J. B. Lippincott Company, 1959.
Castel, Albert. *General Sterling Price and the Civil War in the West.* Baton Rouge: LSU
    Press, 1968.
Claiborne, Thomas. "William H. Jackson: No. 1748, Class of 1856." *Annual Reunion
    June 14, 1904.* United States Military Academy Library, Special Collec-
    tions. West Point, N.Y.
Comte de Paris. *History of the Civil War in America.* Vol. 2. Philadelphia: Porter &
    Coates, 1876.
Cook, V. Y. "Forrest's Capture of Col. R. G. Ingersoll." *Confederate Veteran* 15
    (1907).
Cooke, Phillip St. George. *Cavalry Tactics, or Regulations for the Instruction, Forma-
    tions, and Movements of the Cavalry of the Army and Volunteers of the United
    States.* Washington, D.C.: Government Printing Office, 1862.
Costello, John. *Days of Infamy.* New York: Pocket Books, 1994.
Cowan, Luther H. Letter written to Harriet Cowan, 2 September 1862, Galena
    Public Library Trust. Galena, Illinois.
Cummings. H.J.B. Report. *U.S. War Department, The War of the Rebellion: A Compila-
    tion of the Official Records of the Union and Confederate Armies.* Vol. 17. Part
    2. Washington, D.C.: 1887.
Cupples, Jim. Interviewed by author. Lexington, Tennessee, December 1985.
Daniel, Larry J. *Soldiering in the Army of Tennessee: A Portrait of Life in a Confederate
    Army.* Chapel Hill: University of North Carolina Press, 1991.
Davies, Thomas A. Report. *U.S. War Department, The War of the Rebellion: A Compi-
    lation of the Official Records of the Union and Confederate Armies.* Vol. 17.
    Parts 1 and 2. Washington, D.C.: 1887.
Davis, William J. *The Partisan Rangers of the Confederate States Army.* Louisville:
    George G. Fetter Company, 1904.
Day, Samuel. "From Jackson, Tenn." *Chicago Tribune,* December 21, 1862.
Dengler, Adolph. Report. *U.S. War Department, The War of the Rebellion: A Compila-
    tion of the Official Records of the Union and Confederate Armies.* Vol. 17. Part
    2. Washington, D.C.: 1887.
Dickey, Frank W. Report. *U.S. War Department, The War of the Rebellion: A Compila-
    tion of the Official Records of the Union and Confederate Armies.* Vol. 28. Part
    2. Washington, D.C.: 1887.
Duke, Basil Wilson. *History of Morgan's Cavalry.* Bloomington, Ill.: University Press,
    1960.
Dunham, Cyrus L. Report. *U.S. War Department, The War of the Rebellion: A Compi-
    lation of the Official Records of the Union and Confederate Armies.* Vol. 17. Part
    2. Washington, D.C.: 1887.
Durbin, Marshal. Interview on the history of Estanaula. Summer 1992.
Dwight, Henry. "The War Album of Henry Dwight." Albert Castel, ed., *Civil War
    Times Illustrated* (June 1980).
Emmert, H. D. "U.S. Civil War Cavalry: The Foundations of Its Organization."
    Military Digest (September 1993).
Emmert, H. D. "U.S. Civil War Cavalry: Organization and Tactics." *Military Digest*
    (October 1993).

Engelmann, Adolph. Report. *U.S. War Department, The War of the Rebellion: A Compilation of the Official Records of the Union and Confederate Armies.* Vol. 17. Part 2. Washington, D.C.: 1887.

Ertzgaard, John. "John H. Carter: Company D., 2nd Kentucky Cavalry, C.S.A." *Military Images* (September–October 1986).

Evans, Clement A., ed. *Confederate Military History Extended Edition.* Vol. 9. Wilmington, N.C.: Broadfoot Publishing Co., 1987.

Evans, Rollie. Letter to Mary Evans, 5 September 1862, McLean County Historical Society. Bloomington, Ill.

Fay, Sgt. Edwin H. *This Infernal War.* Bell Irvin Wiley, ed. Austin: University of Texas Press, 1958.

"The Fight at Britton's Lane and Medon, Tenn." *Chicago Tribune,* September 8, 1862.

Ford, C. Y. "Fighting With Sabers." *Confederate Veteran* 30, no. 8 (August 1922).

Forrest, Nathan Bedford. Report. *U.S. War Department, The War of the Rebellion: A Compilation of the Official Records of the Union and Confederate Armies.* Vol. 17. Part 2. Washington, D.C.: 1887.

"From Capt. Gilbert's Company." *The Weekly Gazette* (Elgin, Ill.), September 24, 1862.

"From Jackson, Tenn." *Chicago Tribune,* September 9, 1862.

"From Kentucky and Tennessee." *Chicago Tribune,* December 31, 1862.

Fry, Jacob. Report. *U.S. War Department, The War of the Rebellion: A Compilation of the Official Records of the Union and Confederate Armies.* Vol. 17. Part 1. Washington, D.C.: 1887.

Fry, Speed S. Report. *U.S. War Department, The War of the Rebellion: A Compilation of the Official Records of the Union and Confederate Armies.* Vol. 28. Part 1. Washington, D.C.: 1887.

Fuller, John W. Report. *U.S. War Department, The War of the Rebellion: A Compilation of the Official Records of the Union and Confederate Armies.* Vol. 17. Part 2. Washington, D.C.: 1887.

Gates, John T. "Britton's Lane: Some Interesting Facts Concerning the Battle Grounds." *The Jackson Sun,* August 29, 1897.

Geer, Alan Morgan. *The Civil War Diary of Alan Morgan Geer, Twentieth Regiment, Illinois Volunteers.* Mary Ann Andersen, ed. New York: Cosmos Press, 1977.

Gilbert, C. C. Report. *U.S. War Department, The War of the Rebellion: A Compilation of the Official Records of the Union and Confederate Armies.* Vol. 20. Part 2. Washington, D.C.: 1887.

Grant, Ulysses S. *Personal Memoirs of U.S. Grant.* Vol. 1. New York: J. J. Little & Co., 1885.

Grant, Ulysses S. Report. *U.S. War Department, The War of the Rebellion: A Compilation of the Official Records of the Union and Confederate Armies.* Vol. 17. Part 2. Washington, D.C.: 1887.

Gray, Issac. Report. *U.S. War Department, The War of the Rebellion: A Compilation of the Official Records of the Union and Confederate Armies.* Vol. 28. Part 2. Washington, D.C.: 1887.

Hall, C. Ray. "The Civil War and Kentucky." *The Courier-Journal,* April 9, 1995.

Hancock, Richard Ramsey. *Hancock's Diary, or A History of the 2nd Tennessee Confederate Cavalry*. Nashville: Brandon Printing, 1887.

Hardin, Bayless. *Brigadier General John Hunt Morgan of Kentucky: Thunderbolt of the Confederacy*. Frankfort: Kentucky State Historical Society, 1963.

Harlan, John M. Report. *U.S. War Department, The War of the Rebellion: A Compilation of the Official Records of the Union and Confederate Armies*. Vol. 28. Part 1. Washington, D.C.: 1887.

Harned, Albert. Personal Interview. March 15, 1980.

Hawkins, Issac R. Report. *U.S. War Department, The War of the Rebellion: A Compilation of the Official Records of the Union and Confederate Armies*. Vol. 17. Part 2. Washington, D.C.: 1887.

Haynie, I. N. Report. *U.S. War Department, The War of the Rebellion: A Compilation of the Official Records of the Union and Confederate Armies*. Vol. 17. Part 2. Washington, D.C.: 1887.

Henry, Robert Selph. *First With The Most: Forrest*. Jackson, Tenn.: McCowat-Mercer Press, Inc., 1944.

Herr, Kincaid. *The Louisville and Nashville Railroad*. New Haven, Ky.: Kentucky Railroad Museum, 1943.

Hobson, Edward. Report. *U.S. War Department, The War of the Rebellion: A Compilation of the Official Records of the Union and Confederate Armies*. Vol. 28. Part 2. Washington, D.C.: 1887.

Hoskins, William A. Report. *U.S. War Department, The War of the Rebellion: A Compilation of the Official Records of the Union and Confederate Armies*. Vol. 28. Part 1. Washington, D.C.: 1887.

Hubbard, John Milton. *Notes of a Private*. St. Louis: Nixon-Jones Printing Company, 1911.

Huggins, A. L. "Freeman-Huggins Battery." *The Military Annals of Tennessee, Confederate*. Series 1. John Berrien Lindsley, ed. Nashville: J. M. Lindsley & Co., 1886.

Ichabod. "Letter from Ichabod." *The Carlyle Weekly Reveille*. September 18, 1862.

Ingersoll, Robert G. Report. *U.S. War Department, The War of the Rebellion: A Compilation of the Official Records of the Union and Confederate Armies*. Vol. 17. Part 1. Washington, D.C.: 1887.

"Jackson Reported Captured and the Garrison Massacred." *Chicago Tribune*, December 21, 1862.

Jones, Mary Josephine. *The Civil War in Hardin County, Kentucky*. Vine Grove: Ancestral Trails Historical Society, Inc., 1995.

Jordan, Thomas. Report. *U.S. War Department, The War of the Rebellion: A Compilation of the Official Records of the Union and Confederate Armies*. Vol. 28. Part 2. Washington, D.C.: 1887.

Jordan, Thomas, and Pryor, J. P. *The Campaigns of Lieut-Gen. N. B. Forrest and of Forrest's Cavalry*. Dayton, Ohio: Morningside Bookshop, 1977.

Kennerly, Dan. *Forrest at Parker's Crossroads*. 6th ed. Houston: Parker's Crossroads Press, 1993.

"The Last Roll." *Confederate Veteran* 8 (1900).

Lawler, Michael K. Report. *U.S. War Department, The War of the Rebellion: A Compilation of the Official Records of the Union and Confederate Armies*. Vol. 17. Part 1. Washington, D.C.: 1887.

Leggett, Mortimer. Report. *U.S. War Department, The War of the Rebellion: A Compilation of the Official Records of the Union and Confederate Armies.* Vol. 17. Part 1. Washington, D.C.: 1887.

Logan, Samuel. Report. *U.S. War Department, The War of the Rebellion: A Compilation of the Official Records of the Union and Confederate Armies.* Vol. 17. Part 1. Washington, D.C.: 1887.

Lord, Francis A. "Confederate Cavalrymen Found Revolvers Better Than Sabers or Rifles." *Civil War Times Illustrated* (January 1963).

Lytle, Andrew Nelson. *Bedford Forrest and His Critter Company.* New York: Minton, Balch & Company, 1931.

Malone, Dumas, ed. *Dictionary of American Biography.* Vol. 5. New York: Charles Scribner's Sons, 1961.

Maltby, Jasper A. "The Fight Near Jackson: Operations of The 45th Illinois." *Waukegan Weekly* 13, September 6, 1862.

Martin, David. *The Vicksburg Campaign: April 1862–July 1863.* Conshohoken, Pa.: Combined Books, 1990.

Mathes, Capt. J. Harvey. *General Forrest.* New York: D. Appleton and Company, 1902.

"Matters in Western Kentucky." *Chicago Tribune*, January 1, 1862.

McDonald, G. B. *A History of the 30th Illinois Veteran Volunteer Regiment of Infantry.* Sparta: Sparta News, 1916.

McNeil, E. B. "Monument to Confederates Killed at Britton's Lane in September, 1862." *Confederate Veteran* 2, no. 10 (October 1903).

McPherson, James B. *U.S. War Department, The War of the Rebellion: A Compilation of the Official Records of the Union and Confederate Armies.* Vol. 17. Part 2. Washington, D.C.: 1887.

Miner, Mike. "The Tennessee Bugle Boy." *Military Images* (September-October 1988).

Montgomery, Frank. *Reminiscences of a Mississippian in Peace and War.* Cincinnati: Robert Clarke Company Press, 1901.

Moore, Frank, ed. *Rebellion Record.* New York: Van Nostrand, 1866.

Morgan, John H. Report. *U.S. War Department, The War of the Rebellion: A Compilation of the Official Records of the Union and Confederate Armies.* Vol. 28. Part 2. Washington, D.C.: 1887.

"The Morgan Raid." *Chicago Tribune*, January 1, 1863.

Morton, John Watson. *The Artillery of Nathan Bedford Forrest's Cavalry.* Nashville: Smith & Lamar, 1909 (original edition) reprint, Oxford: Guild Bindery Press, 1992.

Murchison. Diary account. (unpublished). Property of Mrs. Minnie Byrum, Denmark, Tenn.: September 1862.

Neville, Fonville. "Battle of Britton's Lane was Fought For High Ideals." *The Jackson Sun*, August 26, 1962.

Noyes, E. F. Report. *U.S. War Department, The War of the Rebellion: A Compilation of the Official Records of the Union and Confederate Armies.* Vol. 17. Part 2. Washington, D.C.: 1887.

Operations. Field Manual 100-5. Washington, D.C.: Dept. of the Army, 1993.

Palmer, Innis. Report. *U.S. War Department, The War of the Rebellion: A Compilation of the Official Records of the Union and Confederate Armies*. Vol. 17. Part 2. Washington, D.C.: 1887.

Pentagraph. McLean County, Illinois. September 17, 1862.

Preston, R. A. "A Letter From a British Military Observer of the American Civil War." *Journal of Military History* 16 (1952).

Price, Sterling. Report. *U.S. War Department, The War of the Rebellion: A Compilation of the Official Records of the Union and Confederate Armies*. Vol. 28. Part 2. Washington, D.C.: 1887.

Ramage, James. *Rebel Raider*. Lexington: University Press of Kentucky, 1986.

"The Rebel Raid Toward Columbus." *Chicago Tribune*, December 23, 1862.

Reece, J. N. *Report of the Adjutant General of the State of Illinois*. Vol. 2, 1861–1866. Springfield: Phillips Brothers State Printers, 1900.

Reed, W. P. "Service With Henderson's Scouts." *Confederate Veteran* 37, no. 1 (1929).

Richards, Charles H. "Forgotten Campaign: The Story of Armstrong's Raid." Unpublished monograph. Jackson: Britton's Lane Battlefield Association, 1990.

Rieger, Paul. *Through One Man's Eyes: James G. Theaher of Company F, 50th Ohio Volunteer Infantry*. Collection of letters. Louisville Public Library. Louisville, Ky.: 1989.

Rinaker, John. Report. *U.S. War Department, The War of the Rebellion: A Compilation of the Official Records of the Union and Confederate Armies*. Vol. 17. Part 2. Washington, D.C.: 1887.

Robb, T. P. "Military Affairs in Tennessee." *Chicago Tribune*, September 18, 1862.

Rogge, Robert E. "Wrecking on the Railroad." *America's Civil War* (September 1995).

Rosecrans, William S. Report. *U.S. War Department, The War of the Rebellion: A Compilation of the Official Records of the Union and Confederate Armies*. Vol. 20. Part 2. Washington, D.C.: 1887.

Ross, Leonard. Report. *U.S. War Department, The War of the Rebellion: A Compilation of the Official Records of the Union and Confederate Armies*. Vol. 28. Parts 1 and 2. Washington, D.C.: 1887.

Sickles, John. "Soldiers in the War Between the States." *Military Images* (November-December 1991).

Sifakis, Stewart. *Who Was Who In The Civil War?* New York: Facts on File, 1988.

Slemons, W. F. Letter to Martha Slemons, 24 September 1862. Arkansas History Commission. Little Rock, Arkansas.

Snead, Thomas L. Report. *U.S. War Department, The War of the Rebellion: A Compilation of the Official Records of the Union and Confederate Armies*. Vol. 29. Part 2. Washington, D.C.: 1887.

Soldiers of the State of Ohio. Vol. 2. Columbus: Ohio State Archives, 1883.

Sullivan, Jeremiah. Report. *U.S. War Department, The War of the Rebellion: A Compilation of the Official Records of the Union and Confederate Armies*. Vol. 17. Part 2. Washington, D.C.: 1887.

Sylvia, Steve and Read, Mark. "Cavaliers & Orphans: Kentuckians in the Civil War." *North South Trader's Civil War* (January-February 1995).

"The Third Morgan Raid." *Chicago Tribune*, January 2, 1863.

Thompson, Robert L. "Morgan's Raid Into Kentucky." *Confederate Veteran* 13 (1905).

Walden, Geoffrey R. "Hardin County's Railroad Was Heavily Guarded During American Civil War." *Kentucky Explorer* (January 1995).

"The War In Tennessee." *Chicago Tribune*, December 24, 1862.

"The War In West Tennessee." *Chicago Tribune*, January 6, 1863.

Warner, Ezra. *Generals in Gray*. Baton Rouge: Louisiana State University Press, 1959.

Warner, Ezra. *Generals in Blue*. Baton Rouge: Louisiana State University Press, 1964.

"West Tennessee Army." *Chicago Tribune*, September 13, 1862.

Williams, Emma Inman. *Historic Madison*. Jackson, Tenn.: McCowat-Mercer, 1946.

Witherspoon, William. "Reminiscences of '61 and '65." Robert Selph Henry, ed. *As They Saw Forrest*. Jackson, Tenn.: McCowat-Mercer Press, 1956.

Wood, Jack D. "The Battle of Salem Cemetery." *Jackson and Madison County—A Pictorial History*. Emma I. Williams, ed. Norfolk: The Donning Company, 1988.

Wright, Horatio. Report. *U.S. War Department, The War of the Rebellion: A Compilation of the Official Records of the Union and Confederate Armies*. Vol. 20. Part 2. Washington, D.C.: 1887.

Wyeth, John Allan. "Trials With Gen. John H. Morgan." *Confederate Veteran* 19 (1911).

Young, J. P. *The Seventh Tennessee Cavalry: A History*. Dayton, Ohio: Morningside Bookshop, 1976.

Index

Adams, Col. Wirt, 33; capture of Dennis' artillery, 55–67, 65 n.4; later life, 188

Adams' Mississippi Cavalry Battalion, 16, 33, 43, 48

Alabama Cavalry, 4th, 71, 79, 89, 106, 119–20

Allen, Dr. Joe, 53

Arkansas Cavalry, 2nd, 16, 22–28, 48, 58, 59

Armstrong, Brig. Gen. Frank C.: appointed to lead Price's cavalry, 12; background of, 9–10; decision at Medon, 43–44; decision to fight at Britton's Lane, 54; intent of going to Denmark, Tennessee, 48; later life, 187; leadership style, 185; relationship to the railroad, 180; report on Britton's Lane, 62–63

Artillery: description of, 154; importance of, 183–84

Ayers, Lieut. O. C., 86, 100, 101, 111, 127; confrontation with Gen. Sullivan, 112–13; death of, 190; later life, 190; takes charge of wagon train, 120

Bacon Creek, Kentucky, 141–46. *See also* Hutcheson, Col. John B.; Morgan, Brig. Gen. John Hunt

Balch's Battalion, 29, 33, 34, 52

Barteau, Col. C. R., 41

Baxter, Lieut. Nat, 118

Beall, Capt., 49, 62

Beard, Dan, 111, 116

Beauregard, Gen. P.G.T., 10

Bennett, Col. James D. (13th Tennessee Cavalry), 142

Biffle, Col. J. B., 71, 81, 88, 97, 110, 112, 120

Bills, John H., 19

Blanchard, Ira, 38, 54, 60

Boundurant, Capt., 56

Boyle, Brig. Gen. Jeremiah T., 141, 142; criticism of, 162, 171

Bradford, John, 53

Bragg, Gen. Braxton, 10, 15, 69, 73; plans cavalry raids, 133; praises Forrest, 130; view of Morgan, 134

Breckenridge, Col. William K.M., 128

Breckinridge, Col. William, 137, 169, 172

Brisoe, Sgt. Maj. Lee, 56

Britton's Lane: battle at, 49–63; location of, 49

Brown, Lieut. Col. Billy, 161

Bullock, Maj., 166

Burton, Thomas J., 169

Carter, John Hibble, 138 n.1; later life, 191

Cavalry: classic mission of, 136; condition of Armstrong's, 13, 62; condition of Forrest's, 127; condition of Morgan's, 137, 177; role and organization of, 2–4

Champion, Capt. Rock, 26

Chandler, Capt. Zachariah M., 30

Chenault, Col. David Walter, 142, 165, 172

Clifton, Tennessee, crossing at, 74–77

"Clinton Rangers," 49, 65 n.3

Cluke, Col. Leroy S., 5, 142; at Elizabethtown, Kentucky, 152–53

Columbia, Tennessee, 71–72

Command and control, 120

Cook, V. Y., 81

Cooke, Col. Phillip St. George, 2

Corbett, Capt. C. C., 152–53

Counterattack, 167–68

Courtland, Alabama, Armstrong's fight at, 14–15

Cox's Tennessee Battalion, 71, 89–90, 97, 106, 120; capture of a portion of, 124

Crocker, Col. Marcellus M., 19–21

Croxton, Col. John Thomas, 147, 164

Cummings, Col. H.J.B., 120

Cunningham, Rev. J. W., 173

Davidson, Capt. Henry G., 14

Davies, Brig. Gen. Thomas A., 78, 94, 102–4, 108 nn.2,3; later life, 190

Davis, President Jefferson, 12, 133; view of Forrest and Morgan, 134

Deception: Duke's use of, 167, 174–85; Morgan's use of compared with Forrest's use of, 144

Decisive engagement, 151, 179–80

Dengel, Lieut. William, 51, 57, 184; later life, 189

Dengler, Lieut. Col., 85, 88–89, 99

Dennis, Col. Elias S., 32, 36, 38–40, 42, 49–60, 180, 181; association with W. H. "Red" Jackson and Wirt Adams, 65 n.4; later life, 187–88;

leadership, 60; return to Jackson, Tennessee, 63–64

Dibrell, Col. George G., 71, 89–90, 97, 121, 122, 128; later life, 189

Dickey, Capt. Frank W., 140

Dodge, Brig. Gen. Grenville, 77, 86

Double envelopment, 119–20

Dozier, Joseph, 129 n.4

Dozier, Pvt. Nathan Bell, 129 n.4; later life, 189

Duckworth, Lieut. Col. W. L., 22

Duke, Col. Basil Wilson, 142; attack on Elizabethtown, Kentucky, 152–54; background, of 142; at Bardstown, Kentucky, 172–73; capture of Nolin, Kentucky, 145–146; later life, 190; rear guard action at the Rolling Fork River, 167–69; tactics of, 177

Duncan, Henry, 44 n.4

Dunham, Col. Cyrus, 108, 110, 111–28, 128 n.2; claim of victory at Parker's Crossroads, 127; view of surrender at Parker's Crossroads, 121–22

Dupree, T. J., 59

Dwight, Lieut. Henry, 20, 23, 30 n.4

Electronic warfare, 142–44, 162, 181

Elliot, Capt., 101

Ellsworth, Charles "Lightnin,' " 143–44, 162, 185; background of, 142; later life, 191

Engelmann, Col. Adolph, 85–86, 88–89, 99

Estanaula, Tennessee: Confederate withdrawal through, 60; Federal camp at, 36–39; history of, 35

Fay, Pvt. Edwin H., 14, 17 n.1, 19, 31, 34, 52, 62

Fink, Albert, 159

Firepower, 104, 114, 117, 136, 183; at Elizabethtown, Kentucky, 154

Flexibility, 124–25

Fontaine, Lamar, 83 n.1

Force, Col. Manning, 23–24, 181; later life, 188

Ford, C. Y., 26, 30, 52

Forrest, Brig. Gen. Nathan B.: background of, 69–71; caught by surprise, 122–23; Davis' view of, 134; deception plan of, 96; estimate of the situation, 90; later life, 189; leadership style, 185–86; leads by example, 97, 107; presses the attack, 121; reports to Bragg, 105; soldiers' perception of, 81; version of Dunham's surrender, 122

Forrest, Jeffrey, 71, 89, 97

Forrest, William, 71, 110, 115, 129

Fort Boyle, 159, 161, 183

Fort Sands, 159, 161, 183

Foster, Capt. John S., 36

Freeman's Battery, 71, 79, 87–89, 94, 120, 128, 129 n.4

Frisbee, Capt. Orton, 5l, 63; later life, 188–89

Fry, Brig. Gen. Speed S., 169

Fry, Col. Jacob, 94–95, 99

Fry, Maj. John, 20–21

Fuller, Col. John W., 86, 90, 99, 100, 108, 122; closing on Forrest, 111–12; later life, 190; relief of Dunham, 124–25

Gano, Col. R. M., 142, 166, 177

Geer, Alan Morgan, 36, 59, 63

Gilbert, Capt. Franklin, 38

Gilbert, Gen. Charles C., 160; criticism of, 162; view of value of stockades, 176

Glasgow, Kentucky, 139–41. *See also* Quirk's Scouts

Grant, Gen. Ulysses S.: grand plan for Vicksburg, 69; orders to stop Forrest, 86; prods Sullivan to action, 104; response to Forrest crossing the Tennessee River, 77–78

Gray, Col. Issac P., 140–41, 148

Gurley, Capt. Frank B., 80–82

Guthrie, Capt., 64

Halisy, Col. D. J. (6th Kentucky Cavalry, Union), 173–75

Halleck, Gen. H. W., 10, 102–3

Hamilton House, 165–66, 179 n.2

Harlan, Col. John M., 15, 17 n.2; background of, 147; frustration with the railroad, 148; later life, 191; at Munfordville, Kentucky, 149, 156 n.1; ordered to pursue Morgan, 41; at the Rolling Fork River, 164–66

Harned, Albert, 164–65, 168

Harned, Wilford Lee, 165

Haynie, Gen. I. N., 77, 101–2, 108 n.1; later life, 190; near capture of, 115

Henry, William, 61, 64

Hobson, Col. Edward, 148

Hogg, Lieut. Col. Harvey, 24, 30, 180; leads saber charge, 26–28

Holly Springs, Mississippi, attack on Union supply depot, 100

Hoskins, Col. William A., 172; defense of Lebanon, Kentucky, 173–75

Hubbard, John M., 41, 47, 62

Huffman, Lieut. Col., 145, 165

Huggins, Lieut. A. L., 118

Hutcheson, Col. John B., 142, 165; at Bacon Creek, Kentucky, 145–46

Illinois Artillery, Battery E, 2nd Light, 51–63

Illinois Cavalry: 2nd, 24–30, 180; 11th, 20, 78–81, 85; 12th, 38, 49–51

Illinois Infantry: 18th (Mounted), 112–14; 20th, 36, 49, 54–56; 30th, 36, 58–59; 43rd, 85–89, 99; 45th, 32–33, 41–43; 54th, 104; 61st, 85–89; 78th, 160; 91st, 145,150, 155–56; 122nd, 112–20, 129

Indiana Artillery: 9th, 20, 23; 14th, 79–81. *See also* Kidd's 14th Indiana Battery

Indiana Cavalry: 4th, 140–41; 5th, 140–41

Indiana Infantry: 6th, 78; 10th, 14, 164, 167, 169; 13th, 78; 50th, 112–20; 71st, 159–62; 74th, 164; 78th, 20–24

Ingersoll, Col. Robert Green, 78, 180; background of, 79; battle with Forrest, 79–83; capture of, 82–83; later life, 189; paroled, 102

Iowa Infantry, 39th, 86, 100, 101, 112–22

"Jackass Cavalry," 20–24, 108 n.2, 181
Jackson, Col. W. H. "Red," 17, 42, 43, 181; later life, 188
Jackson, Tennessee, target of Armstrong's Raid, 16
Jefferson, Sanderson, 64
Johnson, Col. Adam, 138 n.2, 142; at Lebanon, Kentucky, 174–75

Kelley, Maj. D. C., 71
Kentucky, loyalties of the State, 136
Kentucky Cavalry: 2nd, 138 n.1, 139, 142; 3rd, 142, 166–67; 8th, 142, 152, 165–66; 9th, 142, 152, 165; 10th, 138 n.2, 142, 147, 174, 178 n.1; 11th, 142, 165. See also Chenault, Col. David Walter; Cluke, Col. Leroy S.; Gano, Col. R. M.; Hutcheson, Col. John B.; Johnson, Col. Adam; Morgan, Brig. Gen. John Hunt; Stoner, Col. Robert G.
Kentucky Cavalry (Union): 6th, 173; 9th, 173; 12th, 148, 149, 163–65. See also Shanks, Col. Warren
Kentucky Infantry (Union): 4th, 147, 164, 169; 10th, 164; 13th, 148. See also Croxton, Col. John Thomas
Kidd's 14th Indiana Battery, 79

Lawler, Col. Michael K., 40, 60, 129, 180
Leggett, Col. Mortimer, 20–30, 180–81; later life, 188
Lexington, Kentucky, 134
Lexington, Tennessee, battle at, 78–82
"Lexington Rifles," 134, 142
Little, Gen. Henry, 12
Llewellyn, Maj. D. H., 155
Logan, Capt. Samuel B., 104
Logan, Gen. John, 63
Lowe, Col. W. W., 78, 86

McCreary, Lieut. James, 137, 139, 156

McCulloch, Col. "Black Bob," 17, 22, 48, 51, 65 n.6; saber battle with Lieut. Col. Hogg, 27–28
McCulloch, Gen. Ben W., 10
McDonald, G. B., 39, 58, 63
McLemore, Capt. William S., 115, 123, 126, 182; later life, 190
McNeil, E. B., 55
McPherson, Maj. Gen. James B., 100
Maltby, Col. Jasper, 32, 33, 34, 44 n.2
Manson, Gen. Mahlon D., 171
Mass, 104, 119, 181
Maury, Gen. Dabney, 12
Matson, Lieut. Col. Courtland, 159–61
Meek, Lieut. Col., 85
Metcalf, James, 96, 109, 118, 126, 129 n.5
Michigan Cavalry, 2nd, 140
Middleburg, Tennessee, battle near, 22–28
Military discipline, 134
Mississippi Cavalry, 1st, 16, 41–43, 48–50
Missouri Cavalry, 2nd, 16, 22–28, 51
Missouri Infantry (Union), 7th, 41–43, 182
Montgomery, Lieut. Col. Frank, 42, 48, 60
Morgan, Brig. Gen. John Hunt, 104, 133; achieves objective, 162; background of, 134–35; at Bacon Creek, Kentucky, 145; compared to Forrest and Armstrong, 151; death of, 191; description of, 173; knowledge of Forrest's Raid, 138 n.3; later life, 190; leadership style of, 185–86
Morgan, Henrietta Hunt, 142
Morton, Governor O. P. (Ohio), 162, 176
Morton, Lieut. John W., 71, 79, 81, 93, 122
Morton, Maj. George, 41
Mounted Infantry, 4, 116; Federal need for, 176; Morgan fights as, 177. See also "Jackass Cavalry"
Muldraugh Hill, 169 n.1. See also Trestles (Muldraugh Hill)

Murchison Diary, 61–62

Napier, Col. Thomas Alonzo, 105, 127, 128 n.2; death of, 119
Napier's Battalion, 103, 105, 121; capture of a portion of, 124
Negroes: in Union camps, 40; Union view of, 38–39; used by Federals to build barricades, 86
Nolin, Kentucky, 144, 146. *See also* Duke, Col. Basil Wilson
Noyes, Col. E. F., 122

O'Connell, Lieut. Charles, 49, 65 n.3, 182
O'Hara, Capt., 79
Ohio Artillery, 1st, 164–68. *See also* Southwick's Battery
Ohio Cavalry: 1st, 14; 4th, 36; 5th, 78, 85–89
Ohio Infantry: 14th, 174; 20th, 20–24; 27th, 100, 122; 29th, 124; 39th, 100, 122; 50th, 160; 63rd, 122

Palmer, Capt. Baylor, 152
Palmer's Battery, 142; at Elizabethtown, Kentucky, 152–54; at the Rolling Fork River, 165–66
Parker, Rev. John A., 120, 124
Parker House, 122, 123, 124, 128 n.3
Parker's Crossroads, battle of, 111–26
Partisans, 134
Pemberton, Lieut. Gen. John C., 69
Pendleton, Capt. D., 167–68
Pinson, Col. Richard A., 17, 33, 43
Pipkins, Shedrick, free Negro, 61, 64
Price, Gen. Sterling, 12, 15–16
Prindle, Pvt. Charles, 49; later life, 189
Puterbaugh, Maj. S. D., 20–24, 188–89

Quirk, Capt. Tom, 137, 183; personality of, 140–41, 151; rescues Col. Duke, 168–69
Quirk's Scouts, 137; at Bardstown, Kentucky, 172–73; at Elizabethtown, Kentucky, 151; at Glasgow, Kentucky, 139–41, 144; at the Rolling Fork River, 165–66

Raid, definition of, 3
Railroads: construction of, 4; used to reinforce, 35, 180–81
Railroad workers, support of Harlan's pursuit, 148
Rambaut, Maj. G. V., 96
Ready, Miss Mattie, 134
Reconnaissance, comparison of the role of, 182–83
Reed, W. P., 61
Reynolds, Brig. Gen. J. J., 141
Rinaker, Col. John I., 117; wounded, 119, 126
Robb, T.B. (journalist), 42
Rosecrans, Maj. Gen. William, 133; complains about guerrillas, 156 n.4, 171
Ross, Gen. Leonard, 32, 33, 40, 42–43, 180
Rouse, Capt., 33–34, 40
Russell, Col. A. A., 71, 90, 119–20, 124, 190

Salem Cemetery, battle at, 85–91
Seize the initiative, 118, 124–25, 149; failure to, 167–68
Shanks, Col. Quintius, 149, 163
Shedd, Col. Warren, 63, 64
Sherman, Maj. Gen. William T., 69
Slemons, Col. William F., 22, 27–28; later life, 188
Smith, First Lieut. Pleas S., 41
Smith, Lieut. Col. Harry S., 150–51; defense of Elizabethtown, Kentucky, 154–55; demands Morgan surrender, 152; surrender of, 155
Southwick's Battery, 164–68
Speed, 104
Starnes, Col. John W., 71, 79; at Parker's Crossroads, 110, 111, 115, 120, 128, 128 n.1; at Salem Cemetery, 88, 90, 97
Steger, Lieut. Emil, 38
Stone, Sgt. Henry L., 161
Stoner, Col. Robert G., 142, 152, 165, 172; failure at New Haven, Kentucky, 174
Strange, Maj. John P., 121, 127

Stuart, Maj. Gen. Jeb, 3
Sullivan, Gen. Jeremiah C., 77; back-
    ground of, 78; claim of victory at
    Parker's Crossroads, 127; criticism
    of, 127–28; defense of Jackson, Ten-
    nessee, 90; later life, 189–90; near
    capture of, 115, 122; at Parker's
    Crossroads, 112–13; pursuit of For-
    rest, 99–101; sends Engelmann
    against Forrest, 85–90
Support by fire, 117
Supporting force, 124

Tennesse Cavalry: 2nd, 41, 48, 181;
    4th, 71; 7th, 16, 22, 47–48; 8th, 71;
    9th, 71; 13th, 142; capture of Col.
    Dennis' artillery, 56–57; at Medon,
    41–43. See also Barteau, Col. C. R.;
    Bennett, Col. James D. (13th Ten-
    nessee Cavalry); Biffle, Col. J. B.;
    Dibrell, Col. George S.; Jackson,
    Col. W. H. "Red"; Starnes, Col.
    John W
Tennessee Cavalry (Union): 1st
    (West), 77; 2nd, 78, 79–81, 85–89,
    94; 6th, 128
Tennessee Infantry, 49th, 105
Theaher, James, 160
Thompson, Robert L., 154, 176, 177
Timing, 126
Trenton, Tennessee, battle at, 94–95

Trestles (Muldraugh Hill), 142, 145,
    149; construction of, 159; destruc-
    tion of, 160–63; forces defending,
    150
Turner, Tom, 27

Union City, Tennessee, capture of,
    104–5
Unity of command, 120, 155

Van Dorn, Gen. Earl, 10, 100–102; as
    part of Bragg's overall plan, 133,
    138 n.3

Weather, role of, 184–85
Wendel, Willie, 53
White's (Capt. B. T.) Battery, 142
"Williamson County Cavalry," 115
Witherspoon, William, 43, 48, 52, 55,
    59, 62
Woodward, Capt. Thomas G., 71, 87–
    90, 91 n.2, 119–20, 124
Wright, Maj. Gen. Horatio, 171
Wyeth, Pvt. John A., 139, 140; bypass
    of Lebanon, Tennessee, 174; de-
    scription of Ellsworth, 144; at Eliza-
    bethtown, Kentucky, 155; at the
    Rolling Fork River, 168; at the tres-
    tles, 161; view of Tom Quirk, 140–
    41

About the Author

JAMES D. BREWER is a longtime Civil War researcher, speaker, teacher, site preservationist, and reenactor. A retired U.S. Army officer with experience in cavalry and mounted operations, Brewer brings both a soldier's and a historian's perspective to his work. A freelance journalist for the past fifteen years, Brewer has written widely about the Civil War.